MW00776970

FOR
Isaac MacPherson Hager

CONTENTS

ACKNOWLEDGMENTS

I want to begin by thanking Ken Wissoker. He is a wonderful editor and it has been a pleasure and a privilege to work with him on this book. I am especially grateful to Ken for sending my work to two excellent readers who gave the manuscript a close reading and provided detailed and insightful recommendations for revision that vastly improved the coherence and persuasiveness of my argument. I also owe special thanks to Mary Ann Doane, under whose supervision this project began when I was a doctoral candidate at Brown University. Thanks also to Lloyd Michaels, who inspired and cultivated my interest in film studies, first in his course "Film as a Narrative Art" and then by hiring me as an editorial assistant for *Film Criticism* while I was an undergraduate at Allegheny College.

At various times throughout the past ten years, friends and colleagues have taken valuable time away from their own work to read drafts of chapters or essays that eventually found their way into this book. Others provided comments and suggestions or posed challenging questions at conferences and other presentations. I am particularly grateful to (in alphabetical order) Richard Abel, Jennifer Bean, Giorgio Bertellini, John Caughie, Mark Cooper, Anne Friedberg,

Lee Grieveson, Tom Gunning, Isaac Hager, Bambi Haggins, Frank Koessler, Sheila C. Murphy, Diane Negra, Philip Rosen, Mark Sandberg, Gaylyn Studlar, William Urrichio, Eva Warth, and Linda Williams.

My research was greatly aided by Rosemary Haines in the Motion Picture Reading Room at the Library of Congress, Charles Silver at the Museum of Modern Art, Philip Hallman of the Donald Hall Collection at the University of Michigan, Ann Arbor, and the library staff at the Buffalo and Erie County Historical Society. Katrina Mann kindly supplied me with pages from the program for Buffalo Bill's Wild West published in 1900. Andrew Moisey provided essential help in acquiring images and printing frame enlargements for my illustrations. Portions of the research material in chapter 2 have been published in a substantially different version in "Placing the Spectator on the Scene of History: The Battle Reenactment at the Turn of the Century, from Buffalo Bill's Wild West to the Early Cinema," in *Historical Journal of Film, Radio and Television* 22, no. 3 (2002), 225–43.

I would like to thank my family and friends for the support they have provided over the years. My parents, Thomas and Sandra Whissel, have given me more love, encouragement, and security (financial and otherwise) than any daughter might reasonably expect. Thank you for the excellent education and for making sure I was not burdened by student loans while in graduate school and starting my career as an assistant professor. I am grateful for the fact that no matter where my teaching and research took me, I could always return to the considerable comforts of home whenever and for however long I needed. Thanks also to Bonnie and Richard O'Connor for their love, support, and ruthless competition on the croquet court. I am also grateful to Eugene, Cathy, Caitlin, and Michelle Whissel and to my fabulous friend Michelle Anwar Eckstein for their hospitality and excellent company when I spent time in Washington, D.C., to carry out research.

I am most deeply grateful to my husband, Isaac Hager, who has happily watched every film I watched and, since graduate school, read every sentence I wrote (often several times). Thanks for accompanying me on the film studies odyssey that has taken us from Providence and New York to Glasgow, Ann Arbor, and (finally) Berkeley and for saving the ticket stubs from all the films we saw along the way. I am really glad I made that phone call in high school to tell you that *Rear Window* was playing on TV.

The final stages of this book's revision and preparation coincided with the arrival of my daughter, Isla Hager, who has given every sign of loving film at a very early age—from her utter fascination with *Stella Dallas* while attending one of my undergraduate screenings to her (wonderfully inappropriate) gleeful applause in response to a shot of a captive, frozen Luke Skywalker hanging upside down in a cave in *The Empire Strikes Back*. I can't wait to take you with me to the movies.

INTRODUCTION

In this book I use the concept of "modern traffic" to investigate the relationship between the American cinema and technological modernity from the late 1890s to 1916. In so doing I aim to answer the following questions: How did the moving pictures help audiences make sense of, and find pleasure in, the experience of modern life? How did the cinema address the profound social, cultural, and political changes associated with modernity and its myriad and oftentimes unpleasurable consequences? How did the cinema's modernity—its imaginary mobilizations, its machine-made vision, its annihilation of space and time, its "reality effects," and its status as a form of urban, commercialized leisure—contribute to its pleasurable articulation of modern life? How did the cinema help shape and define a sense of the national specificity of the American experience of modernity—those aspects and features that made it different yet inseparable from, say, European or Asian modernity? To answer these questions, I focus on the silent American cinema's representation of four well-known, broadly covered (inter)national events that foreground the deeply ambivalent character of technological modernity in the United States: the Spanish-American War, the Philippine-American War, the Pan-

American Exposition, and the so-called white slavery scandal. Each event was linked to new forms of circulation and hence the increasing power and progress of the nation; yet all precipitated high-tech crises that brought into relief various reasons to lament or resist the changes wrought by modern life. Early and transitional-era films made each of these events visible, knowable, and pleasurable to the audiences with which they were extremely popular. In turn, as documents of modernity, the films under examination here reveal much about the early and transitional cinema's various modes of address and visual pleasures, its formal and generic transformations, and its capacity for and response to change.

The decade in which the moving pictures emerged onto the field of commercialized leisure witnessed the culmination of a number of processes that constitute the hallmarks of technological modernity. By the 1890s, industrialization had intensified and accelerated the transformation of the United States from an agrarian economy to an urban one and in the process mobilized many Americans from small towns and farming communities to cities. This shift precipitated a way of life in which families and individuals no longer themselves produced the things they needed to sustain life—food, clothing, modes of transport, and even homes—but instead satisfied their needs by purchasing mass-produced goods made by anonymous others in factories. As the industrial economy expanded and contracted, it took Americans through harrowing cycles of boom and bust: half of the twenty-five years spanning from 1873 to 1898 were years of depression.[1] In 1877, 1886, and 1894 there were massive strikes against unfair labor practices that were violently suppressed by state militias and the army.[2] Rather than producing and enjoying directly the fruits of their labor, more and more Americans experienced the alienating effects of the abstraction of their work into time and into wages that for many were low enough to make survival difficult and urban existence miserable. Moreover, many who worked in factories and mills could not afford to buy the goods they produced, and many found it difficult to save enough disposable income to spend on leisure.[3] New technologies of production, transportation, and illumination were celebrated as agents of progress and national power and made life easier and labor more efficient; however, they also subjected bodies to accidental electrocution, deadly accidents, and horrifying injuries in the workplace. Railways, steamships, and streetcars brought the distant near, but they also fragmented entire families and communities by dispersing their members across regions, states, and for many immigrants, across the Atlantic or the Pacific Ocean. In the very act of bridging the distance between sender and receiver, the telephone and telegraph simultaneously emphasized separation and the lack of face-to-face interaction.[4] Women and members of newly arrived immigrant groups claimed a presence in public life and politics, much to the distress of native-born, white, middle- and upper-class men. Members of different classes, ethnicities, nationalities, and races who fifty years earlier might only rarely have encountered one another in public space suddenly found themselves sharing—and often struggling over—housing, transportation, labor, amusements, local politics, and city sidewalks.[5]

All of these changes are inseparable from the development of a highly efficient system of modern traffic. Urbanization and industrialization demanded a radical expansion of the transportation infrastructure to circulate natural resources and workers to factories, as well as finished commodities and a new class of consumers to department stores and commercial thoroughfares.[6] Hence the railroad increased from 30,000 miles of track in 1860 to 200,000 miles in 1900, and between 1890 and 1902 electric streetcar traffic went from constituting 15 percent of urban transit to 94 percent.[7] In turn, the telephone, telegraph, and stock ticker transcended the constraints that space and time placed on the circulation of information about markets and economies, and so further accelerated the traffic in bodies, commodities, and machines.[8] At the same time, the modern steamship gave rise to a new navy able to extend the reach of American "interests" (political and economic) around the globe and to a new fleet of privately owned passenger liners that brought millions of immigrants to U.S. shores from Europe and Asia.[9] Electrification spread weblike through cities: it sped workers and consumers by streetcar through spaces of commerce and leisure; it powered assembly lines; and it illuminated moving picture screens, "great white ways," theater marquees, department stores, amusement parks, world's fairs and expositions, office buildings, and the private homes of the well off, thereby uniting all into an expanding electric network of circuits and currents.[10] And throughout this era, leisure was increasingly commercialized and consumed en masse in dime novels, penny arcades, vaudeville houses, amusement parks, moving picture shows, phonograph parlors, dance halls,

Wild West exhibits, and stage melodramas. Hence, entertainment that had previously been enjoyed in the privacy of the home became a part of the public sphere that kept thoroughfares in cities and towns animated with bustling commercial traffic.

Indeed, the *Oxford English Dictionary* indicates that by the early twentieth century "traffic" had acquired the multiple meanings that make it an ideal concept for tracing the various ways in which the new patterns of accelerated circulation shaped the contradictory experiences of modernity. As Jürgen Habermas notes, the emergence of "traffic" into the English language in 1506 roughly coincided with "three monumental events—the discovery of the 'New World,' the Renaissance, and the Reformation," which, he argues, "around the year 1500 constitute the epochal threshold between modern times and the Middle Ages."[11] The origins of "traffic" were, of course, commercial, and the meanings of the term multiplied along with the development and diffusion of transportation and communications technologies that accompanied the expansion of industrial capitalism until it eventually came to encompass most forms of modern mobility. The eighteen-page definition found in the OED provides numerous meanings of the term.[12] "Traffic" initially identified the circulation of goods between "distant or distinct communities" and thereby implied the development of new forms of spatial, temporal, economic, and social intercourse around emerging commercial practices. It came to include not only the commodities but also the vehicles, bodies, and disembodied communications that move, in one form or another, through the landscape, as well as the rate charged for such circulation and the profits derived therefrom. Traffic eventually incorporated the various technologies—such as the railway, steamship, telephone, and telegraph—that precipitated the annihilation of space and time and gave rise to new forms of "panoramic perception" that historians such as Wolfgang Schivelbusch have defined as central to the experience of modernity.[13] Importantly, the concept of traffic simultaneously accommodated legitimate transactions along with "dealings of an illicit or secret character; to deal, intrigue, conspire." It manifested itself as one of the most public and visible aspects of modern life (i.e., "the passing to and fro of persons, or of vehicles or vessels, along a road, railway, canal, or other route of transport") while simultaneously providing an avenue for and a clandestine means of carrying out conspiracies and forms of trade "with sinister or evil connotation: dealing or bargaining in something which should not be made the subject of trade." In the examples provided by the OED, the virtue of young women (from 1903: "Fruits of 'the [white slave] traffic' occupy a prominent place in today's Metropolitan police court reports") and "honor" (from 1702: "They make a Traffick of Honour, and pay for it with the wind of fair words") are as easily trafficked as more legitimate, saleable merchandise. In turn, in a single space traffic could simultaneously accommodate and bring into relief the old and the new, the modern and everything displaced by it (from 1868: "Cadiz . . . where the ancient and modern systems of traffic were blending like the mingling of the two oceans"). "Traffic" at once implied the efficient circulation of workers and consumers through city streets and the chaotic flurry of speeding vehicles that made urban life difficult to negotiate (from 1886: "The traffic of omnibuses, cabs, carriages, and carts at this point is greater and more confusing than in any other part of London"). The multiple and often contradictory definitions of "traffic" make it emblematic of an era in which, as Karl Marx argued, "everything seems pregnant with its contrary."[14]

For some observers of U.S. culture at the turn of the century, modern traffic was the defining feature of American technological modernity. One particular example is so germane to the argument made here that I would like to discuss it briefly before I outline the structure of this book. In 1899 the Rev. John Watson, an English visitor to the United States, published an article in the *North American Review* entitled "The Restless Energy of the American People — An Impression." Writing under the pen name Ian Mac-Laren, he describes in rather astonished terms the degree to which life in the United States seemed integrated into a highly efficient system of modern traffic. After describing the United States as a place "where the atmosphere is charged with electricity, and every second man is a 'hustler from way back,'" Watson continues by comparing British and American traffic: "The stir of the New World affects the visitor and quickens his pulse as he goes up the Hudson and gets his first glimpse of New York. Your steamer had waited for hours at Queenstown for the mails, but the same mails were transferred to the United States tender as the steamer went up the bay. It is said that some day one of the great railway companies whose connections are broken by the Mersey, will utilize the underground tunnels for goods trains; but on the Hudson you see huge ferryboats carrying across the river the freight trains of the Pennsylvania Railway Company. Little tugs dart about on all sides with feverish speed, and larger steamers pass with their upper machinery exposed as if there had not been time, or it had not been worthwhile, to cover it. Buildings of incredible height line the shores, and suggest that the American nation, besides utilizing the ground, proposes also to employ the heavens for commercial purposes."[15]

Watson's first impression of the United States echoes many descriptions of the overwhelming impression made by the speed and volume of urban traffic upon the newly arrived visitor, immigrant, or rural émigré to cities like New York and Chicago. The efficiency of American traffic amazed Watson (he seems particularly impressed by the sight of railway cars ferried across the Hudson) and the vertical articulation of traffic aided by electricity made circulation in his native country seem both sluggish and retrograde in its insistent horizontality: "It is only yesterday that elevators were introduced into English city buildings," he laments, and then he adds with sarcasm that "there are many London offices to which you still have to make an Alpine ascent of four stairs; but New York regards the stair as a survival of barbarism . . . The higher buildings have several sets of elevators, like the four tracks that railways lay down to work the swift and slow traffic."[16]

For Watson, Americans themselves appeared to be individual nodes to and through which modern traffic found further means of acceleration. Indeed, Americans appeared incapable of idleness and, quite contradictorily, they seemed most at ease when plugged into electricity grids spanning urban landscapes and immersed in the flurry of machines and communications that seemed to circulate with breathtaking rapidity to every corner of the nation. In the United States, he observed, "No man goes slow if he has a chance of going fast, no man stops to talk if he can talk walking, no man walks if he can ride in a trolley car, no one goes in a trolley car if he can get a convenient steam car, and by and by no one will go in a steam car if he can be shot through a pneumatic tube. No one writes with his own hand if he can dictate to a stenographer, no one dictates if he can telegraph, no one telegraphs if he can telephone, and by and by when the spirit of American invention has brought wireless telegraphy into thorough condition, a man will simply sit with his mouth at one hole and his ear at another, and do business with the ends of the earth in a few seconds, which the same machine will copy and preserve in letter books and ledgers. It is the American's regret at present he can do nothing with his feet while he is listening at the telephone, but, doubtless, some employment will be found for them in the coming age."[17]

Always preferring to keep pace with the speediest form of transit or communication available, the modern American keeps traffic in motion even while confined to an office. Even factory workers seemed capable of functioning at alarming speeds. In comparing the British laborer to the American one, he claims that "there seems no doubt that an American workman will do from twenty-five to thirty-five percent more than an Englishman in the same time, and that the higher wages of the American have their compensation for the capitalist in a workman's quickness of mind and sleight of hand."[18] To be sure, Watson also noted the accelerated rate of consumption that spurred the nation's production and circulation of goods and capital. The average newspaper reader, he notes, "flings paper after paper upon the floor. Three minutes or, in cases of extreme interest, five minutes suffice for each paper, and by and by this omnivorous reader, who consumes a paper even more quickly than his food, is knee deep in printed information or sensation."[19]

At the same time that he praised the American capacity for speed in all matters, Watson recognized that the seemingly thorough incorporation of modern life into traffic had its perils as well as its benefits. Drawing from contemporary European and American theories of the body as a repository of a limited amount of "nerve force" that powered human "batteries of life,"[20] Watson explains that "the American climate is an electric climate, and the electricity has passed into the people, who are simply vessels charged up to a certain number of volts." And he continues by noting that "the vessels as sources of motive power can then be attached to pulpits, or offices, or workshops, or politics. Of course, a day will come when the vessels will have been completely discharged, and that day arrives very frequently without warning. A little confusion in the head, and a slight numbness in the limbs, and the man has to go away to Colorado Springs or to Los Angeles. If he's fortunate, he can be recharged and run for another five or ten years; then nature does not give any warning, but simply stops the heart or darkens the brain, and you must get another man."[21] Thus while Watson marvels at the restless energy of the American people and their capacity to function as dynamic subjects of and agents within modern traffic, he also makes it clear that like trains, trolleys, and steamships, Americans are subject to catastrophic breakdown and subsequent replacement by a similar "vessel." This pattern of electrification, expenditure, and collapse is the rule rather than the exception in the United States, where, "no one, unless he leaves the country or becomes a crank, can escape from this despotism of activity; he is part of a regiment and must march with his fellows."[22]

Though written with some hyperbole, Watson's essay provides an excellent portrait of American modernity at the end of the nineteenth century: it is defined for the reader as an exceptionally efficient, highly coordinated *system* of traffic kept in rapid circulation by a broad range of technologies, workers, and consumers. While this rapid circulation thrills Watson and seems to encompass the "miraculous" aspects of technological modernity, it is also profoundly linked to the more dystopian aspects of modern life at the turn of the last century. Watson thereby confirms Schivelbusch's assertion that "by the end of the nineteenth century, the capitalist world's recomposition on the basis of modern traffic had been completed. From then on, traffic determined what belonged where. The pre-industrial contexts of location and space-time relations were no longer valid. Only the general context of traffic assigned and dictated positions to the individual elements."[23]

To be sure, early film scholars have analyzed the relationship between new forms of mechanized mobility created by traffic and the cinema's imaginary visual mobility in order to theorize and historicize the cinema's modernity. Anne Friedberg's influential concept of the "mobilized virtual gaze"—a mediated form of seeing provided by a range of visual amusements that transported the spectator spatially and temporally "to an imaginary elsewhere and an imaginary elsewhen"—is inseparable from urban traffic.[24] As Friedberg explains, "The city itself redefined the gaze. New means of transport provided an unprecedented urban mobility, the broadened boulevards produced unimpeded forms of urban circulation, and shop windows invited passersby to engage in imaginative new sites of looking."[25] In turn, Lynne Kirby has shown how the pleasurable convergence of the cinema and the railway derived from the transformation of the journey into an optical experience based on the perception of shifting and changing "en-framed" views that endowed the viewer with visual mobility in exchange for his or her bodily stasis.[26] More recently, scholars have shifted their attention from perceptual mobility to hyperkinetic bodily motion. Historians such as Shelley Stamp, Ben Singer, and Jennifer Bean have shown how the early film serial provided audiences with dynamic images of daring female mobility as stars like Pearl White and Helen Holmes jumped from moving trains, commandeered airplanes, and careened about in speeding motor cars.[27] In doing so, film serials dramatize some of the contradictions central to women's increased presence in the public sphere and their corresponding absorption into modern traffic. In Singer's words, "With its repudiation of domesticity and its fantasy of empowerment, the serial queen melodrama celebrated the excitement of the woman's attainment of unprecedented mobility outside the confines of the home" while at the same time envisioning "the dangers of this departure."[28]

In this project I continue such lines of research by historicizing and theorizing the cinema's imbrication within a complex of technological "directions in motion" that increasingly incorporated everyday life into modern traffic. Rather than focus on the cinema's relation to a single technology, such as the railway or automobile, I focus on the cinema's place within a broader network of multiple forms of traffic. Indeed, the defining feature of modern technologies was their generation of, and function within, networks and grids that linked individual technologies into expanding systems and integrated a range of technologies into patterns of interdependence. Not only did films exploit the visual and narrative potential of the telephone, railway, and telegraph, but the day-to-day operations of the moving picture industry depended upon its exploitation of transportation and communication systems: exhibitors increasingly relied on their ability to plug into electricity grids to illuminate marquees and screens and to power projectors; the mass distribution of films depended heavily on the railway system; and exhibitors placed orders to film companies by telegraph.

This emphasis on the networks and systems formed by modern technologies opens up new avenues of inquiry into the relationship between cinema and modernity. Some of the most important work on this topic has focused on the profoundly urban nature of both the moving pictures and modern life.[29] Much of this research draws from Walter Benjamin's and Georg Simmel's analyses of the new sensory and bodily experiences to which the modern city subjected the individual. For example, in 1903 Simmel characterized the subjective experience of the modern urban landscape as follows: "The rapid crowding of changing images, the sharp discontinuity in the grasp of a single glance, and the unexpectedness of onrushing impression: these are the psychological conditions which the metropolis creates. With each crossing of the street, with the tempo and multiplicity of economic, occupational and social life, the city sets up a deep contrast with small town and rural life with reference to the sensory foundations of psychic life."[30]

I begin this book by looking beyond the urban settings familiar in early film studies and outward toward broader systems and networks of traffic. By the turn of the century in the United States the commercial traffic that circulated through cities such as New York and Chicago implied (and was ultimately inseparable from) a broader network of imperial traffic made up of shipping lanes, naval bases, and coaling stations located on newly won colonies and protectorates such as the Philippines, Puerto Rico, Guam, and Cuba that stretched from the Caribbean to the Pacific and beyond. In 1898, as fighting broke out in the Spanish-American War these distant locations became sites of shifting, disorienting images, onrushing impressions, and intense bodily "shocks" (indeed, this term has military origins). High-tech imperial traffic brought traditional and rural ways of life on these islands into violent conflict with the hypermodern, and thus subjected the bodies and perception of those caught up in the war to machine-made shocks and a barrage of stimuli exponentially more intense than anything experienced in an urban setting. And just as other forms of traffic produced new optical experiences, imperial traffic created a broad network of "looks" across space and time (between civilians and the military, old and new imperial powers, officers and soldiers, colonizers and colonized, cameras and spectators) into which moving picture audiences were incorporated by the cinema.

Thinking about modernity and the cinema in terms of expanding networks of traffic also brings the ambivalence of modern life into sharper focus. Historians have recently shown how the breakdown and failure of technologies of transportation and communication provided compelling subject matter for sensation melodramas that represented the perils and terrors of modernity as well as its possibilities and pleasures.[31] Tom Gunning argues in an article on *The Lonely Villa* (Biograph, 1909) that the same telephone connection that unites a married couple across the distance between the suburban home and the urban office serves as a narrative device for staging the violent severing of that connection by a malevolent force.[32] I find Gunning's analysis particularly provocative because it demonstrates how the very same features that made new technologies and new narrative devices pleasurable might also create new machine-made terrors. It also suggests that modernity's capacity for bringing about alarming reversals without warning demands that we invert normal lines of inquiry, particularly when thinking about modern technological networks and the individual's relation to them. For example, catastrophic breakdowns and accidents are often cited as the negative outcomes of mechanization while the annihilation of space and time, the extension of human perception, and efficient circulation are often cited as its triumphs.[33] Yet, as I will show, films from the transitional era such as *The Lonedale Operator* (Biograph, 1911), *Traffic in Souls* (Universal, 1913), and *Suspense* (Rex, 1913) dramatize the ways in which interconnecting lines of high-tech modern traffic might be exploited to nefarious and tragic ends. And while historians have revealed how an entire culture coalesced around the spectacle of the cataclysmic breakdown of transport technologies and its (traumatic) effect on the human body, less attention has been paid to the ways in which, as Anson Rabinbach has shown, modern culture also reconceived the human body as a machine powered by a human motor.[34] This project shows how discourses on the working poor woman's absorption into a pulsing system of commercial traffic, from Lois Weber's *Shoes* (Bluebird Productions, 1916) to Jane Addams's *A New Conscience and an Ancient Evil*, detail the features of industrialization that caused the catastrophic breakdown of the *human* motor and made "moral breakdown" a corollary to modern life.

In this study my most significant departure from previous studies on cinema, modernity, and mobility is the close attention I pay to the national specificity of the experience of *American* modernity. Importantly, the formation of the nation-state and the rise of nationalism are cited by historians as two significant hallmarks of modernity. Hence, as Richard Abel argues in his scholarship on the American film industry's deployment of nationalism in moral debates about the content of imported films: "Rethinking the history of early American cinema requires a further reframing . . . through the contexts of modernity (or modern consumer society) and what Homi Bhabha has called 'the ideological ambivalence' of the 'nation-space.' For it was during this period that the cinema as a specific instance of modernity—a new technology of perception, reproduction, and representation; a new cultural commodity of mass production and consumption; a new space of social congregation in the public sphere—was inscribed within the discursive fields of imperialism and nationalism and their conflicted claims, respectively of economic and cultural supremacy."[35]

Early nonfiction films often represented current events of national interest to audiences and thereby functioned, as Charles Musser argues, as visual newspapers.[36] In doing so, they worked with print media to bind American audiences into what Benedict Anderson famously describes as the "imagined community" of the nation.[37] Hence, while early actualities certainly provided images of local street scenes and regional life, they also gave audiences unprecedented visual access to well-known events that, though taking place in a specific city or region or on a distant war front, nevertheless resonated across the country and demanded new interpretations of what it meant to be "American." By bringing these frequently distant events "near" to audiences in cities and towns across the country, the cinema participated in the self-conscious constructions of present and future national identity that were necessary in an era of rapid change. As I will discuss in detail, the cinema provided astonishing visual dispatches from military camps prior to the outbreak of fighting in the Spanish-American War, as well as allowed audiences both to delight in images of the Pan-American Exposition and to mourn the assassination of President William McKinley there. Another early film genre, the reenactment, provided spectators with imaginary visual access to bloody battles fought overseas during the Philippine-American War. In turn, early "features" of the cinema's transitional era offered sensational dramatizations of the scandalous "traffic in souls" that threatened to absorb the nation's young women into a thriving and lurid trade. The cinema made these events compellingly visible to audiences in cities and towns and in the process entered into, by varying degrees, "the discursive fields of imperialism and nationalism."

This book comprises four chapters: the first two focus primarily on imperial traffic, the last two primarily on commercial traffic. Certainly, the separation of commercial and imperial traffic is done here primarily for organizational purposes; for, like two sides of a coin, the two are ultimately inseparable. Not only did the new imperialism help expand American commercial enterprise but new forms of commercialized leisure made participation in imperial culture pleasurable for many Americans and profitable for a few, even when imperial traffic remained an implicit and even unnoticed part of the everyday experience of modern life. However, I have separated these lines of modern traffic in order to bring various parts of a complex system into view—much like the technique of an iris-in isolates part of a detailed image in order to direct the spectator's attention to an important element that might otherwise go unnoticed. As the OED definition of traffic makes clear, commercial traffic encompasses the broad, everyday circulation of bodies, goods, machines, and communications that is a defining feature of modernity. Commercial traffic includes the means used for achieving and expanding circulation (such as new technologies of transport and new forms of consumption and production) and the various representations of technological modernity that celebrated and lamented the various social, political, and cultural effects of new forms of mobility. By imperial traffic I mean the materiel and personnel required to execute a war as well as the images and narratives that always subtend conquest and circulate broadly within a society to constitute a collectively experienced imperial culture. Imperial traffic encompasses those "official" military technologies, goods, and individuals mobilized to a space of conquest, such as battleships and trains, cavalries and pack mules, as well as officers, soldiers, nurses, and the supplies they need to execute a war. The term also includes the journalists, photographers, camera operators, and illustrators and the stories, photographs, films, and sketches they produce for eager audiences at home. Imperial traffic circulates back and forth between the war front and the domestic front, and it includes the agents and technologies of war, the always-profitable discourses (pro- and anti-imperial) that shape prevailing conceptions of empire, and the audiences and readers who flock to sites of commercialized leisure to participate in imperial culture through such representations.

Chapter 1 discusses how in 1898 the Spanish-American War transformed and intensified the social and political meanings attached to modern traffic and its various movements as the United States began constructing what Amy Kaplan calls the "disembodied" overseas empire.[38] Detached from the continental "body" of the nation, its purpose was to accelerate and expand the flow of commercial traffic into and out of the United States by securing greater control of markets in Asia, the Caribbean, and South and Central America and to provide an outlet for the surplus production that was depressing the domestic market.[39] As the United States prepared for war with Spain, moving pictures gave audiences visual access to war camps in Florida and in doing so endowed them with a mobile disciplinary gaze that provided multiple opportunities to review, inspect, and observe new military machinery and robust martial masculinity. War actualities allowed curious audiences to observe soldiers engaging in drills and marching in formation in military camps and to inspect battleships manned by new naval recruits who are seen fueling at coaling stations and speeding through the Caribbean to demonstrate the "restless energy" of the U.S. military that, one year later, the Reverend Watson argued was a general attribute of American culture as a whole. This chapter shows how such films functioned in a mode of revelation by giving audiences the opportunity to see highly mobile, dynamic, and disciplined bodies for the first time as they were harnessed to the project of extending around the globe the reach of the U.S. military and industry. To do so, these films diverged somewhat from other actualities (such as the travelogue) by conflating the optical "journey" with the military mission and both, in turn, with the visual pleasure of operating, however temporarily, as a functional relay in the military's scopic regime.

If the actualities shot in the days and weeks leading up to the war confirmed the cinema's power to annihilate space and time and to extend the spectator's perception into new and previously unseen spaces, the conditions of modern warfare eventually revealed the limitations of the cinema's power to circulate (within) imperial traffic. As the ground campaign got under way first in Cuba and later in the Philippines heavy, bulky motion picture cameras proved difficult to transport across the campaign trails that troops carved out of rain-soaked tropical landscapes. Moreover, the conditions of modern warfare placed limits on both human and machine vision. In Cuba, Spanish forces had the advantage of knowing the terrain and were able to camouflage their positions and movements, thanks in part to their use of smokeless gunpowder. In contrast U.S. soldiers still used black gunpowder, which obscured the soldier's vision upon firing and revealed his position to the enemy via telltale clouds of smoke. As a number of accounts confirmed, American forces experienced much of the conflict in a terrifying state of highly visible battlefield blindness. Naval battles posed a different set of challenges to camera operators: the long trajectory of cannons, the speed of the new fleet, the smoke given off by burning ships and gunpowder, and the temporal contingencies of surprise attacks all conspired to make battle actualities difficult if not impossible to record. However, rather than resulting in an absence, these limitations to the cinema's capacity to circulate within the paths of imperial traffic ultimately proved to be astonishingly productive. To represent battles, production companies resorted to filming reenactments.

The number of battle reenactment films produced in the United States during and after the Spanish-American War and the Philippine-American War suggests that the very artificiality of this genre provided the pleasurable means for audiences to circulate visually within imperial traffic that actualities could not. To explain the pleasures and peculiar authenticity of the reenactment and its particular strategies for picturing American modernity, in chapter 2 I place the battle reenactment film within the broader context of the culture of live reenactments from which this film genre emerged and diverged. William F. "Buffalo Bill" Cody's Wild West was one of the most popular and enduring amusements based on battle reenactments. Programs sold before the show explain that the peculiar pleasure of the Wild West reenactments derived from their simulation of spectacular historic events *and* the spectator position from which these spectacles were "originally" perceived. By placing an "original" spectator on the scene of a historical event and then replicating such a position for spectators at its simulation, the Wild West made the reenactment highly pleasurable and in the process intensified its reality effects. In this chapter I discuss how the cinema borrowed the reality effects of the live reenactment to place its own spectators on the simulated "scene" of history, and I show how the iterable structure of the genre made it ideal for repeating and hence mastering the historical trauma of high-tech modern warfare. In the process, reenactments (both live and film) helped construct the discursive interchangeability of U.S. overseas conquest with the relief of trauma and suffering caused by the soldier's incorporation into imperial traffic.

In chapter 3 I focus on the intersection of electricity, modern traffic, and the cinema at the Pan-American Exposition in 1901. Moving picture technology was only one of several new technologies that provided an outlet for the electric currents that incorporated modern life into a system of circuits that kept electrified traffic in motion. As an invisible source of energy sensible through its effects (light, heat, and motive force), electricity was experienced primarily through whatever (signifying) machinery completed its circuit. Moreover, electricity was a highly profitable commodity and its rapid circulation through expanding urban grids constituted a form of meta-traffic that contributed to technology's annihilation of space and time. At the turn of the century, world's fairs and expositions functioned as the primary sites where amusement seekers could observe the functioning of a broad range of electric technologies during the day and then delight in massive electric illuminations at night.[40] To demonstrate and celebrate the nation's new imperial and industrial power, the organizers of the 1901 Pan-American Exposition staged a massive electric light display that used 350,000 incandescent light bulbs and was called the City of Living Light. The brilliance of this illumination allowed Edwin S. Porter to film what the Edison Manufacturing Co. called "marvels in photography" and claimed were the first films shot at night in the United States. In chapter 3 I discuss how Porter's films of the City of Living Light enacted and aestheticized industry's transcendence of the natural order, celebrated electricity's extension of human vision across space and time, and helped teach amusement seekers how to perceive the power of American technology and industry.

Before the closing of the Pan-American Exposition, however, the cinema would make both the vulnerability and the visibility of this power evident to moving picture audiences after Leon F. Czolgosz, described by newspapers as an unemployed laborer with ties to the anarchist movement, shot President William McKinley on the Exposition grounds. In the aftermath of the assassination another new technology, the electric chair, would join the cinema to help reinforce the close association of national-industrial progress with electric power and the boundedness of modern American life and death with the circuits of technological modernity.

Chapter 4 analyzes the American cinema's participation in the early-twentieth-century moral panic concerning the so-called white slave trade as it created sensational films in which otherwise virtuous young women are detoured into a life of prostitution. White slavery films are based on the premise that to participate in modern life is to be absorbed into traffic. Such films and the source material from which they drew (including government reports, immigration commission investigations, and magazine articles authored by reformers such as Jane Addams) express deep misgivings over the socioeconomic changes wrought by industrial capitalism, the factory system, and the proliferation of new technologies. The films and materials were often as concerned with the methods used by traffickers to procure new victims as they were with the destinies of working poor women. Hence, in keeping with the OED definition cited above, "traffic" rather than "prostitution" serves as the organizing figure for this chapter simply because the various meanings it possessed in the early twentieth century provide a common conceptual framework that ties together the various aspects of American modernity dramatized in one- and two-reel films and the emergent "long feature."

Two feature-length films that directly address the question of prostitution and traffic, George Loane Tucker's *Traffic in Souls* (Universal, 1913) and Lois Weber's *Shoes* (Bluebird Productions, 1916), provide important insight into the experience of modern traffic and the cinema's position within it. Both are melodramas that feature store-clerk heroines from urban working-class families who find themselves detoured into the white slave trade thanks in part to a corrupt patriarch who profits from the exploitation of working poor women. Whereas *Traffic in Souls* melodramatizes the perils of an efficiently functioning network of streetcar, steamship, telegraph, automobile, and urban pedestrian traffic that supports and conceals the illicit traffic in women, *Shoes* focuses instead on a single unit of modern traffic—the young working poor woman who "passes to and fro" along city streets each day in an effort to support her family—and the harsh economic conditions that drain her "batteries of life." Her pedestrianism appears as a more dystopian incarnation of the "flanerie" discussed by scholars such as Friedberg, Lauren Rabinovitz, and Giuliana Bruno in their works on women, urban streets, and the early cinema.[41] Moreover, the particular structure of modern traffic that each film envisions and the model of feature-length storytelling that each employs provide important insight into the new narrative strategies that emerged during the cinema's transitional era, particularly when considered alongside debates waged in the trade press about the long feature and the effects it had on film exhibition and the viewing habits of audiences defined primarily as traffic—that is, as the unscheduled flow of patrons into nickelodeons and moving picture theaters from surrounding commercial thoroughfares.

Throughout this volume I place the films under analysis in the social contexts from which and into which they emerged. This includes paying attention to the intertextual relationships that obtained between the cinema and other forms of commercialized leisure as well as analyzing the relationship between films and the surrounding industrial discourse, particularly film catalogues and trade periodicals. Chapters 1 through 3 make use of the descriptions of films found in the catalogues that circulated between manufacturers and exhibitors. In acting somewhere between advertisements and captions, catalogue descriptions help us to understand how films were promoted by the companies that made them. They provide an interpretive horizon for these films simply because they often select and highlight the formal features and content that presumably constituted what companies thought would be each film's appeal to exhibitors and audiences alike. Hence catalogue descriptions are as important for *what* they describe as for *how* they describe the features of individual films or a group of films. Moreover, as Charles Musser explains, they provide us with important clues as to how lecturers, via their verbal accompaniments, might have guided audience interpretation of individual films.[42] Chapter 4 shifts from catalogues to the pages of the trade press and the debates waged therein over increasing film lengths; this material can tell us much about changing modes of representation, exhibition, and reception and the relationship between these changes and the broader context of the experience of modernity and modern traffic.

Moving outward from the intertextual relations between industry print culture and films to the relationship between films and other forms of commercialized leisure fleshes out the discursive terrain onto which the cinema staked its representational claims and helps distinguish the specificity of the early cinema's various modes of address, its capacity to "picture," its reality effects, and its visual pleasures. As I indicated above, this book analyzes the cinema's intersection with other mass cultural forms—namely, the Pan-American Exposition, William S. "Buffalo Bill" Cody's Wild West, and popular magazines and periodicals. The organizers of the Pan-American Exposition and the Wild West provided their audiences with detailed guidebooks and programs that prepared them for the spectacles they were to encounter and how they should see and understand them. In the case of the Wild West, programs reveal much about the modes of address and reality effects of the live battle reenactments that constituted a major portion of each show and so provide important insight into the cultural origins of the early reenactment film. Similarly, numerous guidebooks for the Pan-American Exposition provided fairgoers with interpretive cues on how to perceive its massive nighttime electric illumination. As such they give insight into cinematic representations of the City of Living Light and the cinema's participation in the Exposition's construction of the "technological sublime."[43]

In turn, chapters 1 and 4 make use of monthly magazines, which, as Richard Ohmann has shown, by 1900 had "become the major form of repeated cultural experience for the people of the United States."[44] Circulation numbers for magazines tripled between 1890 (18 million) and 1905 (64 million), thereby exceeding the combined circulation of newspapers and weekly periodicals (57 million by 1905).[45] As the United States prepared for, entered, and then won the Spanish-American War, numerous articles written by correspondents, soldiers, officers, and Red Cross nurses filled the pages of magazines such as *The Century*, *Everybody's Magazine*, and the *Atlantic Monthly* to satisfy the broad appetite for, and fascination with, information about the war. Similarly, magazines printed numerous articles and fictional stories written by government officials, law enforcement officers, and reformers about the question of prostitution, women's labor, and city life. These publications not only served as the source for a range of discourses on the scandal but also provided source material for films about white slavery and prostitution. Analyzing films and industry discourse alongside these other forms of mass culture fleshes out the broader contexts in which films were made and consumed and reveal how commercialized leisure addressed the changes in identity in gender, race, class, and nation that the new era demanded. At the same time, they help foreground the specificity of the visual pleasures provided by the cinema as it demonstrated its capacity for picturing American modernity.

THE EARLY CINEMA
ENCOUNTERS EMPIRE

War Actualities, American Modernity,
and Military Masculinity

In August 1898 *The Century* magazine published accounts of naval battles fought during the Spanish-American War in which the United States defeated Spain to establish military, political, and economic dominance in the Western Hemisphere. As Captain John W. Philip of the USS *Texas*, after detailing the courage, efficiency, and technological mastery of his crew in battle, lamented: "I shall ever regret that the snap shot of the crew of the boat . . . proved to be a failure, the films being ruined by sulphur. The crew was muscular and well developed, stripped to the waist and their bodies were besmeared with perspiration and the refuse of burnt powder. They were a mild and well-disposed set of men, but they looked angry."[1] Although Captain Philip regretted the destruction of this particular photograph, the early cinema more than compensated for the loss. The Edison Manufacturing Co.'s war actuality films provided civilians with numerous life-size moving images of military men (at times "muscular and developed" and "stripped to the waist") who promised to rescue Cuba from an oppressive Spanish colonial regime and in the process deliver the United States from the ills of technological modernity. With the ability to reproduce "life-size" images of bodies in motion and views of disparate and distant points around the globe, moving pictures were particularly well suited to give new and compelling visibility to an emergent imperial masculinity. Following the declaration of war, the Edison Manufacturing Co. dispatched its newly licensed cameraman William Paley to military camps in Tampa, Florida (which served as a point of departure for troops and ships headed for Cuba and Puerto Rico), and then later arranged for Paley's transport to Cuba on one of the *New York Journal*'s news yachts.[2] The resulting films found in Edison's *War Extra* catalogue promised exhibitors films that "are sure to satisfy the craving of the general public for absolutely true and accurate details regarding the movements of the United States Army getting ready for the invasion of Cuba."[3] Focusing on short bursts of "purposeful" movement, films shot at the military camp in Tampa make visible the kinetic movement and circulation of the male body in motion preparing for the conquest of the new overseas empire. In turn, naval views exhibit battleships adorned with "bustling" activity and the flag, thereby displaying in a single image the synthesis of militarized masculinity, powerful technology, and patriotism. Such films proved to be exceedingly popular with the audiences that flocked to venues such as New York's Eden Musée to see them, thereby "bringing moving pictures into an unprecedented number of metropolitan theatres" and revitalizing a flagging film industry.[4]

In doing so, the moving pictures joined a range of other mass cultural forms in generating images of disciplined white male bodies harnessed to military technologies that came to represent a newly forged national-imperial identity based on an amalgamation of social Darwinism, the imperatives of industrial capitalism, the myth of the frontier, and the ideology of manifest destiny.[5] The proliferation of such images in the sphere of commercialized leisure was joined by a resurgence of claims to an Anglo-Saxon virility that had led the "English-speaking race" to conquer and civilize vast areas and populations around the world. These discursive constructions provided compelling counternarratives to the all-too-familiar image of an enervated male body exhausted and effeminized by the demands of industrial capitalism and technological modernity that circulated throughout popular American culture. Moreover, they seemed to provide evidence that despite the increased participation of the New Woman in suffrage, reform, and anti-imperialist movements and the increased presence of immigrants in politics, the workplace, and the spheres of commercialized leisure, native-born Anglo-American men might once again strengthen their privileged grip on political legitimacy, cultural authority, and social control.[6]

The emergence of this new image of martial masculinity on moving picture screens arrived at an opportune moment, for alarmists had repeatedly warned their fellow Americans that if native white masculinity declined as a result of the exigencies and excesses of modern life, so too would American "civilization."[7] In the last decades of the nineteenth century, such concerns had brought American masculinity under the scrutiny of an older generation of male scientists, adventurers, psychologists, reformers, military veterans, and educators who described the younger generation as "unnatural," "degenerate," "effeminate," "over-civilized," "neurasthenic," and therefore in need of reform. As Gaylyn Studlar has shown, this group of specialists promoted a range of semicompulsory activities (scouting, competitive athletics, hunting trips, etc.) that would revitalize and strengthen individual character.[8] As part of this trend, the discipline of military life was promoted as a corrective for the modern ills that plagued the male body and the national body. T. J. Jackson Lears has shown that a culturally powerful "martial ideal emerged as a popular antidote to over-civilization. Joining transatlantic currents of romantic activism, it animated cults of strenuosity and military prowess; it influenced literature and social thought, education and foreign policy. Though conventional wisdom dismissed war as an anachronism, many Americans began to hope that the warrior might return to redeem them from enervation and impotence."[9] Hence, in 1898 war with Spain was welcomed in newspapers (especially William Randolph Hearst's *New York Journal*), magazines, and vaudeville houses as an opportunity to build male bodies and, in the process, national character.[10]

The actuality films described in the Edison Manufacturing Co.'s *War Extra* catalogue give insight into how the early American cinema's encounter with empire helped reformulate the relationship between modern technology, masculinity, and national-racial identity in late-nineteenth-century American culture. In many respects, these war films drew from and transformed existing early film genres with which moving picture audiences were perhaps already familiar. To be sure, like travelogues and panoramic views war films gave audiences visual access to distant spaces and sights of great topical interest, and so participated in the cinema's characteristic annihilation of space and time. However, the cinema's "mobile virtual gaze" (to use Anne Friedberg's term) took on the added feature of allowing civilians illusory participation in the mass mobilization of troops first to Florida and later to Cuba and the Philippines, thereby conflating the cinematic "journey" with the military mission to incorporate audiences visually into the circuits of imperial traffic. The film *Morro Castle, Havana Harbor* (Edison, 1898) provides a case in point. Made after the sinking of the battleship *Maine* in Havana Harbor, this film provided audiences with a view of the old fortress shot from the deck of a moving vessel. The catalogue description for the film explained that "an excellent view is afforded of the entire fortress. Waves are seen dashing up against the rocks at the foot of the abutments. The lighthouse and sentry box are so near that the guard is plainly seen pacing up and down. The photograph is excellent, and in view of a probable bombardment, when the old fashioned masonry will melt away like butter under the fire of 13-inch guns, the view is of historic value."[11]

Not only did this film bring audiences to the site of impending conflict, it also provided a visual context for imagining the potential destruction to be wrought by the navy in upcoming battles. However, the absence of any visible trace of the agents of the military power of the United States makes *Morro Castle* different from most of the other films in the *War Extra Catalogue*. More often than not, the primary attraction displayed by war films were the spectacles of an ideologically powerful and visually compelling imperial masculinity harnessed to new military technologies. In this chapter I analyze the participation of Edison's Spanish-American War pictures in a broader cultural project that subjected American masculinity to a scrutinizing gaze. As I will show, the visual pleasure provided by these films derived not simply from their topicality but also from their ability to invest curious audiences with a disciplinary gaze able to observe and inspect soldiers as they prepared for war, marched in formation, engaged in drills and target practice, or simply carried out the everyday activities of camp life such as bathing and eating. By positioning audiences this way, the moving pictures endowed them with the illusory power of circulating alongside imperial traffic and operating, however briefly, within the military's scopic regime.

Attention to catalogue descriptions is crucial to establishing the broader interpretive horizon in which these films were projected and consumed. As Charles Musser argues about early nonfiction films, "A simple viewing of these films might suggest a comparative 'value-free' depiction of events. The catalogue descriptions, however, indicate that this was not the case. Such texts were often adapted for a lecture to accompany the film's screening. In any case, they articulate the framework within which contemporary spectators were viewing the films."[12] Indeed, catalogue descriptions point to the features and details that the films' producers themselves sought to trade upon.

Though extremely valuable, catalogue descriptions alone cannot flesh out the broader social, political, cultural, and interpretive context in which these films resonated; and so I turn to articles and personal accounts found in the magazines that were such an important part of the world of commercialized leisure at the turn of the century. As Richard Ohmann has shown, the broad circulation of monthly magazines in the 1890s helped integrate the nation into what Benedict Anderson calls an "imagined community" based on shared experiences of leisure and consumption.[13] Together these sources suggest that the war actuality played a significant role in shaping the early cinema's ability to allow audiences to see (and perhaps make sense of) American modernity, the new overseas empire, and the place that the United States would occupy on the world stage. As part of this process, the cinema participated in the struggle over changing definitions of nation, gender, and race resulting from complex and often contradictory social, cultural, economic, and political changes that stemmed from processes of industrialization taking place at home and around the globe. In what follows, I will focus on the war actuality's discursive construction of a rejuvenated white masculinity that was manufactured in response to such changes, oftentimes at the expense of African American masculinity, the New Woman, and newly conquered overseas populations. Significantly, the war actuality helped refashion the image of American military masculinity into one of modern mobility that was iconic of the efforts of the United States to expand its commercial and political power around the globe.

Curing the Ills of Industrialization: Overseas Empire,
Modernity, and American Masculinity

The historian Amy Kaplan has argued that following the closing of the American frontier in the 1880s the prospect of a new overseas empire helped refashion concepts of the nation: "With the end of continental expansion, national power was no longer measured by the settlement and incorporation of new territory consolidated into a united state, but instead by the extension of vaster yet less tangible networks of international markets and political influence."[14] Such changes led the naval officer and theorist Captain Alfred Thayer Mahan to urge Americans to turn their "eyes outward, instead of inward only, to seek the welfare of the country," for, he noted, "there is a restlessness in the world which is deeply significant if not ominous."[15] To protect the United States from foreign restlessness, and, moreover, to take advantage of distant markets overseas, Mahan argued that the United States needed to build up its naval power and establish "points of support" and "means of influence" on the islands peppering the Caribbean and the Pacific.[16] To justify such endeavors, Mahan invoked what he called a "fundamental truth": "That the control of the seas, and especially along the great lines drawn by national interest or national commerce, is the chief among the material elements in the power and prosperity of nations. It is so because the sea is the world's great medium of circulation."[17] For Mahan, the strength and integrity of the nation's continental core depended upon the circulation of modern American power and commodities throughout a strategically mapped network of naval bases, markets, annexes, and protectorates linked by the supporting technologies of the steamship, railway, and telegraph. This web of commercial and military technologies would help establish a vast commercial empire that would open up new Asian markets—particularly in China—as outlets for the surplus production that was depressing the domestic market.[18] In short, Mahan advocated extending throughout much of the globe the traffic network that spanned the continental United States, thereby accelerating the circulation of commodities and machines to new and highly profitable markets.

This bid for an overseas empire necessarily entailed a shift in the technology of American expansionism, and in the early 1890s the United States began to build its modern battleship fleet.[19] In pro-imperial discourse the railway lost its status as the primary vehicle for expansion, and thus it functioned less to extend the nation's continental boundaries than it did to bind the nation into a commercial-industrial unity. For example, in comparing the railway to the steamship following the close of the continental frontier, Commodore G. W. Melville argued in the *North American Review* that "on the land, rails of steel, traversing valley, plain, and mountain, make easy the path of the flying express and the fast freight, which, together, conquer time and distance in the binding into a homogeneous whole of the many States which form a republic almost continental in extent; but the railroad is a fixed, permanent way, whose direction varies only with new constructions. The sea, on the contrary, gives a track—fluid, mobile, universal— which turns wherever swift prows may point, and on which massive hulls, much too huge for any form of land transit, may pass with ease from port to port."[20] Thus, following a "fluid, mobile, universal" track the steamship emerged in the 1890s as the primary vehicle for circulating military and commercial traffic in the United States and hence for imagining and acquiring a commercial and territorial overseas empire.

Yet new naval technology alone could not fulfill this desire, for overseas empire demanded the production of a specific type of masculinity. Kaplan notes that as "politicians, intellectuals and businessmen . . . were redefining national power as disembodied—that is, divorced from contiguous territorial expansion . . . masculine identity was reconceived as embodied—that is, cultivated in the muscular robust physique."[21] Overseas imperialism demanded a new martial masculinity that could master simultaneously the physical demands of "frontier life" and new military technology. As a result, the military recruit came to embody a newly idealized modern American masculinity. For example, in the pages of the *Overland Monthly*, Lieutenant William F. Fullam of the U.S. Navy detailed the sights on offer at the Naval Academy. He explained that "visitors to the Naval Academy . . . are impressed with the well-groomed, athletic and manly appearance of the cadets, and their bearing and courtesy," and that "the regular life, the great variety of drills and outdoor exercises, and a good, wholesome diet keep the whole battalion in a state of 'training' throughout the year." Unlike his parlor-bound civilian counterpart, the naval cadet was isolated from the ostensibly enervating effects of overcivilization, wealth, and feminine influence: "There are no luxuries, no excesses, and no shirking at the Naval

FIGURE 1 Illustration accompanying the "The United States Naval Academy," in *Overland Monthly*, May 1898. COURTESY OF THE BANCROFT LIBRARY, UNIVERSITY OF CALIFORNIA, BERKELEY, BANC: F850. 045

Academy. The effect of the routine is very marked, as shown by the rapid physical development of the 'plebes.'"[22]

This revised masculinity must be placed in the context of a broader shift in the constructions of "ideal" American masculinity in the 1890s.[23] According to Gail Bederman, the Victorian ideal of "manly" self-restraint lost some of its purchase in a survival-of-the-fittest social and economic milieu marked by economic depressions, labor unrest, and challenges to the native white claim to political authority by immigrant groups and suffragettes.[24] Even worse, such self-restraint was diagnosed as one of the causes of neurasthenia, a nervous affliction that resulted from an unhealthy privileging of "the labor of the brain over that of the muscles" demanded by industrial capitalism.[25] According to George Miller Beard, the accelerated pace of American capitalism combined with the rapid circulation of information via the telegraph, pneumatic tube, and the press worked to drain "civilized" men of their "reserve of nervous energy and life force" and leave them "as weak and useless as a worn out battery."[26] Symptoms of this illness included fatigue, listlessness, and a lack of will and seemed to support claims coming

FIGURE 2 Illustration accompanying "The United States Naval Academy," *Overland Monthly*, May 1898. COURTESY OF THE BANCROFT LIBRARY, UNIVERSITY OF CALIFORNIA, BERKELEY, BANC: F850. 045

from various corners of American culture, particularly those aligned with jingoism, that American men had become overcivilized. The professor of pedagogy and psychology G. Stanley Hall argued that overcivilization could be cured through the recovery of a latent "masculine primitive" that had been submerged beneath the veneer of civilization by allowing boys and young men to engage in what Hall's friend Teddy Roosevelt called "the strenuous life," which included physical and outdoor activities such as hunting, riding, competitive athletics, and body building.[27]

The project of cultivating a more virile and vigorous native white masculinity was inseparable from efforts to prevent what Roosevelt and others referred to as race degeneration.[28] In the 1890s, reformers argued that if native white masculinity declined then so too would the "American race."[29] As they scrutinized native white boys and men, anthropologists and eugenicists measured, quantified, and photographed populations around the world and placed them into racial categories that were then arranged into hierarchies of civilization.[30] By placing the Anglo-American race at the apex of such hierarchies, these discursive projects justified the cultural, military, and economic domination by the United States of those placed lower on the scale. According to imperial discourse, the fact that American and British culture had reached a high degree of technological development and civilization gave these English-speaking cultures the responsibility and even the "duty" to embark upon so-called civilizing missions.[31] Thus, as Bederman stresses, the "masculine primitive" was valued most when combined with a good measure of the "virtues" of Anglo-American civilization. But it was the racially inherited bodily strength and Anglo-Saxon virility that gave "the English-speaking race" the power to prevail in physical battles that were understood to be part of an evolutionary struggle between nations and races.[32] Thus, as Kristin Hoganson has shown, the ostensible need to reclaim masculine primitivity in Anglo-American men dovetailed with the pro-imperialist discourse that promoted the therapeutic benefits of empire for both colonizer and colonized.[33]

The naval events that took place on February 15, 1898, offer perhaps the greatest insight into this particular moment in the history of American modernity, when new relationships were being forged in popular culture between nation, gender, technology, and empire. That night, a mysterious explosion sunk the U.S. battleship *Maine* in Havana Harbor, thereby marking the inception of overseas imperialism by the United States with an extraordinary example of modern technology's capacity for catastrophic breakdown.[34] As an assertion of American military power, the *Maine* had been sent to Havana Harbor in order to protect American commercial interests in Cuba threatened by the ongoing armed conflict between Cuban freedom fighters and Spanish colonial rule.[35] The 260 men killed in the explosion represented a type of masculinity increasingly defined as the perfect embodiment of a culturally powerful "martial spirit."[36] Thus the explosion challenged the sense of historical and evolutionary inevitability on which narratives of national-racial destiny and progress were based. Crucially, the cause of the explosion was never decisively determined (either it derived from an internal technological failure or from a mine planted by the Spanish). This indeterminacy, along with descriptions and images of the wreck cast suspicion on the new military technology. Even the description of the explosion published by the ship's captain, Charles Sigsbee, reads like a technological apocalypse: "To me, in my position, well aft, and within the superstructure, it was a bursting, rending, and crashing sound

FIGURE 3 Illustration accompanying Sigsbee's "Personal Narrative of the 'Maine': First Paper," in *The Century*, November 1898, featuring members of the crew of the battleship *Maine*. COURTESY OF THE DOE LIBRARY, UNIVERSITY OF CALIFORNIA, BERKELEY

or roar of immense volume, largely metallic in character. It was followed by a succession of heavy, ominous, metallic sounds, probably caused by the overturning of the central superstructure and by falling debris. There was a trembling and a lurching motion of the vessel, a list to port, and a movement of subsidence. The electric lights . . . went out. Then there was intense blackness and smoke."[37]

Here, the mysterious explosion appears as nothing less than a ferocious and lethal surprise attack launched by the ship against its own crew. Sigsbee's description of what he saw upon inspection of the ship might have confirmed technophobic suspicions that the new military technology was, at best, an unreliable ally in the quest for a disembodied empire and, at worst, a treacherous foe of American civilization. Explaining that the ship's central superstructure had been torn away, Sigsbee continues: "The broad surface that was uppermost was the ceiling of the berth-deck, where many men had swung from beam to beam in their hammocks the night before. On the white paint of the ceiling was the impression of two human bodies—mere dust—so I was told afterward. The great piece was so torn, twisted and confused with structural details that the identification of visible parts was only possible after careful study."[38] In reducing the bodies of two sailors to charcoal imprints on the berth-deck ceiling and twisting the battleship to an unrecognizable mass of wreckage the explosion that sunk the *Maine* had the hallmarks of technological modernity's deadliest assault on American military masculinity and thus made clear the perils of imperial traffic. Such accounts would have fed into an already burgeoning trade in sensational representations of technological accidents in illustrated weeklies that, Ben Singer argues, represented modern life as "defined by chance, peril, and shocking impressions rather than by any traditional concept of safety, continuity, and self-controlled destiny."[39] William Paley's film *Wreck of the Battleship "Maine"* (Edison, 1898), which displays a spectacle of the destroyed ship through a panoramic point-of-view shot from a moving vessel, undoubtedly helped feed anxious speculations about this unprecedented instance of modern "shock." The catalogue description encourages exhibitors to emphasize the catastrophic extent of the damage done to the ship: "Taken in Havana Harbor from a moving launch . . . [the film] shows the wreck of the 'Maine' surrounded by wrecking boats and other vessels. The warped and twisted remains show how thoroughly the immense mass of iron and steel was blown out of all semblance of a vessel."[40] Such spectacles foregrounded modern technology's fearsome ability to disrupt as well as aid the nation's pursuit of its "manifest destiny" to expand, and in the process it returned the contemporary notions of "shock" to its military origins. As Wolfgang Schivelbusch notes, by the end of the nineteenth century "shock describes the kind of sudden and powerful event of violence that disrupts the continuity of an artificially/ mechanically created motion or situation, and also the subsequent state of derangement. The precondition for this is a highly developed general state of dominance over nature, both technically (military example: firearms) and psychically (military example: troop discipline). The degree of control over nature and the violence of the collapse of that control, in shock, are proportionate: the more finely meshed the web of mechanization, discipline, division of labor, etc., the more catastrophic the collapse when it is disrupted from within or without."[41] The explosion onboard the *Maine* took place within one of the nation's most highly mobile, mechanized, and disciplined spaces, thereby making the ship's catastrophic collapse all

FIGURE 4 *Wreck of the Battleship "Maine"* (Edison, 1898). COURTESY OF THE LIBRARY OF CONGRESS MOTION PICTURE READING ROOM

the more devastating. The *Maine* explosion linked imperial traffic to the spectacle of violent mechanical breakdown and suggested that the high-tech endeavor of empire building by the United States was, perhaps, over before it had even begun. A June 1898 article in the *Atlantic Monthly* sought to ameliorate the public's anxiety over the technological mysteries of the modern battleship, lamenting that "in the mind of the non-technical citizen, the battleship has become almost the synonym for disaster. This huge machine is considered uncertain, unwieldy, and unsafe. . . . The newspapers have contained many illustrations of terrific conflicts, in which ships have been drawn crashing into one another, and plunging into the depths, carrying men and guns down with them. One of the pictorial weeklies has gone so far as to represent the battle ship as a huge sphinx."[42] Ultimately, though, the explosion that sunk the *Maine* acted as a catalyst for transforming the chance, peril, and violent shock associated with imperial traffic back into a narrative of national continuity and self-controlled destiny. The sensationalist press broadly promoted the idea that the explosion was caused by a Spanish mine, thereby allowing blame to be displaced from new American technology to Old World treachery.[43] Whatever the cause of the explosion, the sunken battleship seemed to demand a counterdisplay of technological military power that would compensate for this spectacle of catastrophic breakdown and shore up narratives on naval power, masculinity, and imperial expansion that had been written around the increasingly complex involvement by the United States in the Spanish-Cuban conflict. And so, the United States declared war on Spain on April 25, 1898.

Soon thereafter, war films emerged to provide audiences with a surrogate vision that allowed them to see inside the enclosed and apparently utopian homosocial disciplinary space of battleships and military camps isolated from the ills of modern civilian culture. In these films, the camera's point of view appears as a manifestation of a more ubiquitous disciplinary gaze that penetrates a range of military enclosures to review, inspect, and observe the functioning of military machinery and masculinity. In some of these films the camera observes the unloading of a supply train, or troops disembarking from a transport, or a battleship being coaled and thereby incorporates audiences visually into the emerging routes of imperial traffic. In others, the action seems orchestrated for the camera: soldiers march in formation in front of the camera or recruits having a "morning wash" look directly into the camera and laugh—performing before its gaze and for its approval. In this sense the camera seems to align audiences with the disciplinary regime of observation that thoroughly penetrated military life by aligning the audience's point of view with an authoritative disciplinary gaze that appears to observe and assess the wartime behavior and appearance of men and machines.[44] At the same time, these films operate according to a mode of revelation by allowing audiences to see such spaces and activities for the first time. The point of view they offer, then, is double: although structurally aligned with the point of view of an "insider," curious civilian audiences would consume such images and narratives from the position of an outsider. This double perspective endowed audiences with the imaginary capacity to undertake a novel and hence "fascinated inspection" of a range of new military masculinities and technologies as they prepared to extend the reach and power of American industry through the establishment of new networks of high-tech traffic.

Naval Views and the War Actuality's
Promotion of "Fascinated Inspection"

Edison's naval views brought audiences to individual ships from the new fleet as they made their way toward Cuba and Puerto Rico and were frequently shot from a vessel moving alongside the ships. The effect of this tendency is twofold: the distance of the camera helps convey the astonishing size of the new battleships (which always exceed the frame) while at the same time making visible for inspection a number of activities taking place on board. For example, Edison's *War Extra Catalogue* promises that the *US Battleship "Iowa"* (1898) "shows the US Battleship 'Iowa' at anchor at the rendezvous near the Dry Tortugas. The camera was placed on the small yacht, which approaches and passes the battleship, thus giving a complete view of one side of this mammoth war machine. The picture was taken on the sailors' washday, and on the line stretched along the fore part of the vessel is hung their apparel. The picture is exceedingly sharp and the cannon are plainly shown as they project from the different turrets and portholes. The American flag is flying from the mast and waves in the breeze. Some distance from the stern of the vessel are two targets, and a number of sailors are seen rowing in small boats. This is a most excellent picture of the vessel and is exceptionally good from a photographic standpoint."[45]

As part of a fleet of ships that Captain Philip described as "majestic in their suggestion of irresistible power,"[46] this view of the "mammoth war machine" was meant to inspire awe rather than the anxiety provoked by the sphinx-like mystery of naval technology only several months earlier. War actualities such as this one offered a reassuring glimpse into the everyday disciplined routine of the men that inoculated them against the physical and sensory shocks of modern warfare and transformed them into the embodiment of what Captain Philip later called "mechanical precision fortified by intelligent patriotism."[47] The noncentered quality of the image allows the eye to roam across and inspect a range of activities (from laundry to target practice) that characterized the regimented routine of everyday military life, thereby positioning the viewer as the subject of a disciplinary gaze. And while the camera's distance allows the viewer to watch without being seen, it would be inappropriate to characterize this look as voyeuristic, or simply to classify films in which soldiers acknowledge the camera's

FIGURE 5 *US Battleship "Indiana"* (Edison, 1898) COURTESY OF THE LIBRARY OF CONGRESS
MOTION PICTURE READING ROOM

presence as exhibitionist. For the proper functioning of the disciplinary gaze in a military setting depends upon the soldier's knowledge of the fact that he exists in a state of perpetual visibility and surveillance, whether or not the subjects of the disciplinary gaze are visible to him.[48] Hence in some of these war actualities the camera is acknowledged, while in others it is not. In either case, the war actuality aligns the viewer with the disciplinary gaze of the imperial apparatus via the camera's look of fascinated inspection, and thereby charges this mode of viewing with historically specific visual power and pleasure.

The film *US Battleship "Indiana"* (1898) provides a similar sort of view. Shot from a moving vessel, the camera moves along the starboard length of the ship to reveal a gradually unfolding view of the battleship, thus manufacturing a visual tension between the sight of the massive battleship and the various activities taking place on deck. Lecturers at venues such as the Eden Musée could explain to audiences that the spectacle before them was "taken at the Dry Tortugas and shows the most powerful fighting machine in the world today as she lies at anchor taking on coal. The decks are covered with marines and sailors. An immense barge lies along side, from which a large gang of negroes are hustling 'King coal' into the battleship, on whose decks the coal passers run to and fro. The view is taken from a moving yacht and gives the effect of the vessel itself passing though the water. As the yacht passed the starboard quarter, the powerful 13-inch, 8-inch and 6-inch guns bristle from their turrets. She looks every inch of her great length, 348 feet. The photograph is excellent."[49] As the camera slowly peruses the length of the ship it allows audiences to observe the coaling process taking place onboard, thereby displaying a pleasurable spectacle of the disciplined activity and energetic "hustle" that naval experts argued provided a seamless continuity between peacetime and wartime activity onboard the battleship. For example, Captain Henry Taylor's description, published in *The Century* magazine, of action on board the "Indiana" leading up to the Battle of Santiago emphasized the physical strength and endless energy required to sustain a battleship: "The morning of July 3, 1898, found the battleship 'Indiana' holding the eastern end of the line of battleships and armored cruisers off Santiago. For two days and two nights the labor of the officers and crew had been intense: they had coaled ship at Guantanamo until midnight of July 1, and had then hastened to the fleet off Santiago to take part in the spirited engagement of July 2 . . . Signalling our arrival to the flagship before day break, the answering signal flashed back, 'Take position between flagship and "Oregon" and clear ship for action.' The coal dust was still thick on the deck and on the faces of officers and crew, and most of them had not had more than an hour or two of sleep, caught hurriedly and without undressing; but at this stirring and welcome signal, fatigue of body and mind vanished, and all sprang to their stations with a cool exultation of spirit characteristic of our ship's company."[50]

This article and Edison's actuality promote the fantasy of continuous action carried out by men and machines propelled by endless energy and a capacity for limitless mobility: the energetic men coal the ship to fuel its "fluid, universal" mobility and in turn the ship mobilizes the men to the new frontier. Moreover, the temporal nonclosure characteristic of the early film actuality provides a (perhaps fortuitous) formal support to the idea of endless, restless imperial energy: while the inspection itself is limited to the length of the film, the fact that the camera captures activity in medias res allows it to be perceived as ongoing, without beginning or end.[51] So great is the impulse to display the kinetic energy of imperial traffic's agents and machines that even "at anchor," the catalogue assures, the ship seems to be in motion, thanks to the moving point of view from which the film was shot. In turn, by making available scenes of everyday military life, the war actualities circulating through civilian life undoubtedly helped to normalize the type of military masculinity on display.

The fascination with military life evidenced by both moving pictures and magazines suggests that imperialism joined technology to native white masculinity in a way that revitalized the popular perception of both. Although the battleship mobilized American men to the new "frontier," it was a space that intensified, rather than provided escape from, the shocks, incursions, and draining "brainwork" of modern life. Organized horizontally into different "specialist" departments and vertically into a strict hierarchy of command, the battleship bore greater resemblance to the modern corporation than to the more familiar frontier of the wild West. In 1897 Admiral P. H. Colomb of the Royal Navy explained to curious readers of the *North American Review* that the advent of steam power reorganized the battleship into departments structured according to specialist training, thereby distributing power and knowledge once concentrated in the hands of the captain across different segments of the battleship. This new mechanical environment transformed the battleship from "a private firm to a limited liability company" where it was "instinctively felt that it was the correct working of each department in harmony with all others that made the ship and gave her a good name." New technologies had the added effect of acting like "a great roller pressing out individualities" and "leveling all into one smooth plane." This homogenization of the naval "workforce" unified activity around a coherent ideology: whereas in the past "the junior obeyed the senior because he was afraid of him," now "he obeys because loyalty to a great cause demands it."[52] In 1898 the "great cause" to which sailor and officer alike were loyal was the acceleration by the United States of commercial and military traffic overseas. These endeavors were linked to a sense of national honor piqued by assertions to "remember the *Maine*."

Colomb's article was prescient in its description of the terms upon which the naval officer and recruit would come to embody an ideal modern masculinity; both officer and recruit emerged as modern subjects able to transform the potential chaos of warfare into "a splendid co-ordination and order."[53] As it turned out, the navy was absolutely instrumental in the victory over Spain by the United States as it triumphed decisively in the naval battles fought in both the Caribbean and the Philippines. On the morning of May 1, 1898, Admiral George Dewey of the U.S. Navy's Asiatic Squadron launched an attack against the Spanish fleet in Manila Bay. By nightfall, Dewey's squadron had decimated Admiral Montojo's fleet with very little damage to Dewey's own fleet and only nine of his men slightly wounded. In an article titled "Why We Won at Manila," Lieutenant B. A. Fiske noted that observers onboard any U.S. battleship during the Battle at Manila Bay "would have seen about fifty Tom Bowlings, all doing the same things in the same way. He would have seen fifty guns' crews all eagerly, yet cooly, working their guns, and he would have seen each division of guns, and each turret under the charge of an officer responsible for it . . . The spectacle of the orderly decks, the ardent but controlled enthusiasm, the well-drilled crews working their guns or providing ammunition, or caring for the wounded, or extinguishing fire, might lead him to ask himself, 'Is not this excellent shooting I see merely one sign of a discipline and instruction and drill without which it could not be?'"[54] The unmistakable signs of effective discipline—uniformity of movement and purpose; subdivision and distribution of specialist knowledge, activity, and power; the exercise of physical dexterity and bodily strength; and the docile subordination to hierarchy—reveal themselves to the eyes of the pleased observer and mark out the naval officer and recruit as ideal modern subjects.

On July 3, on the other side of the world, Admiral Sampson's squadron, led by Commodore Schley, defeated Admiral Cervera's fleet near Santiago, Cuba. This event brought great relief to the U.S. Army, which had been suffering under heavy fire at the battles of El Caney and San Juan Hill. While Spain suffered approximately four hundred killed and wounded, the U.S. fleet lost only one man. Though Spain's defeat resulted largely from the fact that their ships had wooden decks that went up in flames when hit by U.S. fire, this victory seemed to confirm suspicions that the outcome was due to the synthesis of a powerful new military masculinity and naval technology. By most accounts, military discipline seemed to fortify the naval recruit against shock and generate a surplus of the "nerve force" lacking in his Spanish counterpart. As the commander of the *Gloucester* said of his crew's performance at the Battle of Santiago: "Our small loss of life can be accounted for, humanly speaking, only by our constant target practice and superior nerve. Our constant target practice gave magnificent fire discipline and correct aiming . . . Our superior nerve (not courage, for there was ample courage on both sides), gave us the ability to hold our range once it was obtained. Nerve in the engine- and fire-rooms, nerve at the helm, and nerve behind the guns, will account for the complete victory, with the loss of only one American sailor."[55] If, as Beard and others contended, the absorption of everyday life into modern commercial traffic depleted the "nerve force" of civilians, absorption into imperial traffic seems to have fortified the recruit's supply. Indeed, reports from the warfront provided further testimony to the apparent immunity of the U.S. Navy to the physical and sensory shocks of modern warfare. In the pages of the August 1898 issue of *The Century*, the surgeon of the flagship *Olympia* described the Battle of Manila Bay as a nightmare of modern shock: "The noise of the explosions was stunning, and a number of officers and men had their ears plugged with cotton as a safeguard. They could still hear commands, but were saved the shock of rapid-firing guns. A private of marines was made deaf for several days and powder smoke made many choke and caused watering of the eyes among all. When the eight-inch guns went off the noise in the sick bay was terrible and . . . the ship heaved as if in the grip of a tidal wave, and one felt as though nothing could withstand the concussion."[56]

Yet high-tech modern warfare ultimately emerges as the condition of possibility for the emergence of a model modern masculinity. As the *Olympia*'s surgeon goes on to assert: "I saw no fear shown by anyone. After the battle began the coolness of the men and officers was as real and as great if they were at target practice. They aimed their guns with the ease and steadiness of men shooting partridges, and cheered each shot home to its mark. Exclamations of satisfaction when some specially valuable target was hit were frequent, and all executed their manoeuvers with the sang-froid of veterans."[57] Rather than suffer trauma in the face of high-tech warfare, the naval officer and crew emerge as unflappably immune to shock and fearlessly "cool." The postwar idealization of the navy seems to have derived in part from overseas imperialism's demand for a combination of modernity's disparaged "brain work" and the physical discipline of "strenuous" military life, yielding a spectacle of modern mechanized masculinity that could be displayed before the eyes of the nation and the rest of the world as the culmination of Anglo-American civilization and power.

The film *Victorious Squadron Firing Salute* (Edison, 1898), shot by James White during the Atlantic Squadron's celebratory naval parade on the Hudson River on August 20, 1898, promoted just such a perception as it revealed to curious audiences images of the victorious fleet firing their guns as they made their way up the river. *The Phonoscope* described the film as follows: "The flagship 'New York' reached Grant's Tomb at precisely 11:30, and four seconds after the picture begins fired the first shot of the national salute of 21 guns. The 'Massachusetts' follows example, close behind. As she approaches, the smoke thickens. The 'Oregon' now comes into sight. By this time the firing has become general; and as she looms up through the thickening smoke her outlines grow more and more distinct until she finally emerges into full view. The effect is magnificent. One can only wonder how the 'men behind the guns' could have aimed so accurate and with such deadly effect in the victorious fight with the Spanish ships. Not only are the smoke effects superb, but the detail and definition of the picture leave absolutely nothing to be desired."[58] Over and over again, the modern battleship increasingly appears in these war actualities as a floating microcosm of a more perfect homosocial industrial "civilization" where the perils of modernity were mastered and exploited by "men behind the guns" whose disciplined training and accurate firing might only stimulate wonder as the sublime battleships come into sharp focus. The aesthetic of astonishment that Tom Gunning argues was the effect of the cinema of attractions arises here from cinema's ability to display with detail and definition the ship's size, speed, and firing power.[59] Such films gave audiences the opportunity to see American modernity by visually mobilizing them through the new circuits of imperial traffic by mechanically reproduced moving images characterized by startling reality effects.

War Preparations, Camp Life, and Racial Constructions of Imperial Identity

Prior to outbreak of hostilities between Spain and the United States, only 25,000 men were enlisted in the army. However, the call for volunteers was so successful that many of the men who clamored to enlist had to be turned away, and by the time the fighting began 250,000 men eager to engage in

FIGURE 6 *Troops Making Military Road in Front of Santiago* (Edison, 1898).
COURTESY OF THE LIBRARY OF CONGRESS MOTION PICTURE READING ROOM

warfare on the nation's new imperial frontier had been mustered in. Many of these troops were mobilized first to military camps in Tampa, Florida, and then on to Cuba. Films shot by William Paley in the camps and on the campaign trail in Cuba offer audiences a closer view of wartime activities. Some of the films shot by Paley include commanding officers within the frame, and thereby reinforce the camera's own power to undertake a fascinated inspection of military activities. For example, *Packing Ammunition on Mules, Cuba* (Edison, 1898) displays the soldiers' arduous task of unloading supplies and ammunition from the transport ships that had landed at Daiquiri, Cuba, under the supervision of "an officer [who] stands by bossing the job."[60] *Troops Making Military Road in Front of Santiago* (Edison, 1898) similarly shows an officer on the scene. *The Phonoscope* described the efforts of the 34th Michigan Regiment as follows: "Under Command of Captain Dodd of Troop E, 3rd Regular Cavalry, they are road making that the siege guns may go to the front. The chaparral and thick underbrush has been cleared away and the soldiers are working with picks and shovels to make the way passable."[61]

The commanding officers visible in both films act as textual surrogates for the curious spectator and reinforce the disciplinary orientation of his or her fascinated look at the soldiers in the frame. Such films simply make explicit what is implicit in films in which no officer is visible. In doing so, they foreground the idea that, as Gunning argues, "the most character-istic quality" of the "view" provided by the actuality film "lies in the way it mimes the act of looking and observing. In other words, we don't just experience a 'view' film as a presentation of a place, an event, or a process, but also as the mimesis of the act of observing."[62] In the case of these mili-tary "views" of camp life and war preparations, the act of observing takes on the distinct quality of inspection not only of the soldiers but also of the visible commanding officers, thereby placing the camera's point of view, and hence the spectator's, at the apex of a series of looks focused upon the military masculinity that kept the war machine moving toward its goal of expanded mobility and conquest. The camera's disembodied point of view perhaps provided audiences with the pleasurable illusion of operating, if only briefly, as a functional relay in the scopic regime responsible for the supervision and production of the martial masculinity on display.

As the descriptions of the above films suggest, like the naval views the actualities shot in the military camps display a visual orchestration of bodies and machines harnessed to the project of laying down the infrastructure of the new imperial traffic, and in doing so they helped promote the myth of the new martial masculine ideal. As the description for *U.S. Cavalry Supplies Unloading at Tampa, Florida* (Edison, 1898) explains: "Here is a freight train of thirty cars loaded with baggage and ambulance supplies for the 9th US Cavalry. In the foreground a score of troopers are pulling, lifting and hauling an ambulance from a flat car. It slides down the in-clined planks with a sudden rush that makes men 'hustle' to keep it from falling off. Drill engine on the next track darts past with sharp quick puffs of smoke. A very brisk scene."[63] In this scenario, a newly embodied and militarized masculinity masters and prevails over technology and seems to be animated with as much energy as the drill engine that "darts past with sharp quick puffs of smoke." The arrival of the freight train occasions the display of bodily strength and the activities of pulling, lifting, and hauling. Even the contingency of an unpredictable event ("the ambulance makes a sudden rush") is converted into military purposefulness and mastery, as the men "hustle" and regain control of the traffic in supplies and personnel so crucial to conquest. Aided by the catalogue description, this film establishes the space of war preparation as one where the male body prevails over machines now harnessed to the purposeful pace and hustle of the military endeavor. Other films focusing on drills, such as *Trained Cavalry Horses* (Edison, 1898), reveal soldiers' similarly masterful command over "natural" forms of transport: in it, soldiers from Troop F 6th U.S. Cavalry are seen on horseback commanding their horses to lie down and then quickly stand up again. Certainly the perspective that these films provide is a privileged one, for it gave contemporary civilians visual access to otherwise inaccessible military enclosures as the army prepared its troops for mobilization.

Given their emphasis on mastery and control over imperial traffic and their display of physical power and military hustle, these films seem to offer a counterdiscourse to the shock and surprise that film scholars link to the modes of looking and articulation of modernity in early cinema. Lynne Kirby has persuasively shown how preclassical films featuring modern technologies (including the cinema) feature male hysterics traumatized by the violent physical and visual shocks characteristic of the experience of new technologies of transportation, such as the railway, and the "cinema of attractions."[64] Kirby links preclassical spectatorship and modes of representation to an "undoing" of gendered identity that reduces men to traumatized hysterics and mobilizes fantasies of submission as well as pleasure in the machine-made thrill. She argues that the emergence and institutionalization of classical narration brought with it a reassertion of gendered codes and a containment of the visual assaults associated with the early cinema. Yet I would suggest that Edison's war actualities offer an earlier, anti-hysterical mode of representation and spectatorship. If preclassical fictional films offer images of machine-made hysterics and fantasies of assault and shock—if only to generate a stimulus shield for the beleaguered modern subject—war actualities seem to offer up images of an ideal machine-made military masculinity already immune to the pathologies of modern life. At the same time that urban technological modernity created the condition of existence for hysterical, traumatized masculinity, the (highly mythologized) space of imperial warfare emerged as the territory on which American masculinity could thrive by reasserting authority and control over transportation and communication technologies, industry, and the racial/ethnic other. Moreover, by placing the spectator in a position of "fascinated inspection," these actualities invested viewers with an imaginary power simultaneously to scrutinize and delight in the image of a type of masculinity that had mastered technological modernity.

The film *9th Infantry Boys Morning Wash* (Edison, 1898) offers a striking example of the kinds of visual pleasure and fantasies of physical power and mastery promoted by war actualities. This film displays a rejuvenated male body (no sign of neurasthenia here) that popular discourse identified as both the cause and the effect of empire. The catalogue asks exhibitors and audiences to "imagine forty or fifty soldier boys each with a pail of water on the ground before him, sousing and spattering and scrubbing away for dear life. Soap and towels too. Every man jack of them looks as if he were enjoying the wash immensely, and also the novelty of having his picture taken. The big fellow in the center of the picture is laughing heartily. All the figures are clearly outlined, and the whole group is true to life."[65] Here soldiers collude with the camera to display the male body immersed in an idealized homosocial space at the perimeter of the nation, insulated from the overcivilizing effects of domestic culture and the enervating effects of big-city life. Although the promise of "clearly outlined" figures is a common feature of such catalogues, here it is significant—for by making highly visible the details of these strapping, soapy, laughing bodies, the camera allowed audiences to see, examine, and inspect them in detail. Here the turn-of-the-century "cult of the body" charges imperial ideology with pleasure by making available life-sized moving images of the militarized male body in a state of partial undress. Moreover, the catalogue's attention to "the big fellow in the center of the picture" who is "laughing heartily" promotes, in a sense, the ontological pleasure—even joy—of embodying a type of masculinity based on physical discipline, power, and mobility. Indeed, jingoes promoted the war, in part, as an opportunity to develop and display a type of masculinity that would be perceived by the nation and the rest of the world as a general sign of the broader strength, health, and progress of the United States.[66] The cinema participated in this process by capturing and exhibiting the spectacle of the powerful militarized male body in motion.

Catalogue descriptions for these films reveal the degree to which the production of this cinematic body relied on a military *mise-en-scène*. The description for the film *Battery B Arriving at Camp* (Edison, 1898), for example, focuses attention on the material world of the military camp:

"When Battery B of the 4th US Artillery came to Tampa, Fla. it meant business and the picture shows it. One by one the big artillery men pass by in front and reappear in the background, dismounting, unloosing saddle girths and bridles and leading away their mounts. Limbers, gun carriages and caissons in the distance. The sweating horses and the vigorous switching of tails tell a mute story of hot weather and fly time."[67] This description evidences a fascination with the soldier's body undertaking any task at all within a military *mise-en-scène*. Surrounded by horses, gun carriages, and caissons, every movement and gesture down to the smallest detail of loosening a bridle is observed and incorporated into the purposefulness of military "business" and the broader project of expansion. The rather banal activities represented here certainly fall short of the romantic tales of imperial adventure found in yellow journalism and the historical novel circulating through popular culture at this time.[68] Yet the very *absence* of anything other than the more mundane activities of military preparation allows the camera to focus and linger over the image of native white masculinity as it made itself into a new embodiment of national identity and imperial mobility.

Such focus on the details of the material *mise-en-scène* and bodily rhetoric of soldiering suggests that rather than simply document war activities, these actualities participated in the active discursive construction of a martial masculine ideal. Indeed, *mise-en-scène* and a focus on everyday routine is as important to the militarization of the white male body as it is to the eroticization of the female body in the protocinematic motion studies and early films. Linda Williams has shown how, in Eadweard Muybridge's motion studies, female subjects are surrounded by decorative objects—cigarettes, transparent veils, vases, bed linens—that create incipient narrative diegeses that aestheticize and fetishize their bodies. Here, surplus *mise-en-scène* has the effect of implanting the female form with sexuality, which in turn appears to be the "truth" of femininity.[69] Similarly, Constance Balides has persuasively shown how early films use quotidian objects and activities—trying on shoes in *The Gay Shoe Clerk* (Edison, 1903), hanging laundry in *A Windy Day on the Roof* (AM&B, 1904), and walking down the street in *What Happened on Twenty-Third Street, New York City* (Edison, 1901)—to stage exposures of the female body that normalize the eroticization of women's bodies in everyday life.[70] At the same time that

Williams and Balides note that a particular deployment of setting, looks, and fictional *mise-en-scène* is fundamental to the eroticization of femininity, they also note an absence of superfluous gestures and props in presentations of the male body. Thus Williams observes that in Muybridge's motion studies "naked and semi-naked men, for example walk, run, jump, throw, catch, box, wrestle, and perform simple trades such as carpentry," and that when the male movements require props, "these props are always simple, such as a saw and some wood for carpentry."[71] In turn, Balides notes, for example, that in *Al Treloar in Muscle Exercises* (AM&B 1905), the body builder Treloar wears trunks and appears on a stage decorated only by a stand with cards that indicate the type of exercise on display, giving the mise-en-scène a didactic rather than erotic function.[72] Yet if in such films and motion studies "men's naked bodies appear natural in action: they act and do,"[73] it is only thanks to the amount of discursive and cultural labor that went into naturalizing ostensibly "male" activities precisely at a time when other activities—brain work, office work, novel reading, tea sipping—were being identified by specialists as unnatural and effeminizing. Indeed, films featuring Al Treloar and Eugene Sandow were part of the broader promotion by "specialists" of the strenuous life as essential to the cultivation of "healthy" American masculinity, as were the activities of boxing, running, jumping, and wrestling executed by the university athletes that Muybridge employed as models of normative male movement. I would argue, then, that the selection and display of the bodily rhetoric of specific activities (running, wrestling, jumping, boxing, sawing wood, bodybuilding) in "functional" settings in proto and early cinematic images was an integral part of the turn-of-the-century production and naturalization of a "strenuous" masculinity that was meant to be perceived as the opposite or antithesis of (an equally manufactured) static, fetishized femininity.

Thus in war actualities and their catalogue descriptions acute attention is paid to the details of bodily rhetoric and costume so necessary to the discursive construction of a martial ideal linked to the hyperkinetic mobility of imperial traffic. Films documenting the arrival of the 10th U.S. Infantry are instructive in this sense. The films themselves simply display the disembarkation process of the troops upon their arrival by train; however, the description for the film *10th US Infantry Disembarking from Cars* (Edison,

FIGURE 7 *10th US Infantry Disembarking from Cars* (Edison, 1898). COURTESY OF THE
LIBRARY OF CONGRESS MOTION PICTURE READING ROOM

1898) promises "a stirring scene; full of martial energy. No ordinary dress
parade this, but a picture full of soldiers—men with a high purpose. They
march up the platform in fours, and left wheel just in front of the camera, passing out of sight in a cloud of dust. The customary small boy is
in evidence in great numbers, while the rear guard, the train pulls out of
the station. Literally 'out of sight.'"[74] The catalogue describes a similar
film, *10th US Infantry, 2nd Battalion, Leaving Cars* (Edison, 1898), with a
"Hurrah—here they come! Hot, dusty, grim and determined! Real soldiers,
every inch of them! No gold lace and chalked belts and shoulder straps,
but fully equipped in full marching order: blankets, guns, knapsacks, canteens. Trains in the background."[75] Both of these descriptions contrast the
bodies onscreen with the ornamented body of symbolic military display
that might signify precisely the "Old World" decadence and effeminacy
that had increasingly been linked to Spain.[76] Thus *10th US Infantry, 2nd
Battalion, Leaving Cars* focuses attention on the accoutrements of imperial
conquest ("blankets, guns, knapsacks, canteens") as the props needed to
charge with power the militarized body in motion. This list again seems
to promote and support a disciplinary gaze, one that inspects and peruses
the bodies for guns, knapsacks, and canteens even as such a sight is offered

up to audiences for the first time. Yet it also suggests the importance of the material *mise-en-scène* of the imperial adventure to the construction of martial masculinity and its inseparability from a landscape animated by interconnected systems of high- and low-tech traffic. Settings featuring either dusty landscapes filled with horses, trains, military equipment, and uniformed bodies, or seascapes dotted with battleships increasingly appear as the condition of existence for this idealized form of masculinity. Both films endow the spectator with a privileged look at an exceptional form of American masculinity propelled by "martial energy" and "high purpose" through an emergent network of imperial traffic that already extends far beyond the edges of the frame, "literally out of sight."

The importance of setting and the emphasis on vitality and purposeful activity in the films shot at the military camp in Tampa is somewhat surprising in light of the broader representation of the preparations for the Cuban campaigns reported in newspapers. Most historians agree that the period of preparation intervening between the declaration of war on Spain by the United States on April 25, 1898, and the landing of the first troops in Cuba on June 22, 1898, was extremely disorganized, even chaotic. Regular troops and volunteers along with supplies, equipment, arms, and provisions needed to be gathered and transported from various locations across the country to Florida, where the troops were encamped. Then, all of these had to be reorganized and transported to Cuba. Major General William Shafter was responsible for these preparations, and he was fairly ill suited to the task of managing the complex logistics of organizing for war: a corpulent and apparently unhealthy man, he seemed to suffer increasingly from nervous exhaustion and physical collapse as the campaign progressed. The task of trafficking volunteers, supplies, and weapons by railway proved overwhelming as cars transporting supplies and weapons were separated from cars carrying troops, while other cars simply went astray.[77] The journalist Richard Harding Davis dubbed this period of waiting as "the rocking-chair period"—a phrase that did little to bolster the sense of transformation in American masculinity and national character that the prospect of war seemed to promise. Indeed, the term "rocking-chair period" connoted a repetitive, static movement and the confinements of domesticity and femininity—precisely the formations that men seeking the "strenuous life" sought to escape. To reinscribe this phase of the

FIGURE 8 *Major General Shafter* (Edison, 1898). COURTESY OF THE LIBRARY OF CONGRESS MOTION PICTURE READING ROOM

war back into narratives of national progress and imperial purpose, the disorderly standstill created by the complexities of military mobilization needed to be recuperated into scenarios that displayed a purposeful male body, eagerly moving toward the frontiers of the new empire. The Edison Manufacturing Co.'s war actualities participated in this process by joining the tendency of the media to place blame upon the lumbering figure of General Shafter, whose appearance contrasted sharply with the image of brawny physicality and energetic hustle that had been linked to the circulation of imperial traffic.[78] The description for the war actuality *Major General Shafter* (Edison, 1898)—a film that shows him riding slowly past the camera on horseback—describes the general as wearing "a white helmet, a broad expanse of shirt bosom and a general air of avoirdupois," thereby defining him as a conspicuously anomalous figure in the bustling military setting.[79] More generally, though, the brevity and the selective framings of the camp views extract images of soldiers and supplies from the surrounding context of massive disorganization and protracted periods of tedious waiting in a way that restores order and progress to the "rocking-chair period." In turn, the documentary status of these actualities, coupled with what can be called an impulse to show that "this is being done," gives these films a compelling evidentiary status that may well have challenged journalistic accounts of disorder and low morale among the troops. In this respect, the early cinema acted as a crucial cog in an imperial war machine that labored in part to convert the logistical nightmare and high-tech spectacle of breakdown, confusion, and delay into images that displayed the restless energy of the militarized male body and the coordinated movements of imperial traffic. Hence, just as the disciplinary gaze of the camera undertook a fascinated inspection of ideal military masculinity, it also sought out and subjected to scrutiny masculine types who apparently fell short of this ideal and were deemed in need of further discipline and training. To be sure, the body in motion displayed in these films is a racialized body, an idealized version of native *white* masculinity. The rest of the description for the *10th US Infantry, 2nd Battalion, Leaving Cars* makes it clear that the idealization of native white masculinity depended upon the production of a range of racialized male bodies that might be compared, contrasted, and ranked in relation to one another. Thus these films create what Mark Cooper and, elsewhere, Richard Dyer have respectively referred to as a visual differential system of racialized and gendered bodies, without which an idealized whiteness cannot exist.[80] As the catalogue goes on to describe: "Crowds of curious bystanders, comical looking 'nigger dude' with sun umbrella strolls languidly in the foreground and you can almost hear that yaller dog bark. Small boys in abundance. The column marches in fours and passes through the front of the picture. More small boys of all colors. The picture is excellent and full of vigorous life."[81] This description seems to suggest that the visibility of the 10th Infantry's "vigorous life" required the presence of the "comical looking" African American "dude" marked out as precisely the kind of ornamented, overcivilized masculinity that the catalogue argues the 10th Infantry do not themselves embody. In this film, the particular attraction of the African American dude's racial difference derives from the way in which his body is made to contrast with the "martial energy" and "high purpose" of the 10th Cavalry. While they march, he strolls languidly. While the accoutrements of imperial masculinity—canteens, guns, knapsacks—are disavowed as decoration and made to signify the strenuous life of imperial conquest, his sun umbrella is made to signify a sharply contrasting ornamentation and delicate effeminacy. Indeed, the catalogue positions

FIGURE 9 *10th US Infantry, 2nd Battalion, Leaving Cars* (Edison, 1898). COURTESY OF
THE LIBRARY OF CONGRESS MOTION PICTURE READING ROOM

the African American as a diegetic spectator of the newly embodied masculine ideal and makes an attraction of his failure to be incorporated into
this spectacle of national-imperial unity. Moreover, the language used to
describe this figure was part of a racist pro-imperial discourse that sought
to consolidate definitions of the new empire around a newly unified whiteness that smoothed over the sectional and economic differences between
whites while exacerbating racial divisions between whites and blacks. According to Hoganson, the "dude" was a "stereotypically effeminate wealthy
man, usually from the Northeast" who was often depicted as a symbol "of
the corrupting power of money" and the tendency to privilege class comfort over national honor.[82] Highly publicized participation in the Cuban
campaign allowed many upper-class white men to refashion their "dude"
image by demonstrating their courage and patriotism on the warfront and
thus their right to claim a share in the political legitimacy attached to war
veterans. For example, the well-publicized exploits of Roosevelt's Rough
Riders in the Battle of San Juan Hill gave New Jersey's Republican senator

William Sewell the opportunity to affirm the dude's right to political and social power: "The darling of the parlor, the athlete at Yale, Harvard, or Princeton are lined up today on the picket line before Santiago with the farmer and the mechanic, each equal, each claiming no more right as an American citizen, and each anxious and eager for the fray. It is the most sublime spectacle, I say to the Senate of the United States, that ever has been witnessed that our very best blood, our brightest young men claim the right of citizenship to the extent that they go to the front line of battle and die with anybody and everybody, no matter from what rank of society."[83]

Such sentiments represented a broader tendency in American culture to regard the war with Spain as an opportunity not just to reunite white men of the upper classes with white men of the lower classes but also to unite the "Blue" with the "Grey" and the city dweller with the farmer in common effort under the same flag.[84] Hence war actualities such as *Roosevelt's Rough Riders* (AM&B, 1898), which shows "a charge full of cowboy enthusiasm by Troop I, the famous regiment" directly toward the camera,[85] participated in a broader mass-mediated process that transformed troops such as the Rough Riders into "walking advertisements" for what Bederman calls "a collective imperial manhood for the white American race."[86] Thus it is quite important that the catalogue description for this film marks out — even manufactures — the racial and class difference of the "African American dude," for in doing so it reveals the discursive strategies used to position black Americans outside new imperial constructions of the nation.

While mustering in was promoted as a magical process that erased perceivable class, ethnic, and regional differences between white Americans, the resulting spectacle of this newly unified martial ideal intensified racial and class differences between black Americans and whites.[87] The incorporation of black regulars and volunteers into the campaign was based in part on the assumptions of scientific racism, which reasoned that African Americans would make up a contingent of "immune troops" whose genetic constitution would act as a prophylactic against tropical diseases. These troops were forced to fight under white officers and were subject to segregation, Jim Crow laws, and racial violence once they reached camp in the South. Significantly, the question over black participation in the Spanish-American and Philippine-American wars was a matter of debate in the

FIGURE 10 *Roosevelt's Rough Riders* (AM&B, 1898). COURTESY OF THE LIBRARY OF
CONGRESS MOTION PICTURE READING ROOM

black community. According to the historian Willard B. Gatewood, some
quarters of the black community argued that participation in American
imperialism would demonstrate the undeniable patriotism of black men
and would legitimate the claims to the full and equal citizenship that they
had been violently denied in the post-Reconstruction era. Others argued
that the acquisition of colonies would provide black Americans a new context in which to pursue opportunities for prosperity denied to them in the
continental United States, for countries like Cuba were perceived as being
relatively free of the American racism that proved to be a major obstacle to
blacks. Yet soon after the wars had ended, many African Americans noted
that the occupying forces had very quickly imposed Jim Crow–styled segregation in the colonies. Meanwhile, from the beginning, anti-imperialists
in black communities pointed out the hypocrisy of white pro-imperial discourse that described intervention by the United States in Spanish colonies
as a rescue mission, for the same federal government turned a blind eye to
state-endorsed racial violence and the denial of black civil rights. Some
of those black soldiers who considered staying in the colonies soon real-

FIGURE II *Colored Troops Disembarking* (Edison, 1898). COURTESY OF THE LIBRARY OF CONGRESS MOTION PICTURE READING ROOM

ized that Cubans and Filipinos regarded them as no different from white Americans and thus simply as agents of U.S. imperialism.[88]

Another Edison actuality reveals the processes through which cinematic discourse might have participated in the positioning of African Americans outside the newly forged national-imperial identity by manufacturing interpretive frameworks that define the black soldier as in need of further discipline. *Colored Troops Disembarking* (Edison, 1898) shows the 2nd Battalion of the 24th Colored Infantry disembarking from a transport in a manner that is no different from those scenes featuring whites: it simply projects an image of soldiers, outfitted in the accoutrements of military life, arriving in Cuba, and thus it appears to inscribe the 2nd Battalion of the 24th into the circuits of overseas American imperialism. Yet the catalogue encourages exhibitors and audiences to perceive the black body as one that is comically at odds with the martial energy and serious "high purpose" embodied by, for example, the white 10th U.S. Cavalry: "The steamer 'Mascotte' has reached her dock at Port Tampa, and the 2nd Battalion of colored infantry is going ashore. Tide is very high, and the gangplank is extra steep;

and it is laughable to see the extreme caution displayed by the soldiers clambering down. The commanding officer struts on the wharf, urging them to hurry. Two boat stewards in glistening white duck coats are interested watchers—looking for tips perhaps. The picture is full of fine light and shadow effects."[89] The catalogue description acts as an early example of what Daniel Bernardi calls "the voice of whiteness," an intervention that encourages exhibitors and audiences to perceive this film as a contrast between black and white.[90] Unlike descriptions that define white soldiers in terms of orderly purposefulness and hyperkinetic motion, this description defines the black body in motion as a comic spectacle—as overly cautious, timid, and unable to circulate rapidly within imperial traffic. In turn, the catalogue's interpretation of the image of the white officer who, we are told, urges the 24th to "hurry," suggests that the black troops are out of synch with the accelerated pace of the new imperialism. In contrast to the bodies appearing in *10th US Infantry, 2nd Battalion*, whose movements, the catalogue suggests, demonstrate that they "meant business" and thereby provoke hurrahs, the bodies on display in *Colored Troops Disembarking* are transformed into a type of minstrel masculinity meant to provoke laughter. However, the provocation of such responses would have depended largely upon the lecturer's accompaniment to the program, which might eschew the overt racism of catalogue descriptions. Indeed, some catalogue descriptions participated in the promotion of the African American involvement in the war effort as evidence of the need for granting equal rights and full citizenship to black Americans. For example, the F. M. Prescott catalogue provided the following description for *Colored Invincibles* (1898): "Here is a famous colored troop, the so-called immunes, who went away to fight with as much zeal as their white brothers. The boys look well, and from appearances stood the strain in splendid form. This is one of the scenes where the colored man is accepted as a brother in arms, for his work in the field was equal, if not superior at times, to his white companions.' A very fine picture."[91] Hence, the war actuality participated not only in the broader discursive construction of a range of masculinities coming out of the war but also entered into the debates taking place around the question of the extent to which incorporation into imperial traffic might refurbish the image of a particular group. When individual films, catalogue descriptions, and lecturer's accompaniments inscribed African Americans as either spectators in the text or as military subjects in need of further discipline, they participated in the broader discursive and political marginalization of blacks from the newly forged conceptions of national unity coming out of the war and helped consolidate a dominant whiteness at the expense of newly colonized and African American populations. In such instances, the war actuality worked in tandem with a range of late-nineteenth-century visual forms—chronophotography, the museum exhibit, world's fairs and exhibitions, zoos, travelogues, and early ethnographic films—to classify difference according to what Fatimah Rony calls "the narrative of evolution which slots humans into a hierarchy of color-coded categories and places the white race at the apex."[92] However, when they championed black participation in the war, the actualities provided evidence against the racist politics of Jim Crow and even the segregationist policies of the military.

To conclude, I will return to Captain Philip's regret over the loss of the postbattle photograph of his crew, which seems to stem in part from the ensuing loss of the audience that would have accompanied this image's mass-mediated display. Philip's desire for spectators was more than fulfilled by the audiences—made up of both women and men—that in 1898 packed the Eden Musée and vaudeville houses to see war pictures.[93] Charles Musser notes that soldiers returning from the war front flocked to the Eden Musée to see the war films.[94] A newspaper announced that "the Eden Musée is becoming a headquarters for the soldiers in this city. Since they returned scarcely a day passes that at least 500 do not visit the Musée. The majority of the Rough Riders have been there. They praise the war groups and take the greatest interest in the war pictures. The pictures taken in and about Santiago are cheered, and often have to be shown again. The other visitors take almost as much interest in the soldiers as in the attractions at the Musée."[95]

And while the latter might present an early example of the narcissistic identification that feminist scholars link to the masculinized spectatorship of the cinema's classical era, one suspects that these soldiers found added pleasure in watching female audiences consume and cheer life-size moving images of themselves and their comrades. The cultivation of a female audience at war programs was part of a broader process also at work in the historical novel and popular press, which, as Kaplan argues, "sought to enlist women in the traditional male realm of what Edward Said has called

FIGURE 12 *Cuban Refugees Waiting for Rations* (Edison, 1898). COURTESY OF THE
LIBRARY OF CONGRESS MOTION PICTURE READING ROOM

the pleasures of imperialism."[96] Part of this pleasure, Kaplan notes, derived
from the inscription of women into fantasies of chivalric rescue and protection so characteristic of imperial culture.[97] The film *Cuban Refugees Waiting
for Rations* (Edison, 1898) suggests how the presence of native white female
spectators in war films and at moving picture programs contributed to the
broader cultural inscription of overseas imperialism by the United States as
a benevolent rescue mission. The catalogue description for the film states
the following: "A group of escaped reconcentrados, saved from the fate
of starvation imposed by the Butcher, Weyler. They stand in line waiting,
each man with his tin dish and cup. One expects to see just such men as
these, after the centuries of Spanish oppression and tyranny. As they come
forward, their walk, even, is listless and lifeless. The picture affords an exceedingly interesting racial character study. At one side stands a group of
officers from the camp near by, accompanying several ladies who are seeing
the sights."[98]

The apparent chivalry of the officers "accompanying several ladies seeing the sights" on the one hand, and the rather ethnographically oriented

spectacle of the Cuban refugees receiving relief from Spanish tyranny on the other, have the effect of promoting a perception of the military camp as a space that is outside the spheres of colonial oppression. Put differently, the film and its catalogue description encourage audiences to perceive U.S. imperialism as the antithesis of Spain's brutal colonial regime rather than as a mere replacement of it. The exchange of looks and distribution of bodies in this film reveal once again how the discursive production of a native white masculine ideal depended upon the production of a range of differently gendered and racialized bodies. The presence of native white "ladies" confers chivalry on their military chaperones. In turn, the protective glances of both the officers and the ladies "seeing the sights" combined with the catalogue description marks the ostensibly "listless and lifeless" Cubans as in need of protection and further intervention, discipline, reform, and rejuvenation by the United States. In enclosing and protecting its new and not-so-new dependents, the military camp emerges in this film as a space capable of producing virile native white masculinity as a bastion of benevolent racial and patriarchal protection. Women who saw this film would have seen projected before them the positions to be occupied by native white women in the new empire. While this film inscribes women as spectators in awe of imperial masculinity, it also glimpses their coming function in imperial discourse: as I show in the next chapter, the participation of women in the war as Red Cross nurses would be crucial to the emerging discursive constructions of the war as a mission for the relief of trauma and suffering in the (former) Spanish colonies.

Missing from this particular picture are the forces of resistance to U.S. imperialism, such as the American anti-imperialists who protested expansion and the colonial subjects who resisted U.S. imperialism in the new colonies. While the former were disparaged in the new imperial culture in gendered terms, the latter were deemed savage, ungrateful, and in need of civilization.[99] The moving pictures participated in the rearticulation of gender, race, nation, and empire at the end of the nineteenth century as they displayed life-sized moving images of physically developed bodies and powerful machines working efficiently to extend the nation's political and commercial power around the globe. These films offered a vision of unity and order that allowed white, middle-class audiences to indulge in fantasies of power, mastery, and control over the conditions of technological modernity and over the populations (women, African Americans, and "native" colonials) who were increasingly defined by dominant white culture as "problems" in the century to come. Such fantasies relied on the kinds of looking provided by these films, the spectacles they display, and the catalogue descriptions that accompanied them and provided an interpretive framework for them. In 1898, imperial ideology intersected with moving picture technology to make maximally visible the new figure through which American masculinity and national identity were to be imagined as the United States expanded the global circulation of its military and commercial traffic through the establishment of an overseas empire.

This martial ideal based on technological superiority, military efficiency, limitless mobility, and a powerful masculinity immune to the violent shocks of warfare was, of course, highly mythological. The soldiers who went off to fight on the new frontier and the moving picture cameramen who accompanied them were indeed limited in their capacities for mobility and for enduring the hardships of warfare; moreover, they were often limited by the technologies they used to conquer, visually and militarily, the new overseas frontier. Like Major General William Shafter, the cameraman William Paley failed to embody the new martial spirit: he was a corpulent man who suffered greatly in the extreme conditions of heat, rain, and disease experienced in Cuba during the conflict. Moreover, his camera and equipment were heavy, bulky, and difficult to move along the muddy, rain-soaked and often impassable campaign trail: whereas the camera seemed to penetrate the military camps with ease during the long period of preparations, once on the front the early cinema's "virtual mobile gaze" met with insurmountable material obstacles. As a result Paley, stricken with a serious and mysterious fever, had to return to the United States without having captured any moving pictures of battle. The technological limitations of the cinema were joined by the technological limitations experienced by U.S. soldiers who, armed with outdated Springfield rifles and black gunpowder, proved to be perilously visible to the Spanish troops who fought with modern Krag-Jorgensens and enjoyed the invisibility given to them by smokeless gunpowder. In turn, as troops began to return from the front, reports of the army's wide-scale and at times catastrophic disorganization began to feature more prominently in the press. While battleships and sailors appeared to return home in "ship shape," soldiers returning from Cuba appeared neither virile nor invigorated but rather debilitated and alarmingly emaciated; for the massive and rapid expansion of the army left it unable adequately to feed and provide medical care for its own men. Biograph's *71st Regiment, Camp Wikoff* (AM&B, 1898) shows returned soldiers, quarantined at Camp Wikoff on Montauk Point, Long Island, marching in formation. The catalogue description explains that "of the thousand and more men who left New York for the Cuban campaign, scarcely three hundred were able to shoulder their rifles to march before the Biograph camera at Camp Wikoff. The picture shows many of the companies reduced to seven or eight men, and the whole regiment, rank and file, is in sad condition."[100]

At the same time that the United States seemed to bear greater responsibility than Spain for the traumatization of its own troops, it began a campaign of violent military suppression against Emilio Aguinaldo and the same Filipino freedom fighters that had acted as U.S. allies in the war against Spain. The effort to acquire a new overseas empire, and the attempt to represent that effort cinematically, helped to reveal the possibilities and pleasures of American modernity as well as its limitations, paradoxes, and perils. A cinematic counterpart to the war actuality that flourished after the war — the battle reenactment film — gives even greater insight into the early cinema's propensity for enabling audiences to see and perceive American modernity and to be incorporated into the newly established network of imperial traffic; it is to this peculiar genre that I turn in the following chapter.

2

PLACING AUDIENCES ON
THE SCENE OF HISTORY

Modern Warfare and the Battle Reenactment
at the Turn of the Century

In January 1900, after the celebrations of the victory over
Spain by the United States had waned and the Philippine-
American War and the Boer War were escalating, an article
in *Leslie's Weekly* entitled "Pictures That Will Be Historic"
announced that "the American Biograph is taking a prominent part in the two wars which are now occupying the center of the world's stage . . . We are promised some vivid,
soul-stirring pictures of actual, grewsome war, and the conditions under which the Biograph operators in the Transvaal
and the Philippines are working are so favorable that the
promise will probably be made good."[1] The much-hoped-
for fulfillment of the cinema's promise to provide a technologically mediated view that visually placed the audience on
the imperial battlefield echoed speculations about the same
promise made by photography in the middle of the nineteenth century. Writing on the eve of the Crimean War and
the U.S. Civil War, Oliver Wendell Holmes predicted that
"the next European War will send us stereographs of battles.
It is asserted that a bursting shell can be photographed. The

time is perhaps at hand when a flash of light as sudden and brief as that of lightning which shows a whirling wheel standing stock still, shall preserve the very instant of the shock of contact of the mighty armies that are even now gathering. The lightning from heaven does actually photograph objects on the bodies of those it has just blasted—so we are told by many witnesses. The lightning of clashing sabres and bayonets may be forced to stereotype itself in a stillness as complete as the tumbling tide of Niagara as we see it self-pictured."[2]

At both of these cultural-political moments, new technologies of visual representation promised to transform the shock of modern warfare into consumable spectacles available for mass consumption by civilian spectators eager to *see* history. Holmes's anticipation of instantaneous photography by approximately thirty years allowed him to imagine an ideal form of image making analogous to a bolt of lightning and hence able to match the violence of modern mechanized warfare. He describes a form of photography powerful enough to arrest an otherwise unstoppable motion at the point of irreversibility—the spinning of a wheel, a waterfall, a bursting shell, or clashing armies—and thereby make the historically significant moment of military shock visible while diminishing its capacity to harm the observer. Half a century later, the author of the *Leslie's* article asks the reader to return to Holmes's era and to the Civil War and the Crimean and "imagine the historical value of a moving picture of the charge at Balaclava, or of the advance upon Gettysburg." Like Holmes, this author imagines future military history captured and rendered visible at its most dynamic and incendiary moment when charging armies reach the peak of their momentum and collide. Moreover, the technologies they discuss seem to shape their understanding of history—for in each case to "see history" is to see the "vivid" and the "grewsome," or the "moment of the shock of contact" between clashing forces. In short, technologies of vision promised to satisfy curiosity about (the gruesomeness of) modern warfare and a hence desire to participate visually in the *trauma* of history. Photography and film seemed to offer viewers the opportunity to savor what Alan Trachtenberg calls "that pleasurable fright from the safest of distances: that between one's eyes and a photograph,"[3] or between spectator and screen.

Holmes's expectations and the actual outcome of photographic enterprises during the Civil War in many ways parallel the expectations and outcome of cinema and of American imperial wars at the turn of the last century. As Trachtenberg notes, Holmes's prediction of the imminent photographic recording of military shock was belied by the actual output of Civil War photographs. The camera's technological limitations and long exposure times (from three to twenty seconds) excluded "actual battle" from the kinds of events and scenes that photography might record; hence Matthew Brady's photographers captured only war preparations and the aftermath of battles in images of damaged and dismembered bodies, ruins, and war-torn landscapes.[4] In turn, as Timothy Sweet notes, many of the latter were photographic reenactments of sorts: often the pictured scene was arranged or composed by the photographer to yield ideological meanings about the nature of the war, its inevitable outcome, and the future of the Union.[5] Like their counterparts during the Civil War, moving picture cameramen such as Biograph's Billy Bitzer (who landed with U.S. forces in Cuba) and W. K. L. Dickson (attached to British forces in South Africa), C. Fred Ackerman (who was attached to U.S. forces in the Philippines), and Edison's William Paley (who followed U.S. troops to Cuba only to have to depart because of illness), were frustrated by their attempts to record battles on film. The hypermodern condition of contemporary warfare—its unprecedented mechanization of violence and unpredictable, traumatizing shocks; its unstable visual fields; its surprise attacks and blinding smoke; its dispersal of charging, falling, and dismembered bodies across distant, tropical landscapes—made cinematic recordings of real battles difficult if not impossible. As the *Leslie's* article suggests, the same technology of vision that had produced a surplus of films of camp life and war preparations, new military technologies, victory parades, and military drills had also produced a paucity of "vivid, soul-stirring, pictures of actual, grewsome war." To represent this most modern scene cinematically, companies resorted to reenactments restaged after the fact, and on U.S. soil, by national guardsmen or hired actors.

Hence the battle reenactment film seems to have addressed twinned desires linked to the visual consumption of the nation's military-imperial history: the desire to follow the movements of armed forces, even in battle, and the attendant need to "manage" the inevitable trauma incurred by modern warfare. That such desires were paramount in American culture in the late nineteenth century and the early twentieth is not surprising, for

U.S. history had long been inscribed within ideologies of expansion that required the conquest of space by the military, by settlers, and by technologies such as the railway. And, as the previous chapter makes clear, by the end of the nineteenth century the soldier had become a rather celebrated icon of modern mobility within American culture. In turn, new technologies of war enabled the annihilation of space and time in profound new ways that were calculated to accelerate the momentum of clashing forces, thus making military "shock" an effect of new types of mobilization. Live and film battle reenactments addressed the spectatorial desire to be absorbed visually into paths of military traffic as it moved across distant frontiers and to view the "moment of the shock of contact" between clashing forces. In turn, the reiterative structure of the reenactment—its rehearsal and repetition of violent conflict—seems to have made it a powerful form for mastering the trauma of war. The fact that numerous live and filmed reenactments produced in the United States represented military subjects suggests that the very artificiality of the reenactment provided the pleasurable means of knowing and "seeing" military-imperial history that documentary actualities could not, thereby giving rise to an early film genre that continues to challenge any easy classification as fiction or nonfiction film. Hence the feature of the battle reenactment that I seek to address in this chapter is its imaginary circulation of audiences along with imperial traffic to distant frontiers through spectacularly rendered live performances and moving images that blurred the distinction between representation and the "historical" real and in the process annealed the shocks of warfare.

When discussing the generic liminality of early reenactment films, historians tend to agree that, as Richard Abel notes, "imposing the later distinction between documentary and fictional genres . . . is problematic in several respects." As Abel states in his history of early French film, prior to 1908 "the difference between recording a current public event as it was happening and reconstructing a past (or even present) historical event in a studio" was relatively insignificant. More important "was that a representation of the 'historical' differed from a representation of the 'purely fictive' or imaginary—which meant that referential differences mattered more than differences in modes of representation . . . In other words, the 'historical scene' was bound to the actualité within an unbroken continuum uniting historical past and present." This historical continuum allowed

French filmmakers such as Pathé and Méliès to "exploit the shared 'family resemblance' between historical reconstructions and actualités."[6] Miriam Hansen concurs by noting that "many actualities involved reconstructions . . . yet not necessarily with the intent to deceive; as a subgenre, dramatic reenactments of current events were considered legitimate. [While the] boundaries between documentary reality and *mise-en-scène* may have been relative, they seem to have mattered less than the kind of fascination which connects, for instance, the 'realistic imitation' of President McKinley's assassin in the electric chair in *The Execution of Czolgosz* (Porter/Edison 1901) with historical reenactments such as *The Execution of Mary Queen of Scots* (Edison 1895)—or the substitution trick in *Execution by Hanging* (Biograph 1905) with the authentic footage of *Electrocuting an Elephant* (Edison 1903)."[7] For Hansen, then, sensationalist appeal joined to a historical referent helped construct the reenactment's legitimacy in representing "actual" events.

Following on from Abel and Hansen, in this chapter I will turn to the question of *how* or upon what representational, epistemological, and aesthetic grounds the reenactment film achieved legitimacy for articulating the historical real in general and the battle in particular. For while we know that the reenactment film achieved legitimacy as historical discourse, we also know that audiences and reviewers were often able to recognize the (visible) formal and aesthetic differences, as well as the subject matter, that frequently distinguished the two. Though the relationship between the actuality film and the reenactment film tells us much about the reception of the reenactment as a legitimate historical discourse, the significant cultural and aesthetic relationship between the reenactment film and the live reenactment reveals even more. Importantly, the *live* reenactment prepared consumers of urban commercialized leisure for their encounter with film reenactments and, in the process, helped establish what we might call this early film genre's peculiar authenticity. Moreover, like battle reenactment films, live battle reenactments often mobilized audiences to scenes of expansion and spatial conquest while simultaneously addressing the trauma that inevitably resulted from the soldier's—and the spectator's—absorption into this violent form of imperial traffic. In order to demonstrate how it did so, I will analyze the live battle reenactments and military displays featured in Buffalo Bill's Wild West and the particular relations they constructed between "history" and its spectacular simulation, and between the "original" witness of an event and the secondary audience who delighted in its reenactment. After contrasting the mode of address and visual lure of the battle reenactment to that of P. T. Barnum's hoaxes and humbug, I will analyze how many battle reenactment films share the mode of address, spectatorship, and reality effects previously manufactured by the Wild West. Historical evidence suggests that by 1898 the culturally established form of the battle reenactment strongly informed turn-of-the-century notions of what modern warfare would look like to a "witness" on the battlefield. When turn-of-the-century commentators speculated about the appearance of the actuality films of battles, they described texts that featured the point of view, content, and formal features provided by reenactment films. Paradoxically, then, to seem most "real" the turn-of-the-century war actuality had to achieve the "reality effects" that had already been established by the (live and film) battle reenactment.[8]

The Peculiar Authenticity of the Live Reenactment

The reenactment was a prominent and profitable part of live urban commercialized leisure in U.S. culture since the 1880s. John F. Kasson notes that amusement seekers at Coney Island could see spectacular reenactments of famous disasters such as "The Fall of Pompeii" (which simulated the eruption of Mount Vesuvius), another that simulated the eruption of Mount Pelée, and still others that restaged the Johnstown flood of 1889 and the Galveston, Texas, flood of 1900.[9] The reenactment of military campaigns, however, were most popularly incarnated in William F. Cody's traveling entertainment enterprise—Buffalo Bill's Wild West. Between 1883 and 1913 the Wild West appeared before audiences in numerous cities in the United States and Europe, including New York, Atlanta, Manchester, London, Rome, Paris, and also at a number of world's fairs, including Chicago's 1893 World's Columbian Exposition (where it was located just beyond the official grounds) and Buffalo's 1901 Pan-American Exposition.[10] Wild West reenactments and military displays were often promoted as "object lessons" that demonstrated through visually compelling spectacles the higher ideals characteristic of a fast-receding, nostalgically rendered past. Cody's Wild West represented early stages of continental expansion by the United States through reenactments of Indian battles (including Custer's Last Stand), attacks on pioneer cabins, stagecoach ambushes, buffalo hunts, and catastrophes such as prairie fires, stampedes, and cyclones.[11] These high-tech reenactments synthesized the sensationalism of the dime novel (in which Cody made his first mass-cultural appearance)[12] and the popular stage melodrama with the myth of the frontier that had become so compelling for urban easterners mired in big-city life.[13] The resulting "Drama of Civilization" was produced by Steele McKaye, whose stage melodramas, Nicholas Vardac argues, represent the culmination of the theater's late-nineteenth-century drive toward a realist "pictorial ideal" later actualized in the moving pictures.[14] Played out against a backdrop of massive panoramas and cycloramas and accompanied by live music and a lecturer's narration (but virtually no dialogue), Wild West reenactments featured grand spectacles of the dynamic, violent action of frontiersmen, scouts, and cavalry as they circulated through hostile landscapes and subordinated "villainous" native populations to American "civilization."

Though Cody promoted his Wild West reenactments as factual, Richard Slotkin notes that "the Wild West wrote 'history' by conflating it with mythology. The reenactments were not recreations but reductions of complex events into 'typical scenes.' Cody's 'West' was a mythic space in which past and present, fiction and reality could co-exist; a space in which history, translated as myth, was reenacted as ritual."[15] In turn, the moral of the story rehearsed the American stage melodrama's characteristic conflict between "innocence" (civilization) persecuted by villainy (its savage foe), with the former ultimately defeating the latter. As Linda Williams notes, though the Wild West elaborated scenes of expansion and imperial conquest by the United States, it consistently represented the conquerors as victims whose suffering at the hands of Native Americans needed to be displayed and then avenged, over and over again, in racialized spectacles of power and dynamic action.[16] Cody's profitable articulation of national "history" via the conjoined modes of myth, realist spectacle, sensation, and melodrama was nevertheless championed as an example of progressive education about the nation's recent history of continental expansion.[17] Indeed, as Joy Kasson notes, the Wild West became a compelling force for translating Cody's personal memories into broadly embraced historical memories shared by audiences who participated in his reconstitution of the nation's past.[18]

Sold for ten cents before every show, the extensive program for the Wild West gives insight into the modes of address and forms of spectatorship around which Cody and his partner, Nate Salsbury, constructed their reenactments. The program was purchased by those attending the show as well as by those who could not afford to attend, and hence it was a form of mass cultural entertainment in its own right. It provided detailed discourse on the nature of continental expansion and overseas imperialism by the United States, narrative summaries of the reenacted events, brief biographies of Cody and the other featured "historical characters," as well as reprinted reviews of the Wild West and letters of support from military officials and historians who testified to the exhibition's authenticity. In this respect, the program provided a supplementary discourse that helped shore up the claims that the Wild West made about the historical authenticity of its reenactments. Hence, just as it detailed the historical contexts in which the reenacted events "originally" took place, the program also provided cues regarding the attraction-spectator relation on which the visual pleasure of the reenactment relied. The program even provided audiences with a (perhaps already familiar) vocabulary for thinking about the realism and sense of historical presence that the reenactment evoked, deploying terms such as "actual pictures," "living pictures," and "faithful pictures." As explained in the program text, for example: "Our aim is to make the public acquainted with the manners and customs of the daily life of the dwellers in the far West of the United States through the means of actual and realistic scenes from life. At each performance marked skill and daring are presented. Not only from the standpoint of the spectator, but also from a critical point of view, we assure the auditor that each scene presents a faithful picture of the habits of these folk, down to the smallest detail."[19]

In support of this claim of pictorial realism, Brick Pomeroy's review of the Wild West (reprinted in the program) declared that "as a lover of his country" Cody "wishes to present as many facts as possible to the public, so that those who will can see actual pictures of life in the West, brought to the East for the inspection and education of the public. Buffalo Bill has brought the Wild West to the doors of the East."[20] Over and over again the program promoted the reenactment as a visual form able to make available representative "pictures" of a society, culture, or nation that contain the "smallest detail" and have a capacity for circulation. Moreover, the program

FIGURE 13
Cover of *Buffalo
Bill's Wild West
Historical Sketches
and Programme*
(1896).

implied that the reiterative structure of the reenactment captured and pre-
served past events through ritualistic repetition that, unlike photography or
waxworks tableaux, functioned in a mode of presence rather than absence,
and through dynamic rather than suspended movement—both of which
intensified the impression of the past reanimated in the present as "*living*
pictures." Though not the "original," the reenactment professed to be a
form with a special ontological relationship to the original. By bringing
"the Wild West to the doors of the East," the reenactment provided late-
nineteenth-century amusement seekers a credible solution for overcoming
the "aura" of the wild West without destroying it entirely.[21]

The emphasis on framing and circulating "actual and realistic scenes from
life" links Wild West reenactments to a broader scopic regime characteristic of late-nineteenth-century European and Anglo-American imperial
culture in which, Timothy Mitchell argues, can be found the tendency

to render up "the world-as-exhibition." Along with panorama paintings, landscape pictures, wax museums, and "life group" museum displays, and ethnographic exhibitions found on midways at world's fairs and expositions, the Wild West encouraged audiences to perceive "the world as a picture set up before a subject."[22] Mitchell links this latter tendency "to the unusual conception of the world as an enframed totality, something that forms a structure or a system" organized "to evoke some larger meaning, such as History or Empire or Progress."[23] Wild West reenactments evoked History, Empire, and Progress as its "Drama of Civilization" pictured a spectacular history of American continental conquest and expansion, updated in 1899 to dramatize the Battle of San Juan Hill from the Spanish-American War.

To bolster the realism of its reenactments, the program for the Wild West suggested that the (original) wild West often appeared before the frontiersman "as a picture set up before a subject." Hence, the Wild West program insisted that life on the frontier was characterized by participation in—and the visual consumption of—live spectacles of dynamic action, violent conflict, and astonishing displays of power. Put differently, the program included awed *spectatorship* as a component of life on the frontier and the battlefield. Pomeroy's reprinted review of the Wild West suggests that Cody fulfilled his promise to "illustrate life as it is *witnessed* on the plains." He continued by stating: "Could a man now living have stood on the shore of the Red Sea and witnessed the passage of the children of Israel and the Struggle of Pharaoh and his hosts, what a sight he would have seen, and how interested would be those to whom he related the story. Could the man who stood on the shore to see Washington and his soldiers cross the Delaware have lived till now to tell the story, what crowds he would have to listen. How interesting would be the story of a man, if he were now living, who had witnessed the landing of Columbus on the shores of the New World, or the story of one of the hardy English Puritans who took passage on the 'Mayflower,' and landed on the rock-bound coast of New England. So, too, the angel who has seen the far West become tame and dotted under the advancing civilization as the pioneers fought their way westward into desert and jungle. What a story he can relate as to the making of that history and what a history America has, to be sure!"[24]

As an "angel who has seen the far West become tame," Cody occupies the ideal and unique position of one who was simultaneously and somewhat paradoxically a part of the spectacle he witnessed. The claim that the reenactment's spectacular simulation of an equally spectacular real had been tailored around Cody's privileged point of view loaned support to the reenactment's claim to historical authenticity. As Pomeroy's review explained: "Since the railroad gave its aid to pioneering, America is making history faster than any other country in the world. *Her pioneers are fast passing away.* A few years more and the great struggle for possession will be ended and generations will settle down to enjoy the homes their fathers located and fenced in for them. Then will come the picture maker—he who with pen, pencil, and panel can tell the story as he understands it. The millions will read and look at what the pioneer did and what the historian related, wishing on the whole that they could have been there to have seen the original. These are some of the thoughts that crowd in upon us as we view the great living picture that the Hon. Wm. F. Cody ('Buffalo Bill') gives us at the Wild West Exhibition, which every man, woman and child the world over should see and study as realistic fact."[25]

According to Pomeroy, the urge to see the "original" frontier was an effect of industrialization: the railway had accelerated the pace of history itself and annihilated the past with the same rapidity that it annihilated space. The Wild West reanimated an image of pretechnological movement across the frontier and to ritualize forms of motion and transport displaced by new technologies. Yet the Wild West does not simply represent these protomodern forms of frontier traffic as do books and pictures. Pomeroy contends that literary and painterly representations of the West only intensify the desire to see a no-longer-available "original" wild West visible to, observed, and known only by those pioneers who began "the great struggle for possession." The gap left between the pioneer and the picture maker, the "original"/historical real and its inadequate representation in literature, written history, and painting is filled by Cody's historical reenactments. Here, the reenactment claims to achieve the status of a "great living picture" appearing as "realistic fact" precisely by reproducing the point of observation from which this unfolding history—taking the shape of dynamic movement across space—was "originally" seen. The power and the pleasure of the Wild West's live reenactments were predicated on the splitting of Cody's own status as the "agent/witness" of history: to reenact spectacular history, he repeated the (violent, dynamic) actions of the historical agent of continental conquest; however, he passed along the (pleasurable) function of the witness-spectator to the audience.

By first establishing the presence of a spectator as an integral part of the original historical event, Cody made such a position available and seemingly authentic when the event was reenacted before a paying audience. Put differently, by placing an "original" spectator on the "scene" of history and then replicating such a position for spectators at its simulation, the Wild West made the reenactment highly pleasurable and in the process supported its claims of authenticity. Yet central to the pleasure of Cody's live reenactments was the trauma, violence, and shock of the historical scenes they repeated. On one hand, the Wild West insisted that the process of westward expansion it reenacted took place in an extremely harsh context characterized by violent conflict and circulation across the vast spaces of the frontier, and it was therefore *by definition* beyond the scope of any "audience" other than the exceptional pioneer. On the other hand, it insisted that the process of moving through the protomodern paths of frontier traffic was so central to American history and identity that it demanded a national—even international—audience. Hence, the particular visual pleasure and peculiar authenticity of Wild West reenactments seems to have derived from their power to endow audiences with an imaginary presence—or presence by visual proxy—at significant and highly sensational moments and movements in history that by definition precluded their attendance. It was precisely the "proximate distance" of the "agent-witness" that the Wild West aimed to reconstruct for its audiences.

The audience's sense of presence and proximity was intensified by the showman's tendency to martial up "historical scenes" in terms characteristic of the dime novel and stage melodrama. Hence, if Wild West reenactments defined American "history" as a series of grand spectacles of dynamic motion taking place before an agent-witness, so too did they suggest that these historical episodes took the shape of a series of shocking and surprising sensational incidents, defined primarily through violent conflict between (ostensibly morally superior) agents of civilization and (ostensibly morally inferior) obstacles to civilization. The program's introduction to its reenactment of a Native American attack on the Deadwood stagecoach is telling in this respect: "The people of the Eastern States of the Union

FIGURE 14 Illustration of the "Attack on the Deadwood Stage" from *Buffalo Bill's Wild West Historical Sketches and Programme* (1896).

are accustomed to regard the West as the region of romance and adventure. *And, in truth, its history abounds with thrilling incidents and surprising changes.* Every inch of that beautiful country has been won from a cruel and savage foe by danger and conflict . . . *The history of the wagon trains and stage coaches that preceded the railway is written all over with blood and the story of suffering and disaster*, often as it has been repeated, is only known in all of its horrid details to the bold frontiersmen who, as scouts and rangers, penetrated the strongholds of the Indians, and, backed by the gallant men of the army, became the avant couriers of Western civilization and the terror of the red man."[26]

In condensing several attacks into a single event, the spectacle of the "Attack on the Deadwood Stage" (which is figured as the primary vehicle that drove frontier history forward) vividly reenacted scenes in which the "avant couriers of Western civilization" attempted to traverse and settle the West. The "thrilling incidents and sudden changes" on display included an attack by Native Americans as the drivers defended the coach with their lives and as passengers were taken hostage and later rescued. Significantly, the reenactment involved the activation of a number of sensory stimuli (in addition to vision) that intensified the spectator's sense of proximity to, and illusory presence on, "the scene of history": the sounds of galloping horses, the whoops and cries of the attackers, the screams of the stagecoach passengers, the ring of gunshots, and the acrid smell and taste of gunpowder. To further enhance the illusion of the viewer's absorption into protomodern forms of frontier traffic (i.e., the slow, low-tech circulation of populations, goods, and businesses to the West) Cody would select a few members of the audience to ride in the Deadwood stagecoach (usually local politicians and celebrities) during the attack and rescue, thus giving such privileged spectators an even closer yet nevertheless "safe" proximity to the thrilling sensations and deadly shocks of life on the frontier. Like the highly manufactured and controlled thrills of the Coney Island attraction "Loop the Loop," such reenactments promised "The Greatest Sensation of the Age . . . No Danger Whatever,"[27] for the reenactment's reiterative structure allowed for control over "thrilling incidents" and "surprising changes" incidental to frontier traffic.

Through such discursive constructions of U.S. history, Cody's Wild West linked the nation's past to the conquest of space and the act of witnessing history to the act of spectatorship, such that the latter seemed an extension of the former. The link that the Wild West made between national identity and the power to circulate through and conquer hostile landscapes and the connection it made between an "original witness" and spectators were quite important to establishing the pleasures and the legitimacy of the battle reenactment film. Before I turn to specific films, however, I would like to distinguish further Cody's showmanship and reenactments from another form of nineteenth-century popular culture that also placed particular emphasis on questions of authenticity and legitimacy—namely, P. T. Barnum's "Humbug."

The Reenactment's Witness-Spectator
vs. Humbug's Detective-Spectator

With their emphasis on dynamic movement across space and strenuous physicality, the Wild West's live reenactments were part of a shift in late-nineteenth-century popular culture away from a mode of intellection central to the "operational aesthetic" typical of P. T. Barnum's hoaxes and humbug and toward more "vigorous" forms of entertainment that, according to John F. Kasson, had previously "existed only on the margins of American life." Such amusements included prize fighting, competitive athletics, moving picture shows, and amusement parks, as well as litera-

ture that celebrated "masculine toughness" such as Owen Wister's literary western *The Virginian* (1902) and Jack London's *The Call of the Wild*
(1903).[28] This shift is quite important for understanding the cultural history of the popular reenactment and the battle reenactment film's place
in that history, for it is tempting to see the reenactment film as a kind of
hoax or sham. Indeed, at first glance Cody's Wild West reenactments seem
to be in the same vein as Barnum's famous hoaxes. As Barnum had done
before him, Cody's Wild West staged a buffalo hunt, claimed to display
"authentic" relics such as the Deadwood stagecoach, and exhibited feats of
physical skill (notably Annie Oakley's sharpshooting) so astonishing as to
seem impossible and hence the effect of a trick. A closer comparison of the
aesthetic and spectator-attraction relation typical of Barnum's and Cody's
attractions suggests that Wild West reenactments signaled something of a
departure from humbug. However, it is nevertheless worthwhile to think
of Barnum's and Cody's audiences alongside one another; for though each
audience paid to encounter and engage with simulations, neither seems to
have done so naively.

In his study of Barnum's humbug, Neil Harris defines the particular
pleasure and the cultural and social conditions involved in nineteenth-
century audiences' encounter with, and consumption of, attractions such
as the "Feejee mermaid" (a half-monkey, half-fish), a sham buffalo hunt,
the display of Santa Anna's wooden leg, or the ostensibly "ancient" slave
Joice Heth, which made such hoaxes pleasurable for audiences and profitable to purveyors. According to Harris, humbug thrived in a Jacksonian
social and cultural milieu that was insistently egalitarian, rejected "secret
learning and private information" in favor of lecture going, embraced widespread common-school education as "a guarantee for the republic's future,"
and was in the midst of a technological revolution supported by popular
enthusiasm for scientific and industrial progress.[29] As technologies such
as the railway and telegraph became more diffuse in American culture,
so too did mechanical language and a measure of technical know-how.
As Harris notes, "machinery was beginning to accustom the public not
merely to a belief in the continual appearance of new marvels but to a jar-
gon that concentrated on methods of operation, on aspects of mechanical
organization and construction, on horsepower, gears, pulleys, and safety
valves."[30] Popular delight in learning and the widespread acquisition of

knowledge was accompanied by a widespread skepticism—a tendency to "test" anything and anyone for truthfulness. This combination made the American individual susceptible not to deceit and fraud but to the closely related (and more pleasurable) experience of "humbug" organized around a contest of wits between showman and amusement seeker. As Harris explains: "Experiencing a complicated hoax was pleasurable because of the competition between victim and hoaxer, each seeking to outmanoeuvre the other, to catch him off balance and detect the critical weakness. . . . Barnum understood that the opportunity to debate the issue of falsity, to discover how deception had been practiced, was even more exciting than the discovery of fraud itself. The manipulation of a prank, after all, was as interesting a technique in its own right as the presentation of genuine curiosities. Therefore, when people paid to see frauds, thinking they were true, they paid again to hear how the frauds were committed."[31] To exploit the popular propensity for skepticism and truth testing as well as critical evaluation and detection, Barnum encouraged his patrons to approach his attractions fully armed with doubt—ready to match wits with the showman and eager to penetrate the surface deception that cloaked the truth of the matter—and thereby provide a solution to the conundrum on display. In such a milieu, the ideal amusement seeker took up the position of the detective who "enjoyed disentangling the true from the false, the spurious from the genuine."[32]

Like Barnum, Cody exploited a widespread cultural penchant for the provocation and satisfaction of curiosity. However, in contrast to Barnum's hoaxes, Wild West reenactments purported to reveal previously hidden actions occluded not by a false veneer designed to confound the senses, but instead by distance, time, geography, and the forbidding conditions of frontier life. In turn, the *processes* on display and under consideration were not the mechanics of an infernal machine designed to stymie the intellect but rather were the distant processes of nation building and imperial expansion meant to stimulate national feeling.[33] Hence, the exposure of fundamental but hidden relationships—between East and West, frontier and city, native white American and Native American—was the job of the showman-pioneer and not the spectator.

Indeed, even the showmen's strategies for promoting, publicizing, and thereby preparing amusement seekers for their encounter with the attraction are suggestive of the differences between the concealment and doubt central to the experience of humbug and the mode of revelation and "proxy" spectatorship central to the pleasures of the reenactment. To pique his audience's curiosity and truth-testing inclinations, Barnum often publicized alongside more legitimating reviews others that cast serious doubt on the integrity of his attractions. In contrast, Cody used the program for the Wild West to publicize numerous letters of reference from military officers and government officials that confirm his personal honesty, his participation in the events he reenacts, and the realism and authenticity of his exhibition. A letter from a well-known military figure, reprinted in the catalogue and dated January 7, 1887, provides another succinct example: "I take great pleasure in testifying to the very efficient service rendered by you as a 'scout,' in the campaign against the Sioux Indians, during the year 1876. Also, I have witnessed your Wild West Exhibition. I consider it the most realistic performance of the kind I have ever seen. George Crook, Brigadier General, USA."[34] An illustration from the catalogue pictures Cody surrounded by images of the military leaders under whom he served; beneath each picture is a quote attributed to the official, most of which testify to Cody's honesty and integrity or to the realism of his exhibition. Such testimony authorizes Cody as both a credible and even privileged source for the enunciation of an officially sanctioned military history of the American West. Moreover, it provides witness to Cody's own witnessing of the conquest of the West, suggesting a series of credible looks able to confirm the authenticity of Cody's historical reenactments. This crucial difference in promotional strategy is telling, for it points to the difference between spectator-attraction relations typical of the hoax and the reenactment. Whereas the pleasurable experience of humbug depended upon the amusement seeker's incredulity and a competition of wits between showman and audience, the pleasure of Wild West reenactments depended upon the amusement seeker's *willing* and temporary suspension of disbelief that accompanied his or her delight in the simulation. To be sure, this consensual credulity resulted neither in the spectator's confusion of the reenactment with the real nor in being easily duped. Rather, this willing suspension of disbelief helped align the audience's point of view with the showman's, which, in turn, made his position as witness available to them—by proxy—in a thrilling new form.[35] In an effort to orient its

FIGURE 15 Illustration from *Buffalo Bill's Wild West Historical Sketches and Programme* (1896).

spectators away from incredulity and toward fascination, the Wild West program describes a conversion scenario in which the doubts held by spectators on the original scene of one of Cody's buffalo hunts are ultimately transformed into astonishment. Under the heading "The Pawnees Astonished," the program recounts the prehistory of the reenactment of one of Cody's buffalo hunts: "One day a herd of buffalo [was] descried, and Cody desired to join in the hunt. The Indians objected, telling the Major, 'The white talker would only scare them away.' Seventy-three Indians attacked the herd and killed twenty-three. Later in the day another herd was discovered, and Major North insisted that the white chief have a chance to prove his skill. After much grumbling they acquiesced grudgingly, and with ill-concealed smiles of derision consented to be spectators. Judges of their surprise when Cody charged the herd, and single-handed and alone fairly amazed them by killing forty-eight buffaloes in fifty minutes, thus forever gaining their admiration and a firm friendship that has since often accrued to his benefit."[36] Initially skeptical but ultimately amazed, the Pawnees shift from incredulity to fascination. Certainly, this passage was included in the program in order to encourage the audience to take up a similar position while watching Cody reenact his own famous methods used to hunt and ultimately decimate the buffalo on which Native Americans relied for sustenance. The program's description of the Pawnees' shift from incredulity to astonishment provided additional discursive cues for spectatorial identification with the star and charged with pleasure the processes of continental expansion, imperial prowess, and national progress that he reenacted. Once again, the program prepares the Wild West audience for the upcoming reenactment by setting up a reiterative spectatorial structure that places the audience in the (imaginary) position of the witnesses of the "original" hunt that Cody will once again enact.

This is not to say that all spectators agreed with the politics of the Wild West; for example, in one well-publicized instance Mark Twain left in the middle of a performance, disgusted by the spectacle of imperialism he encountered there. I am interested instead in the way Wild West reenactments—and the programs that described them—constructed and then exploited the structural similarities and differences between (original) witness and (secondary) audience in order to establish the peculiar authenticity of the reenactment and its power to transport spectators across space and time. Cody seemed to have done this by suggesting that the audience saw the event repeated as it was originally perceived by the agent-witness and thereby took up a position of (illusory) "presence" unique to the "genuine frontiersman" that was rendered available to (and made safe for) urban consumers en masse. Even the military displays and drills that constituted the portion of the show featuring "The Congress of Rough Riders of the World" seem to have created a powerful impression of revelation and presence—even immersion—in the represented scene. After seeing the Wild West in London, Frederic Remington observed: "The Cossacks will charge you with drawn sabers in a most genuine way, will hover over you like buzzards on a battlefield—they soar and whirl about in graceful curves, giving an uncanny impression, which has doubtless been felt by many a poor Russian soldier from the wheat fields of Europe as he lay with a bullet in him on some distant field."[37] Remington's rapid alignment of his own point of view with that of "many a poor Russian soldier" lying injured on a battlefield suggests that one of the hallmarks of turn-of-the-century battle reenactment and military display was the creation of a perilous point of view that helped audiences imaginatively to place themselves in the crossfire on the scene of history, thereby providing the brief sensation of witnessing well-known dramas of nation formation and imperial expansion.

Live reenactments such as the Wild West helped establish a cultural disposition toward the historical reenactment, its mode of address, the kinds of visual pleasure it might provide, and its peculiar authenticity. In this respect, the Wild West and its detailed program helped to prepare audiences for their encounter with the reenactment film. Certainly, there were crucial differences between the live reenactment and that of the film. The live reenactment promised the presence of real "historical characters" and featured authentic relics, such as the Deadwood stagecoach, bearing scars and auratic traces of their past. However, the thick materiality of the Wild West and its emphasis on authenticity and the physical presence of objects and individuals placed relative limitations (when compared to moving pictures) on its ability to circulate to audiences. And, while its pleasures derived from its power to place its audience on the simulated "scene" of history, its staging in large arenas (such as Madison Square Garden) held the audience at something of a distance from the depicted events and thereby placed limits upon the audience's sensation of immersion or absorption within such scenes. Battle reenactment films, by contrast, rarely featured "historical characters" or authentic relics but instead enlisted the skills of generic substitutes, such as national guardsmen, to reenact battles "originally" fought by the army. To compensate for the absence of live and "real" historical figures and for the filmed image's characteristic "presence of absence," battle reenactment films brought audiences closer to the field of battle, intensifying the sense of the spectator's visual presence on the depicted scene of history by aligning the audience's point of view with that of the camera. Indeed, the point of view provided by battle reenactment films tends to position spectators in the crossfire between enemy combatants as they move through and defend space, making it somewhat comparable to the point of view of those privileged few spectators who rode in the Deadwood stagecoach at the Wild West. And, as we shall see, the battle reenactment film's closer proximity to the historical "scene" of imperial conquest brings into sharper focus one crucial aspect of the cultural "work" done by the reenactment: its tendency to repeat the trauma of history in order to master it. Before turning to this issue I would like first to discuss the close cultural connections between the "historical agents" who carried on Cody's canny negotiation of the gap between the reenactment and the real: namely, Roosevelt's Rough Riders.

Appropriations and Transformations: Rough Riders and Battle Reenactments on Film

Battle reenactments and military display films that focus on the Spanish-American War and on the Philippine-American War share with Wild West reenactments a generic category as well as the themes, historical characters, and an ideology of American imperial expansion that emphasized the military's power to take control of and circulate rapidly through space. In many respects, Cody's Wild West's own celebration of the centrality of the U.S. military—and Buffalo Bill's close affiliation with it—to the violent conquest and settlement of the West created a historical foundation for constructing continuity between these two phases of U.S. imperialism and spectacular representations of them. Hence, in 1898 when Theodore Roosevelt enlisted in the war against Spain and named his regiment the Rough Riders (denying, rather implausibly, the accusations that he had taken the name from the Wild West), he solidified a sense of historical continuity between the new overseas imperialism by the United States and its earlier continental phase and encouraged Americans to perceive the new imperial traffic as an extension of the mobilizations that previously circulated pioneers throughout the frontier.

Just as Cody tailored his reenactments of frontier life in the West to the tastes of urban consumers in the East to create a myth of national expansion, Roosevelt also synthesized what Slotkin calls "the myth of the Frontier" with the modernity of the urban East to create a closely related myth of overseas imperialism.[38] Roosevelt described his regiment of Rough Riders in terms strikingly similar to those used by Cody to describe the scouts, cowboys, and soldiers who appeared in the Wild West. According to Roosevelt, his Rough Riders hailed from

the Four Territories which yet remained within the boundaries of the United States; that is, from the lands that have been most recently won over to white civilization, and in which the conditions of life are nearest those that obtained on the frontier when there still was a frontier. They were a splendid set of men, these Southwesterners—tall and sinewy, with resolute, weather-beaten faces, and eyes that looked a man straight in the face without flinching. . . . In all the world there could be no better material for soldiers than that afforded by these grim hunters of the mountains, these wild rough riders of the plains. They were accustomed to handling wild and savage horses; they were accustomed to following the chase with the rifle, both for sport and as a means of livelihood. They were hardened to life in the open, and to shifting for themselves under adverse circumstances. They were used, for all their lawless freedom, to the rough discipline of the round-up and the mining company. Some of them came from small frontier towns; but most were from the wilderness; having left their lonely hunters' cabins and shifting cow-camps to seek new and more stirring adventures beyond the sea.[39]

The terms used by Roosevelt to describe these Rough Riders echo those used by Cody to describe the original Rough Riders and link new, high-tech forms of imperial traffic to previous protomodern (or "rough") forms of frontier traffic. Hence, when Cody included in his bill a reenactment of the Battle of San Juan Hill, the program mentioned that the regiment's "popular and famous title was borrowed from Colonel Cody's use and application of the term 'Rough Riders,' which was mainly composed of the physical qualities represented so splendidly in Buffalo Bill's Wild West, and which, moreover, included many volunteers from Colonel Cody's camp."[40] These, as Roosevelt explained, were joined by a number of "eager volunteers who did not come from the Territories but who possessed precisely the same temper that distinguished our Southwestern recruits, and whose presence materially benefited the regiment." Such recruits were drawn "from Harvard, Yale, Princeton, and many another college; from clubs like the Somerset, of Boston, and Knickerbocker, of New York, and from among the men who belonged neither to club nor to college, but in whose veins the blood stirred with the same impulse which once sent the Vikings over sea."[41] For many Americans, perhaps, the mobilization of this second generation of Rough Riders to a new frontier seemed to repeat an earlier "drama of civilization" and in the process made historical sense of a new era of imperial traffic.

Films shot before the war of Roosevelt's Rough Riders in camps in

Florida seem to repeat the mode of presentation used by Cody to display his own Rough Riders: they feature images of the celebrated Cavalry charging in formation directly toward the camera. Films of military drills shown before battles might have been viewed as "preenactments" of a sort: they featured actions that would be repeated in combat and so allowed audiences to imagine the shock force that would be unleashed against Spain on the battlefield. *Roosevelt's Rough Riders* (AM&B, 1898) provides an example of the continuity of address, aesthetic, and theme between live and film military displays and reenactments. Though the film does not reenact a specific battle, it showed the famous mounted Cavalry charging directly toward the camera, turning sharply only at the last moment. By orienting the Cavalry charge directly toward the camera and hence the spectator, this "Rough Rider" film places the latter in the direct line of danger, thereby intensifying what Gunning refers to as early cinema's "aesthetic of astonishment" based on shock and surprise.[42] Moreover, the visible trace of the filmed military drill's generic proximity to the battle reenactment—its placement of the spectator in the direct line of danger—is inseparable from the particular visual experience and pleasures it provides. In the tradition of Cody's "Congress of Rough Riders," this film offers spectators a thrilling sense of absent presence and a view of how such a charge might or did appear to soldiers on an actual battlefield, and in doing so it gave curious audiences visual access to an "authentic" image of military shock.

This visual positioning of the spectator in the Cavalry's path is quite important, for it anticipates the battle reenactment film's orientation of action and its articulation of imperial history as trauma. While modern "shock" has been closely linked to urbanization and the traumatic experience of mechanical breakdown in traffic (such as railway accidents) in the late nineteenth and early twentieth centuries the term has its origins in the mechanization of the military. Wolfgang Schivelbusch notes that "shock" emerged in the sixteenth century to denote "the encounter of an armed force with the enemy in charge or onset; also, the encounter of two mounted warriors or joustlers charging one another."[43] "Shock" similarly entered the romance languages via the Middle Dutch *shokken*, meaning "to collide," and eventually accrued the connotations of a strike or a blow. The rise of the modern mass army in fourteenth-century Europe "concretized the entirely specific sense of the word: the clash of two bodies of troops, each of which represented a new unified concentration of energy by means of a number of warriors into one de-individualized and mechanized unit." As Schivelbusch notes, this concentration of energy inevitably changed the meaning of shock, for "the greater the degree of concentration/mechanization of the two colliding bodies of troops, the more violent the shock of their clash, the greater the attrition of the elements that constitute the whole."[44] Just as industrialized traffic created shocks that traumatized the passenger, so too did the increasing mechanization of military traffic create unprecedented shocks on the battlefield.

Roosevelt's Rough Riders appeared in popular culture as the embodiment of the modern shock force required to establish a presence by the United States in the international arena of empire building, just as famous regiments in the U.S. Cavalry before it had executed the shock force required to subordinate the continent to control by the U.S. government. Arthur Wanger, instructor in the "art of war" at the U.S. Infantry and Cavalry School, in his treatise on the history of "tactics and organization" of the army identified the Cavalry as the unit most ideally suited to delivering shock on the battlefield. Defined by its high degree of mobility and concentration of energy and forces, the "most successful cavalry on the battle-field has always been that which possessed the power of giving the most effective shock; in other words, the one which united the greatest mobility with the highest power of cohesion and the most effect use of their weapons in a melée." Hence, the cavalry charge was to be "made in close order, boot-to-boot, the forward movement increasing in rapidity until it finally terminates in a shock delivered at full speed. The effect of the shock depends upon the cohesion, weight and speed of the charging force; in the melée which follows, the result depends upon the weapons of the trooper, and his skill in their use."[45] Just as early films in which locomotives speed toward the camera display transportation technology's annihilation of space and time, films such as *Roosevelt's Rough Riders* communicated the shock force of U.S. imperial traffic by placing spectators in the direct line of the charge as the object of their assault. Filmed in 1898 during war preparations in Tampa, Florida, this film momentarily places the spectator in the structural position of the enemy, thereby endowing audiences with the maximum perception of the mobilized force that promised to deliver the Spanish empire into the hands of the United States and to extend the reach of American military and industrial power around the globe.

Like Roosevelt's redeployment of the "Rough Rider" motif, the cinema's redeployment of the reenactment to represent violent struggle on this new frontier provided audiences with a familiar and familiarizing format for consuming "authentic" representations of national history as military spectacle. Such films promised audiences the (imaginary) proximate position of an agent-witness on the scene of imperial expansion. For example, in a paragraph introducing the section "War Films"—which includes actualities as well as reenactments of the Spanish-American War—the catalogue of the Edison agent F. M. Prescott promised exhibitors and their audiences precisely the sensation of being present as a witness on the battlefield: "In these superior films can be seen the dead and wounded and the dismantled cannon lying on the field of battle. The men are seen struggling for their lives, and the American flag proudly waves over them and can be plainly seen through the dense smoke. The brave American and Cuban soldiers show their valor and superiority in fighting the hated Spaniards. You think you can hear the huge cannon belch forth their death-dealing missiles, and can really imagine yourself on the field witnessing the actual battle."[46] Within this catalogue, the only films that depict battles or any significant "action" are reenactments and films of military drills. Hence, like the program for the Wild West, the Prescott catalogue suggests that the particular pleasure (and profitability) of reenactment films derived from their capacity to inspire the spectator's fantasy of presence on the scene of history, of finding oneself suddenly "on the field *witnessing* the actual battle" and perceiving the shock and trauma of modern history.

Not surprisingly, then, battle reenactment films shot after the war by the Edison Manufacturing Co. in New Jersey continue the tendency to orient the movement of the Rough Riders' "shock force" toward the camera. For example, *US Infantry Supported by Rough Riders at El Caney* (Edison, 1899) shows "a detachment of infantry, firing, advancing, kneeling and firing, again and again. The advance of the foot soldiers is followed by a troops of Rough Riders, riding like demons, yelling and firing revolvers as they pass out of sight."[47] The camera is placed at an oblique angle to the action, just at the side of the road along which the foot soldiers and Rough Riders advance, such that the soldiers fire at and advance toward it. *Skirmish of Rough Riders* (Edison, 1899) similarly angles its action obliquely toward the camera: the film opens with two marksmen lying behind a "dead" horse at the turn of a road, firing at the unseen enemy. In the background of the

FIGURE 16 *US Infantry Supported by Rough Riders at El Caney* (Edison, 1899).
COURTESY OF THE LIBRARY OF CONGRESS MOTION PICTURE READING ROOM

frame, the mounted Rough Riders wait. As the catalogue explains, "Suddenly comes the command, 'Forward,' and the riders dash up the road, out of sight, leaving behind them a great cloud of dust and smoke."[48] An alternating pleasure in power and powerlessness lies at the heart of such films: spectators might thrill in their imaginary placement in the path of this shock force—as its object—while knowing all along that they were (nationally, politically) aligned with the agents of this same force. Military shock and cinematic shock thereby intersected in the battle reenactment film to endow the civilian observer with spectatorial fantasies of imperial power, agency, and mobility. In turn, these films also foreground the mythologizing tendency of American battle reenactments: as it turned out, the Rough Riders saw only dismounted action in Cuba and so were the objects of a different kind of military shock. But perhaps the greatest mythologization effected is the visibility and visuality represented within these particular scenes of history; for, as many soldiers and journalists testified, the experience of modern warfare was defined by high-tech battlefield blindness and scenes of erasure. Just as Roosevelt's appropriation of the

FIGURE 17 *Skirmish of the Rough Riders* (Edison, 1899). COURTESY OF THE LIBRARY OF
CONGRESS MOTION PICTURE READING ROOM

appellation "Rough Riders" suggests his canny use of the "Wild West" to
shape popular perception of the war, it also suggests the degree to which
live battle reenactments and military displays had shaped contemporary
notions about the experience of "actual" battle. Preparations for the war
were highly mediated, and the presence of newspapermen (such as Richard
Harding Davis) and cameramen (such as Edison's William Paley) undoubtedly contributed to the sense of the war as something of an intertextual
spectacle. In describing the moments immediately preceding the outbreak
of fighting on the morning of the Battle of San Juan Hill, Roosevelt recounted: "It was a very lovely morning, the sky of cloudless blue, while the
level, shimmering rays from the just-risen sun brought into fine relief the
splendid palms which here and there towered above the lower growth. The
lofty and beautiful mountains hemmed in the Santiago plain, making it an
amphitheatre for the battle."[49] Roosevelt's description of the plain as "an
amphitheatre for the battle" suggests his own perception of the contested
territory as a stage designed to provide the agent-witness (and, perhaps,
the world as audience) with an optimal point of view on the proceedings,

replete with a "lofty and beautiful" picturesque backdrop. Yet the ensuing battle sharply undermined this expectation, for the Rough Riders experienced it as a terrifying combination of blindness and perilous visibility arising from the development and deployment of new military technologies—specifically the Krag-Jorgensen and smokeless gunpowder—calculated precisely to increase the "shock force" of the salvo.

According to Schivelbusch, the standard issue of firearms in the eighteenth century made possible the "salvo" or "volley"—the simultaneous, "collective, un-aimed discharge of firearms by the entire unit" from a technologically mediated distance. The perfectly timed salvo first razed as many soldiers as possible, and in doing so it created a vast spectacle of simultaneous casualties that terrified and demoralized those left standing in closed ranks on the battlefield. Schivelbusch notes that the salvo's technologically mediated distance meant that "the force of the clash lost its concrete physical manifestation," thereby changing the soldier's sensory experience of war: now the assault "occurred suddenly, invisibly; it came 'out of nowhere,'" denying the soldier the means of preparing himself for the blow. Hence, in comparing the state of mind of the medieval duelist with that of the modern combatant, Schivelbusch notes that "the intense relationship between the state of duelists may be seen as one of alert expectation. The individual combatants were able to see from exactly which direction the possible wound may be caused: they were, as it were, well prepared for it. From the eighteenth century on, such a state of readiness no longer existed."[50] A passive, psychological-perceptual meaning became grafted onto shock's active, physical-mechanical meaning. The salvo's terrifying invisibility and the soldier's inability to prepare for it resulted in his delayed realization of the wound or "overthrow" that had taken place within his body. As the military historian G. H. Groningen explains, this insensate state resulted "not only because of the rapidity of the damage but rather because of the total exertion of all their psychological powers towards other goals. Every sensation requires a degree of attention, however small."[51]

New military technology further denied the U.S. soldier's required "degree of attention": whereas Spain used smokeless gunpowder and Krag-Jorgensen rifles, the U.S. still used Springfield rifles and black gunpowder. Roosevelt described the effect of the smokeless gunpowder used by Spanish soldiers as "remarkable": "The air seemed full of the rustling sound of the Mauser bullets, for the Spaniards knew the trails by which we were advancing, and opened up heavily on our position. Moreover, as we advanced we were, of course, exposed, and they could see us and fire. But they themselves were entirely invisible. The jungle covered everything, and not the faintest trace of smoke was to be seen in any direction to indicate from whence the bullets came." While smokeless gunpowder and thick tropical vegetation gave Spain the military advantage of invisibility, gunpowder smoke coming from the Americans' weapons revealed their position and further obscured their already blocked vision. As Roosevelt concludes, "It was most bewildering to fight an enemy whom one so rarely saw" whose presence was indicated only by the menacing sound of Mauser bullets "singing through the trees over our heads, making a noise like the humming of telephone wires."[52] The invisibility of the Spanish forces, and the state of blocked vision experienced by the U.S. soldiers, found its way into popular representations of the war. As the catalogue description for the Wild West reenactment of the Battle of San Juan Hill explains: "To add to the horror of the situation, the infernal Spanish guerillas, concealed in the treetops and using smokeless gunpowder, which renders it impossible to locate them, make targets of our wounded and the surgeons and wearers of the Red Cross."[53] In turn, Frederic Remington represented this terrifying battlefield blindness in *Scream of Shrapnel at San Juan Hill, Cuba*—in which soldiers are shown convulsively flailing, ducking, dropping, and fruitlessly looking in every possible direction for the source of a salvo. However, as Alexander Nemerov notes, Remington's direct observation of the battle was prevented by the extreme conditions of modern warfare; he therefore described the famous battle as "the most glorious feat of arms I ever heard of."[54]

Hence, American imperialism placed the soldier into an intense "visual topology of modernity," which Gunning characterizes as "fragmented and atomized" and structured around "a gaze which, rather than resting on a landscape in contemplation, seems to be pushed and pulled in conflicting orientations, hurried and intensified, and therefore less coherent or anchored."[55] Indeed, the conditions of imperial conquest and resistance to it were at odds with the desire to see History, Progress, and Empire as an enframed spectacle. As Paul Virillio argues, "The history of the battle is primarily the history of radically changing fields of perception." War does not

FIGURE 18 *Scream of Shrapnel at San Juan Hill, Cuba* by Frederic Remington (1898).

simply consist of "scoring territorial, economic, or other material victories" but also of appropriating "visual fields."[56] Well aware of the importance of such appropriation, Filipinos resisting colonization by the United States following the defeat of Spain fought a guerrilla war in which rebels camouflaged as civilians executed unexpected ambushes on U.S. soldiers. In turn, U.S. soldiers suppressing the Philippine insurgency often found themselves caught up in a fruitless search for an elusive enemy. As one officer wrote to his wife: "I do hope the idiotic newspapers haven't worried you to death about the heavy engagements at Caloocan. 'Battles' out here are greatly exaggerated. The enemy is like a flea you can't see."[57] Letters and diaries written by U.S. soldiers describe the visual terrain of modern imperial warfare as shifting, unstable, and characterized by self-erasure. For example, on one scouting mission to locate insurgents, soldiers from the black 24th Regiment reported seeing in the distance "a body of Filipinos, drilling on extended order, such as used only in fighting." Once they reached the site, however, the dismayed 24th encountered only "peaceful citizens planting rice."[58] The astonishingly nonspectacular imperial landscape refused to take the shape of a clearly rendered "living picture," yielding only disorienting, kaleidoscopic transformations and leaving U.S. volunteers "looking for rebel forces which are nowhere to be found."[59]

On the other side of the world, battlefield blindness also afflicted the motion picture camera's mechanical eye. W. K. L. Dickson in *The Biograph in Battle*, his memoirs of his experiences filming British soldiers in the

Boer War, described his attempt to film a battle in the valley of the Upper Tugela. Dickson used a telephoto lens and set up the Biograph "not fifty feet from the big guns." Though, as Dickson recounted, "the air was full of bursting shells," and though he could see "the flash of a Boer gun that might just probably miss the naval guns and strike us," the resulting film appears onscreen as nothing more than a panorama of the South African landscape: "The depth and vastness of the scene was so great as to some-what disqualify it for a biographic view. I fear very few will be able to discern the shells bursting, or the cavalry and artillery below us . . . As for the foot soldiers in khaki, it will be quite impossible to see them, as they are always invisible from a distance, being the color of the earth. The exact position of our guns and those of the enemy can be seen by studying the accompanying panoramic sketch . . . Every hill and dale and winding of the [valley] is shown, and should one see the Biograph panoramic projection of the valley at the time of the battle he will get a very good idea of the whole thing, even if the distant puffs should be invisible."[60] Khaki-colored uniforms and the battle's massive scale—caused in part by the extended trajectory of modern artillery—conspired to camouflage weapons and sol-diers alike, rendering the battle indistinguishable from the surrounding landscape.[61] Hence at precisely the historical moment that the cinema's panoramic perception and documentary capacities held forth the promise of actuality footage of such battles, the moving pictures encountered some-thing of a limit case. The battle reenactment film emerged as a compro-mise between the at-times-conflicting scopic regimes of early cinema and turn-of-the-century imperial warfare. Like the live reenactments staged by the Wild West, reenactment films of the Spanish-American War and the Philippine-American War transformed the shock, surprise, and con-tingencies of modern imperial warfare into spectacular displays of mili-tary power and progress. In the process, film reenactments carved out the imaginary position of the agent-witness for their audiences by creating the illusion of being "embedded" within imperial traffic, and in so doing they created the pleasurable illusion of presence "on the scene" of history.

Edison's *Advance of the Kansas Volunteers at Caloocan* (Edison, 1899) pro-vides a stunning example of such mediation. Unlike Dickson's failed battle actuality, the landscape in this reenactment film remains subordinated to the action, which in turn remains centered in the frame. The film opens with a line of "Filipino insurgents" firing directly at the camera. Then U.S.

FIGURE 19 A AND B *Advance of the Kansas Volunteers at Caloocan* (Edison, 1899).
COURTESY OF THE LIBRARY OF CONGRESS MOTION PICTURE READING ROOM

troops emerge from behind the camera, firing several rounds as they advance toward the now-retreating Filipinos. The U.S. color-bearer is shot and falls, at which point another soldier picks up the flag and waves it furiously. The U.S. troops disappear into the foliage in the background of the frame, behind a veil of smoke. Nothing in the catalogue description for the film suggests that it was passed off as an actuality to unsuspecting audiences, and the popularity of the live reenactment as a form of commercialized leisure suggests that few would have been easily duped. Indeed, the catalogue description for the film trades upon precisely those formal details that would reveal its generic status to urban, relatively sophisticated turn-of-the-century exhibitors and spectators—the placement of the camera/spectator directly in the crossfire between the Filipinos who shoot directly at the camera and the Americans who charge from behind it: "This is one of the best battle pictures ever made. The firing is first done directly toward the front of the picture, and the advance of the US troops apparently through the screen is very exciting; the gradual disappearance of the fighters sustaining the interest to the end."[62] David Levy notes that the reenactment's perilous point of view led one reviewer to determine such films obvious reenactments.[63] And while such a response provides evidence that some exhibitors might have passed off reenactments as actualities, it also provides evidence that urban spectators were well aware of one of the characteristic features of the battle reenactment: the placement of the audience in an impossible position at the edges of—or in this case in the middle of—military traffic. Indeed, the film provides a mediated sensation of being visible and hence vulnerable to the enemy's frontal assault, yet the camera-endowed disembodied presence in the scene transforms the terror of such a position into the pleasurable satisfaction of curiosity about the shock force of imperial warfare. And unlike the blindness experienced by U.S. troops assaulted by and in search of an elusive enemy, the camera endows spectators with a prosthetic vision that allows them to see the enemy and the source of the salvo, translating the imperial soldier's (and cameraman's) terrifying battlefield blindness into scopic clarity and power. Hence the gunpowder smoke that blinded soldiers on the battlefield here creates an aesthetic effect as the Filipinos retreat from vision, with "the gradual disappearance of the fighters sustaining interest to the end."

Like Cody's reenactments, this film presents military conquest as a spectacle of U.S. power in which soldiers act as agent-witnesses, for the soldiers are revealed to have been "alongside" the spectator, on the other side of the camera, until they charge in front of it to become part of the spectacle—a formal strategy that helps carve out an imaginary presence on the scene of history for the spectator. This illusory placement of the spectator within the circuits of military traffic also entails a positioning vis-à-vis the project of imperialism. The camera's placement has the effect of aligning the audience with the agents of U.S. imperialism, who emerge from behind the camera to protect them from the frontal assault that opens the film. Placing civilian spectators in the line of this frontal assault supported the pro-imperial press's representation of Filipino resistance as an unwarranted, savage attack on the so-called innocent agents of civilization, progress, and uplift. Indeed, reenactments of battles fought against the Filipino resistance consistently begin with Filipinos firing first. For example, both *Capture of the Trenches at Candaba* (Edison, 1899) and *Filipinos Retreat from Trenches* (Edison, 1899) open with the camera in a trench occupied by Filipinos, who fire several rounds at the initially unseen U.S. soldiers who ultimately advance into and take the trench. As with Wild West reenactments, the agents of U.S. imperialism appear as victims who, in the process of defending themselves, aid in territorial expansion as they are seen moving dynamically across the depicted space of a new frontier.

Though battle reenactment films did not show "actual" images of battle, they allowed audiences to "see" ostensible (and highly ideological) "truths" about the overseas expansion by the United States promoted by pro-imperialists in the popular press that dovetailed with the ideology of manifest destiny. *Capture of the Trenches at Candaba* places the camera/spectator in the trenches via a sidelong view of Filipino soldiers defending their possession of a small strip of land. Initiating the movements of the U.S. troops with an act of "aggression," the insurgents fire several rounds as their color-bearer waves the flag of the Philippine Republic in the middle of the frame. Suddenly they retreat, exiting frame left as U.S. troops advance into the trench from frame right. The camera not only creates an illusory visual presence on the scene but also seems to anticipate the historic moment when possession by the United States takes place. In doing so, the camera and the spectator's anticipatory presence in this space marks the trench as *already* conquered, suggesting the inevitable and even unstoppable movement of the imperial traffic of the United States. *Filipinos Retreat from Trenches* repeats this simple narrative of Filipino aggression, retreat, and

FIGURE 20 A AND B *Capture of the Trenches at Candaba* (Edison, 1899). COURTESY OF
THE LIBRARY OF CONGRESS MOTION PICTURE READING ROOM

FIGURE 21 *Filipinos Retreat from Trenches* (Edison, 1899). COURTESY OF THE LIBRARY OF CONGRESS MOTION PICTURE READING ROOM

"inevitable" incorporation of space into the circuits of the new American empire. Much like Cody's Wild West reenactments, battle reenactment films suggested that imperial conquest was not only the fulfillment of destiny by the agents of "progress" but that this destiny, and its long history, was a traumatic one for the imperial agent. Put differently, the reenactment makes clear that circulation within imperial traffic subjected the modern individual to shocks more violent than those experienced in urban street traffic. This suggests that the reenactment appealed not just to the desire to see "actual, grewsome war," but also, as the review quoted at the beginning of this chapter suggests, to repeat via reenactment the trauma of military history.

The Mastery of Trauma: Reenactment, Repetition, and Heroic Femininity

To understand the appeal of reenactment's reiterative structure it is important to note that unlike the actuality film, the remit of the reenactment was not simply to record but, first, to repeat. Moreover, like audiences at

Cody's Wild West, as well as those attending later film reenactments such as *The Execution of Czolgosz* (Edison, 1901) and *The Capture of the Biddle Brothers and Mrs. Soffel* (Edison/Porter, 1902), audiences watching battle reenactments would have arrived at the theater knowing the outcome of the conflicts already widely reported in the press. Indeed, most of the reenacted battles were quite bloody and were treated quite sensationally by the press, which also increasingly reported on the high number of civilian casualties suffered by the Filipinos. The tendency to reenact bloody, notorious, or otherwise well-known battles suggests that the visual pleasure of the reenactment was perhaps uncompromised by its status as a "mimic"—for the reenactment's reiterative structure perhaps promoted the sense of mastery that Freud argues results from the repetition of a traumatic event. Indeed, live and film battle reenactments involved showmen, filmmakers, and audiences alike in the act of replaying the historical trauma of warfare.

In his now famous essay on "Little Hans"—a case study discussed by Freud in the context of theorizing war neuroses—Freud analyzes the relationship between shock/trauma, repetition, and the pleasure principle. To demonstrate the point that the individual derives pleasure from the repetition or reenactment of a deeply unpleasurable experience, Freud describes a game played repeatedly by a young boy that, he asserts, allowed the child to overcome the trauma associated with the departure of his mother. Freud observed Little Hans repeatedly casting a spool attached to a long string over the side of a bed with the exclamation of "Fort" (gone) and reeling the spool back to himself with the exclamation "Da" (here). By doing so, Freud argues, the child restaged his mother's traumatic departure and return via "the disappearance and return of objects within his reach."[64] Freud described the motive behind and the satisfaction derived from the repetitive restaging of this event: "At the outset he was in a passive situation—he was overpowered by the experience; but, by repeating it unpleasurable though it was, as a game, he took on an active part. These efforts might be put down to an instinct for mastery that was acting independently of whether the memory was in itself pleasurable or not."[65] The repetition/reenactment of a traumatic event allows the individual to shift from a passive to an active position of "mastery" that translates unpleasure into pleasure. Freud's analysis of mastery through repetition provides a structure for understanding the reenactment as a form well suited to the task of representing the traumatic shock of battle. For at the conclusion of his essay, Freud makes a connection between Little Hans's repetition compulsion and the "representational arts": "Finally, a reminder may be added that the artistic play and artistic imitation carried out by adults, which, unlike children's, are aimed at an audience, do not spare the spectators (for instance, in tragedy) the most painful experience and yet can be felt by them as highly enjoyable. This is convincing proof that, even under the dominance of the pleasure principle, there are ways and means enough of making what is in itself unpleasurable into a subject to be recollected and worked over in the mind. The consideration of these cases and situations, which have a yield of pleasure as their outcome, should be undertaken by some system of aesthetics with an economic approach to its subject matter."[66]

The battle reenactment film provides a unique opportunity to undertake such analysis, for it is precisely an "artistic imitation" "aimed at an audience" that repeated traumatic *historical* events. We might even speculate that such repetition allowed audiences to shift from a passive position vis-à-vis the event ("this is happening to us over there") to a more active position that seemed to place audiences on the battlefield and in the trenches alongside U.S. soldiers ("'we' must subordinate 'them'"). And, as noted above, live and film battle reenactments revised as they repeated conquest such that each battle begins with an assault on white Americans by a hostile racial foe, followed by a charge/attack that ultimately makes U.S. forces the masters of violent conflict. Hence, reenactments "recollected and worked over" the "most painful experiences" associated with imperial expansion in such a way that made the colonizer both victim (of an apparently unwarranted aggression) and ultimate master (of violent conquest). The very presentation of imperial aggression as trauma is, of course, a mythologization that allowed imperial agents to pose as "innocent" objects of attack even as they engaged in violent conquest. The battle reenactment's placement of the spectator on the "scene" of historical trauma and its mode of repetition provided a cultural form for revealing and mastering the shock of warfare experienced by the soldier on the new frontier and, by extension, the nation as it became an overseas empire.

As many Americans knew, the sources of warfare's traumatic shock were multiple and not necessarily attributable only to the enemy. After the defeat of Spain in the Spanish-American War the American soldier's suffering on the warfront was increasingly attributed to the U.S. government's scandalous lack of "war preparedness" and disregard for its soldiers' welfare. Reports coming from the front provided alarming accounts of soldiers' near starvation on the campaign trail due to the lack of provisions and supplies. The coincidence of the rainy season with the outbreak of fighting in the Caribbean led to an epidemic of yellow fever among the soldiers and, as a result, the military campaign heralded by Roosevelt and others as a project for the reinvigoration of American manhood quickly yielded up horrifying spectacles of bodies laid to waste by the shocks of warfare and disease. An article in the *New York World* dated September 19, 1898, detailed one of the causes of bodily degeneration among the returning soldiers: "When the men of the Second New Jersey Volunteers reach home and are mustered out an exhibition of scandalous official neglect and cruelty will be unveiled to their friends. One of the most popular men in the regiment is an athlete known all over the country and up to the outbreak of the war the occupant of a Government position in Hoboken. This man has written a letter to one of his Hoboken friends . . . 'Such a lot of sick, weak, broken-down and dejected looking men as those of the Second New Jersey Regiment were never seen before. You will not believe it when I tell you the cause is starvation.'"[67]

The F. M. Prescott catalogue described the appearance of returning soldiers in the actuality *3rd Regiment, Philadelphia* in a way that suggested that a very fine line indeed separated the bodily signifiers of regeneration and degeneration effected by participation in the imperial project: "One of our crack Philadelphia regiments, headed by Col. Ralston, is here portrayed as they arrived in Philadelphia from the war. The boys, on the whole, look exceedingly well, which proves how sturdy and patriotic the American soldier is. Everyone is interested in the soldier boys. While, as a whole, the regiment returned in a very healthy condition, the results of four months' life in camps are plainly visible in the appearance of many of the men. A large number of them are exceedingly thin, some being changed so much as to make recognition by friends difficult. Quite a number of the soldiers who have returned with but little flesh were quite stout when they left this city. At first sight even immediate relatives failed to recognize some of the soldiers on account of their bronzed faces. Some had also changed their appearance by raising full beards."[68] This film, then, displays male bodies so transformed by the war that they are unrecognizable to friends and family. And while the catalogue urges exhibitors and audiences to perceive their emaciated bodies as signs of sturdiness and patriotism, its classification of these soldiers' bodies as "exceedingly thin" would have resonated alongside reports in the press that the soldiers had been most traumatized by their own government's neglect to feed, shelter, and provide medical care for the wounded and sick as well as the healthy soldier.

The specter of the physically degenerated soldier was swiftly followed by suggestions of the broader moral and political degeneration of the United States as it began the process of imposing its rule in the new colonies and territories. Indeed, the cinematic representation of the Rough Riders as the agents of a shock force oriented toward Spain in Cuba, on the one hand, and the representation of U.S. soldiers fighting insurgents in the Philippines as objects of trauma, on the other, had much to do with the re-lationship of the United States to its newly subjugated populations in over-seas territories taken from Spain. While American culture gladly embraced the idea that it had defeated a European colonial power and in the process elevated its status in the international arena, it seemed less certain about its violent suppression of the very same Filipino independence movement that Admiral Dewey himself had promised Emilio Aguinaldo that the United States would support. By 1899, reports of atrocities committed by the American military against civilian Filipinos during the so-called pacifi-cation of the insurgency found their way into the press due to the efforts of the Anti-Imperialist League, which was founded by Mark Twain, William Dean Howells, and Jane Addams among others.[69] In 1899, a struggle over the meaning of American imperialism took place in the popular press: while reports of military atrocities by the United States (including the tor-ture of civilians) seemed to suggest that its colonial rule was no different— and indeed even more brutal—than that of Spain, counternarratives of atrocities committed by "savages" against a civilizing force struggling to uplift those that William Taft called "our little brown brother" presented U.S. forces as victims of trauma.

The repetition function of the reenactment and its ameliorative effects were supplemented in many battle reenactment films by images of the be-nevolent forces of empire that assuaged the suffering of U.S. soldiers and enemy combatants alike. Laura Wexler has analyzed the production and circulation of what she calls "domestic images" in American photography after the war, which she argues helped refurbish the tarnished image of U.S. imperialism. Wexler focuses on photographs of sailors at work and play taken by Frances Johnston on board Admiral Dewey's famous battleship *Olympia* in 1899. In deploying simultaneous meanings of "domestic" as a category for signifying the spatial "home" of the nation and of the family, Wexler notes that "the cult of domesticity was a crucial framework for American imperialism in the late nineteenth century. In the United States, apologists for colonialism used conceptions of domestic progress as both a descriptive and heuristic tool. . . . At home, American domesticity was a potent concatenation of ideas of scientific racism, social Darwinism, and economic pragmatism that could be used to orchestrate consent for expansionist policies. In the colonies, and in the institutions and social agencies that dealt with subjugated peoples within the (constantly expanding) borders of the continental United States, such ideals of domestic life were also disciplinary structures of the state."[70] Johnston's photographs displayed "homey" images of sailors engaged in the activities of rest and relaxation—whether fencing or playing with the ship's kitten—images that helped eclipse the *unheimlich* image of imperial violence with familiar, homey images of the naval family. Hence, Wexler argues, domestic images need not necessarily focus on "representations of and for a so-called sphere of family life. Instead, what matters is the use of the image to signify the domestic realm," which "can be figured as well by a battleship as by a nursery if that battleship, as in the case of the 'Olympia,' is known to be on a mission to redraw and then patrol the nation's boundaries, the *sine qua non* of the homeland."[71]

The reenactment film contributed to the circulation of domestic images of imperial conquest and in the process helped restore not only the image of the new empire but also the image of modern femininity. Participation in the war effort gave women the opportunity to construct a female counterpart to images of heroic masculinity coming out of the imperial project. In turn, it mobilized the characteristic features of ideal domestic femininity—benevolence, maternal self-sacrifice, and the relief of suffering—to the warfront. Just as the wounded soldier was at the turn of the century a signifier for the historical shock and trauma of imperial warfare, the Red Cross nurse became a signifier for the mastery and relief of the same. Indeed, as Clara Barton herself noted, the shock of warfare provided the condition of existence for the heroic femininity embodied by the Red Cross nurse at the turn of the century. To contextualize her published memoirs on the activities of Red Cross nurses during the campaign in Cuba, she noted that her book's subject "took its rise in, and derived its existence from, war. Without war, it had no existence." Prior to 1898 in the United States, "War was obsolete—out of date—out of taste—in fact, out of the question: hence there existed no need for providing relief for it; and thus the Red Cross has stood, unrecognized in the shadows of obscurity all the eighteen years of its existence among us, waiting for the sure, alas, too sure, touch of war, to light up its dark figure, and set in motion the springs of action."[72] The repeated appearance of the Red Cross nurse in battle reenactment films suggests her importance within cinematic constructions of empire and gives insight into the way in which the moving pictures helped mobilize women through the circuits of empire. Indeed, the figure of the Red Cross nurse brings into sharp focus women's participation in the "war effort" at home and abroad. For while the nurse might seem like an incidental detail meant to boost the realism of these battle films, she is, in fact, the proverbial tip of the iceberg—a visible bit of an expansive structure of women's wartime work at home and abroad that demanded their increased participation in the public sphere of politics and commerce on the homefront as they kept in motion an unofficial traffic in medical supplies and food. The image of the Red Cross nurse in reenactment films onscreen back home helped create, in the words of Amy Kaplan, "a counter-narrative that turns imperial adventure into the rescue of American masculinity,"[73] and imperial expansion into the relief of trauma. Indeed, within battle reenactments the nurse appears to circulate within imperial traffic in order to ameliorate the effects of its violent shocks.

A pertinent example of this notion is provided by *US Troops and Red Cross in the Trenches before Caloocan* (Edison, 1899). The film opens with the camera positioned in a trench occupied by a commanding officer waving a sword and facing screen right as he urges forward U.S. troops who charge into the trench. They fire several volleys and, waving their hats enthusiastically, charge forward out of the trench and the frame. As they do so, two wounded soldiers fall back into the trench as the officer picks up the flag and follows his charging troops. Before he leaves the frame entirely, however, stretcher-bearing attendants followed by Red Cross nurses

FIGURE 22 *US Troops and Red Cross in the Trenches before Caloocan* (Edison, 1899).
COURTESY OF THE LIBRARY OF CONGRESS MOTION PICTURE READING ROOM

dressed in white enter the trench at screen right and, as the catalogue de-scribes, "tenderly care for the fallen." As the attendants carry away one soldier on a stretcher, a nurse—with her red cross clearly visible on her arm—attends to another as the film ends. The rapid appearance of the nurses on the heels of the charging soldiers creates a parallel between these two kinds of "troops"—one the representative of heroic masculinity, the other of heroic femininity. Importantly, the traumatized body of the fallen soldier—wounded by an unseen enemy—is the figure that calls forth the appearance of heroic femininity, making her emblematic of the reenact-ment's fascination with and repetition of historical trauma and its mastery. Though before its declaration, the war was promoted in the popular press as an opportunity for American men to escape the degenerating effects of too-influential modern femininity, once transferred to the front the very same feminine influence became responsible for the regeneration of the traumatized body of the American soldier. To understand how this figure would have resonated within popular culture in 1899, I will turn to Clara Barton's published accounts of Red Cross activities on the domestic front and on the warfront that appeared in magazines in 1898.

On February 8, 1898, nine days before the destruction of the battleship

Maine, the "President's Committee for Cuban Relief" left Washington for Cuba with, as Barton wrote, "no thought on the part of any person but to do unobtrusively the little that could be done for the lessening of the woes of a small island of people, [afflicted by] adverse circumstances, racial differences, the inevitable results of a struggle of freedom, the fate of war, and the terrible features of a system of subjugation, which, if true, is too dark to name."[74] This "system" of subjugation was, of course, Spanish colonial rule. Through a system Barton termed "organized beneficence," her Red Cross nurses helped rehabilitate hospitals and orphanages and create systems of food distribution among the Cuban populations prior to the military campaign in Cuba, thereby helping to establish a narrative of intervention by the United States as a form of rescue. For example, Barton reported seeing an astonishing spectacle of suffering at the Los Fosos hospital in Havana, where she found

> over four hundred women and children in the most pitiable condition possible for human beings to be in, and live; and they did not live, for the death record counted them out a dozen or more every twenty-four hours, and the grim, terrible pile of rude black coffins that confronted one at the very doorway, told to each famishing applicant on her entrance what her exit was likely to be.
>
> We went from room to room, each filled to repletion—not a dozen beds in all. Some of the inmates could walk, as many could not—lying on the floors in their filth—some mere skeletons; others swollen out of all human shape. Death-pallid mothers, lying with glazing eyes, and a famishing babe clutching at a milkless breast.[75]

Spanish colonial rule had rendered this horrifying spectacle of mass trauma, death, and the decay that seemed to demand intervention by a more benevolent regime, one that might impose the signifiers of domestic order and hygiene in the face of such squalor. As representatives of the "mother heart" of the nation, Barton's nurses demonstrated the ability of the United States to do so. One observer described the nurses' response as follows: "Scrub women were put to work and a plentiful supply of soap, water, and disinfectants soon made a great change for the better. When the place had been cleansed, new cots were brought in and clean bedding put on them . . . those devoted nurses worked faithfully from early morn till late in the day to keep the place decently clean and instill habits of neatness into those miserable beings. Deprived of the pride and care of those trained women, it is easy to believe that within a week after they left, Los Fosos had resumed its former reputation as the most unsavory spot in all Havana."[76] Significantly, relief of suffering slides easily into a progress narrative in which Cuban reconcentrados are already imagined as dependent upon a more benevolent regime of uplift, hygiene, cleanliness, and institutional order mobilized from the ostensibly more civilized colonizing nation to the ostensibly less civilized. Indeed, the author speculates that without the sterling example provided by the nurses, the reconcentrados will slide back into their previous state of helpless suffering. Hence, from the beginning the discourse on the "relief" mission contained within it broad overtones of imperialism's own civilizing mission and progress narratives, in turn presented through domestic images imported from the United States to Cuba.

At times Barton even described her relief mission through military metaphor, in a way that reveals the discursive interchangeability of relief and conquest. Arriving at a small Cuban hospital in Jaruco, Barton and her nurses were driven back by the stench of death and decay they found there. Undaunted, they determined to clean and organize the hospital and save its last four living patients: "Like a body of retreating soldiers, driven but not defeated, we went a few rods out and rallied, and calling for volunteers and picked men for service, determined to 'storm the works' . . . Twenty good soldiers, with only dirt and filth as enemies, can make some progress."[77] The trained nurse thus emerged as a figure that mediated and mastered trauma, making relief the counterpart of conquest. In the process, the presence of the female trained nurse on the frontiers of the new empire helped shape, and even reform, the image of American imperialism. For, as Barton herself explained, "The army and navy embody the power of the government in the Spanish War, but the Red Cross in large degree represented the affectionate regard of the American people, for those who went out to defend the flag of the Union, and their great desire to mitigate in every possible way the sufferings resulting from exposure, disease, and conflict, as well as to relieve distress wherever it existed."[78]

Indeed, the precession of the Red Cross nurse into Cuba—just ahead of official military traffic—and the close association between the military and the Red Cross made the goals and mission of the latter available to the former. The mobilization of these women within imperial traffic had a my-thologizing effect as it allowed imperialism to pose as a mission of benevo-lent "relief" of the trauma inflicted on U.S. soldiers first by Spain and later by newly colonized Filipinos resisting rule by the United States. Hence, by 1899 Red Cross nurses appear on the heels of charging U.S. troops in *US Troops and Red Cross Nurses in the Trenches before Caloocan*; and, as nurses appear to care for the wounded, the film's focus quickly shifts from imperi-alism as territorial expansion in the Philippines to imperialism as the relief of trauma.

Significantly, the actions of heroic femininity on the warfront were doubled by the efforts of women on the home front. In the weeks leading up to the war as 250,000 men were "mustered in," thousands of women joined the "Emergency Corps" of the Red Cross to "take up that branch of work which belongs alone to women in time of war and consists in providing the requisites for a soldier's welfare not laid down in army regu-lations."[79] Organized at local as well as state and national levels, women's organizations raised money to buy medical supplies, bedding, clothing, and food that, by all accounts, the government failed to provide for its soldiers. Miss Caroline Beaumont of the Red Cross of St. Paul, Minnesota, re-ported, for example, that thanks to the Emergency Corps in Minnesota, "the Twelfth, Thirteenth, and Fourteenth, Minnesota Volunteers were first furnished with hospital supplies, delicacies for the sick, and all those nec-essary articles which the government does not supply, or furnishes only in meager quantities. Working headquarters were established, requests for donations were published. . . . women from all over the city gave freely of their means, their time, and their efforts, as they thought of a husband, a son, or a dear one in far away Cuba or Manila. The patriotism and loyalty of the men of Minnesota was shared and often inspired by the women who gave so freely. The women of St. Paul with willing hands and loving hearts, have shared in the glories of war, and the sorrows of personal loss have been mitigated by pride of race, and the love of a country that has borne such soldiers and sailors as our brave boys."[80] Motivated by patriotic "pride of race," such efforts placed women squarely in the imperial project and gave them the right to conflate nationhood with motherhood as they orches-trated and circulated a key component of imperial traffic—the supply of goods, food, and medicine that soldiers required to subordinate the "new frontier."

The absorption of women into imperial traffic also helped transform the perception of their work in the public sphere (associated with the rejection of domesticity and what Roosevelt referred to as the patriotic duty to bear children),[81] making it central to the twinned projects of nation building and empire building. Indeed, even women's participation in consumption and commercialized leisure could be remade as department stores became primary sites for women's "emergency corps" fund-raising activities. For example, on May 14, 1898, in Portland, Oregon, "an offer was made by the firm of Lipman, Wolfe, and Co. to turn over their department store to the Emergency Corps upon any date they might select. The entire charge of this establishment was to be assumed by the organization for one day—ten percent of all sales to go to the regimental fund . . . This offer was unanimously accepted and on May 17 the most novel scene ever witnessed in Portland's business history was presented. Women, prominent in charitable and philanthropic work, leaders of society, sedate and stately matrons, assumed control of the various departments of this large business house, acting as superintendent, assistant superintendent, cashier and floor managers, while a hundred more of Portland's fair daughters from early morning to late at night stood behind counters serving customers. The store was gaily decorated with flags, bunting, and roses . . . Thousands of purchasers who had waited for this day surged back and forth through the aisles, crowded stairways in their haste to give their ten percent to the soldiers' fund."[82] Such mobilization in and through the public spheres of consumption and politics incorporated women into the various forms of commercial traffic that overseas imperialism was meant to accelerate and expand. Hence, women's emergency work during the war demonstrated the mutually beneficial relationship between imperial and commercial traffic: the fund-raiser was declared a success, adding $1,000 to the treasury of the society, "while the remark made by the senior member of the firm that 'it had been the happiest day in a business career of 35 years' left no other conclusion than that a two-fold blessing follows such generous deeds."[83] At home as well as abroad, women's relief work mediated and remade commercial and territorial expansion into the image of domestic benevolence.

In return, the Spanish-American War helped remake the image of modern American femininity. As a highly mobile system of "organized beneficence" that followed disaster—natural, military, or medical—wherever it struck, the Red Cross' primary functions included the anticipation and mastery of the contingencies, shocks, and trauma of warfare. Hence, the scandalous lack of "war preparedness" on the part of the government that astonished civilians and soldiers alike struck Barton as routine, even inevitable: "Those who have seen only this one war will find these uncertainties and shortcomings very strange, and unaccountable; to me, who had seen other wars, they seemed natural, probably largely inevitable, and quite the thing to be expected, the fatal results of which misfortunes I had spent half my lifetime in instituting measures to prevent or lessen."[84] Barton's status as one of the most experienced war veterans on the new imperial frontier (she was seventy-seven years old in 1898, and she had been on the front at the Civil War and the Franco-Prussian War) and the Red Cross nurse's habitual exposure to trauma and suffering made this type of modern femininity ideally suited to the task of reinvigorating and regenerating the traumatized body of the American soldier. In this way, representations of the Red Cross nurse recuperated, in Kaplan's words, "the threat of the white out-of-control New Woman . . . by leashing her new mobility to an imperial order."[85] Specifically, the Red Cross nurse helped transform the New Woman's mobility into the mobilization of American domesticity to the battlefield, where it seemed to be needed most. Upon receiving word of the Rough Riders' engagement at San Juan Hill, Barton wrote in her diary, "It is the Rough Riders we go to, and the relief may also be rough, but it will be ready. A better body of helpers could scarcely be gotten together."[86] Once mobilized to the new frontier, then, the very same feminine qualities that just before the war were associated with the dangerous degeneration of American masculinity now became responsible for its regeneration.

For example, upon reaching the army hospital at Siboney, Barton was confronted with a spectacle of American masculinity traumatized not just by Yellow Fever and Mauser bullets but also by its own government, with the soldiers' suffering parallel to that endured by the Cubans at the hands of Spain: "The sights that met us brought tears to our eyes. There were half a dozen cots in a building where there were, perhaps, fifty or sixty patients, the greater number of whom were lying on the floor, some with a blanket under them, but a great many were lying almost naked. There were some wounded men, and others who were sick with fever; and in the dim light of a few lanterns we could see them turning from side to side in their discomfort and agony and hear their moans."[87] Though military officials initially rejected Barton's offer of help, eventually they relented and the nurses' "bright faces and cheerful voices drove away all feelings of despondency and homesickness among the sufferers, and in this way helped them quite as far on the road to recovery as the medicine that the doctors might prescribe."[88] If Mauser bullets and Yellow Fever were the unseen foes that traumatized the U.S. soldier, the Red Cross nurse was a highly visible force trained to master and relieve trauma. The war was to be retold and remembered at home as an event characterized by the soldier's heroic subjection to the shock of warfare alleviated by the nurse's heroic capacity for charity, benevolence, and relief—qualities that resisted rational analysis or quantification. Hence, one report concluded, "in all the States, the willing hands and loving hearts of the women of America have been among the foremost in affording the relief to the sick and wounded . . . True soldiers of humanity, they have labored earnestly and incessantly."[89]

Mediated representations of heroic femininity on the scene of imperial conquest shaped the way the war was repeated, represented, and hence understood in the private and the public spheres. The appearance of the nurse in battle reenactment films helped to mobilize (native white) women audiences through the circuits of imperial traffic at the turn of the century. However, the interdependent relationship between warfare and "relief" made possible a particularly pernicious mythologization that allowed imperial aggression to masquerade as the relief of suffering. The Prescott catalogue describes another reenactment, entitled *After the Battle* (probably the 1899 Edison film *Red Cross at the Front*), that foregoes representing the infliction of shock and trauma on the soldier's body (and psyche) and instead reenacts the alleviation of suffering and trauma by American women on the front. The Prescott catalogue conveys precisely the notion that the "aftermath" of imperial warfare involved mercy and the relief of the suffering of one patriotic troop by another: "After the fierce fight is over, there is always a number of dead and wounded soldiers left on the field. In this picture you can see the Sisters of Charity and members of the Red Cross Society going about the field caring for the wounded. You can also see the priest as he administers the sacrament to the dying, and can see the dead soldiers carried from the field."[90] The catalogue encourages exhibitors and audiences to perceive the Red Cross nurse seen in this picture as an agent of the American domestic order on the frontier of the new empire, thus extending the home front to the warfront. As the nurses begin the process of regenerating the traumatized male body, their actions translate the passivity of the soldier's suffering to the activity of its relief. The much more succinct description for the film *Red Cross at the Front* (1899) in the Edison catalogue simply states, "Wounded soldiers are lying around, watching the arrival of a poor fellow on a stretcher from the front. The nurses and attendants all wear the red cross on their arms,"[91] and thereby demonstrates how conquest might appear onscreen beneath the sign of benevolence.

In this way, the battle reenactment film helped place audiences on the scene of history in such a way that addressed a range of desires and demands characteristic of American modernity: to circulate visually within imperial traffic as soldiers moved across a new frontier; to "see history" from the position of an "original witness" that is simultaneously marked as innocent and even benevolent; and to repeat and thereby master the traumas that result from imperial expansion. Though the film itself is lost, descriptions of *The Battle of San Juan Hill* (Edison, 1899) suggest that it contained the characteristic features of the battle reenactment film that help explain its generic specificity and its peculiar authenticity. As *The Phonoscope* explained: "This is one of the greatest war films ever placed on the market. The enemy is seen scouting in the underbrush at the foot of the steep hill. Suddenly our own soldier boys appear under the order of 'Forward by rushes,' and gallantly charge up the hill. A struggle takes place, but our boys are victorious and they plant our flag there to stay. The most realistic part of this scene is the explosion of the bombs thrown by the enemy in close proximity to a soldier who has fallen, and who is being cared for by the Red Cross staff, who finally carry him away on a stretcher. A most exciting picture."[92]

As with Wild West reenactments, *The Battle of San Juan Hill* trades upon the reenactment's ability to place spectators in the imaginary position of a witness to highly sensational scenes of dynamic action and violent conflict between "gallant" forces of civilization and villainous forces of disorder, with the former suffering at the hands of, but ultimately triumphing over, the latter. It synthesizes the pleasures and perils of military conquest by endowing spectators with an imaginary presence on the scene of history and, concurrently, by granting them visual access to the shocks of warfare by mobilizing them to the new frontier with U.S. soldiers. Subtending the reenactment's structure of repetition that allows for the mastery of historical trauma is the image of the Red Cross worker, who through a synthesis of Victorian domestic virtue and the attributes of the New Woman helped in-scribe conquest as a more generalized relief of suffering. Battle reenactment films were, then, complex forms that endowed spectators with the illusory ability to enter into the circuits of imperial traffic and "see history"; such films thereby helped "forge moments of public unity by mobilizing multiple and often conflicting fantasies and anxieties" arising from the shift of the United States to an overseas empire.[93]

The Reenactment's Reality Effect and the Ideal Actuality

Despite—or perhaps *because of*—the reenactment's mode of address, reality effects, and illusory presence on the scene of spectacularly rendered trau-matic history, audiences continued to imagine the potential visual effects of future battle actualities. At this point it is helpful to return to the January 1900 article published in *Leslie's Weekly* that expressed the desire for "pic-tures of actual, grewsome war."[94] This revealing article suggests that the (live and film) reenactment's positioning of the spectator as observer on the battlefield had so informed popular perceptions of what the battle actuality might—or should—look like that reenactment's reality effect had become an ideal that the hoped-for actuality might some day fulfill and intensify by its status as document. The author begins by describing two different positions taken up by the camera/spectator in relation to the staged mili-tary parade and the spectacle of war: "The American Biograph is taking a prominent part in the two wars which are now occupying the center of the world's stage, and the pictures which are being shown at Keith's Theatre in New York, and at other leading houses throughout the country, are of intense interest. The Biograph paid a great deal of attention to the soldier-boys of John Bull and Uncle Sam in times of peace, and so many splendid parade pictures have been made that we are all very familiar with the ap-pearance of the American and British soldier in his gorgeous trappings of peace."[95]

Both sentences in this statement describe a distinct positioning of the camera/spectator in relation to these two types of military spectacles. The latter places the Biograph among the crowds at military parades at which there is a fairly sharp distinction between the camera/spectator and the spectacle of "the American and British soldier in his gorgeous trappings of peace." In contrast, the preceding sentence suggests that rather than merely recording war from the position of a spectator cordoned off as audience with the rest of the world, the Biograph now takes "*a prominent part* in the two wars, which are now occupying the center of the world's stage." Like the "original" witness-on-the-scene described in Wild West programs and reviews, the camera occupies the position of a witness that is paradoxically a part of the spectacle it sees and records. From this new position within military traffic, the Biograph promises a military spectacle of a different order: "Now we are to look at [the soldier] as he works in his flannel shirt, muddy khaki trousers and gaiters, with fierce whiskers on his face, and none too much flesh on his bones. We are promised some vivid, soul-stirring pictures of actual, grewsome war, and the conditions under which the Biograph operators in the Transvaal and in the Philippines are working are so favorable that the promises will probably be made good."[96]

In taking up the position alongside the soldier and thus placed in the thick of things, the camera promises to provide images of the imperial soldier intimate enough to let us see his "fierce whiskers" as he engages in "actual, grewsome war." In short, the desired point of view for the camera/spectator is that of the agent-witness of imperialism as he or she struggles to bring the disputed territory under control. This point of view is similar to the one promised by Cody when he claimed that his reenactments reiterated both the historical event and the position from which it was originally seen by the agents of national expansion, only now the camera records the original, iterable event. Like the program for the Wild West, the *Leslie's Weekly* article foregrounds the presence of the source of the spectacle's enunciation at the event. The cinema then displays the spectacle for the audience, which is granted the opportunity to mistake the camera's agent-witness point of view for its own, and thereby places the spectator in the position of an "original" witness to the spectacle of imperial warfare. Just as the Wild West rejected painterly and written accounts of frontier life, the article rejects journalistic accounts of war: "A written description is always and forever the point of view, more or less biased, of the correspondent. But the Biograph camera does not lie, and we form our own judgment of this and that as we watch the magic screen."[97] The transparently rendered spectacle of war seen from the point of view of the imperial agent on the scene becomes the desired mark of the historical real. Rather than the battle reenactment film "faking" or simulating the actuality, *the hoped-for war actuality aspires to achieve that which the reenactment had already accom-*

plished: the illusory placement of the camera/spectator as a witness on the scene of a historical spectacle it records/perceives. Important here is the relationship between history and spectator that the (live and film) battle reenactment made both imaginable and ideal. Once in place, the reenactment's reality effect informed fantasies about what the battle actuality would or should look like—never mind that the defining characteristic of the "actual" perceptual experience of war was battlefield blindness. To become visible as spectacle and hence to seem most "real," then, the battle actuality had to deploy the reenactment's own reality effects.

Quite significantly, the author understands that the battle actuality and spectator-position he describes will in all likelihood remain an ideal and hence the province of the reenactment: "So both the American and British war offices have recognized the possible value of real war pictures, and have given the operators of the American Mutoscope and Biograph Company the privilege of risking their lives to secure actual pictures of the war. They may not be successful. They are handicapped by all the involved processes of photography. Their films, thousands of miles from a developing station, may be ruined before they ever pass from the negative to the positive stage, and what promised to be a wonderful scene may prove a blank strip of film. But the game is worth the candle. Imagine the historical value of a moving picture of the charge at Balaklava, or of the advance upon Gettysburg. There will be other Balaklavas and other Gettysburgs, and the Biograph may get there just in the nick of time."[98] As Dickson's account of the Boer War would soon demonstrate, the mere presence of the camera at a battle did not necessarily bring the latter into focus. The contingencies of modern imperial warfare and film technology made it difficult to incorporate the camera and hence the spectator into the accelerated movements of military traffic and to manage the shocks and trauma that such mobilizations inevitably incurred. It was precisely the reenactment's repetition or reiteration of the imperial battle under conditions that controlled the contingencies and shocks of modern warfare that made the imaginary position of the "witness" both possible *and* an ideal to which the battle actuality aspired. Like the live reenactments staged in Buffalo Bill's Wild West, reenactment films such as *Advance of Kansas Volunteers at Caloocan* suggest that the pleasures provided by the battle reenactment lay precisely in its artificiality.

Undoubtedly, the indexicality of the reenactment film's image further intensified its reality effects, giving support to the turn-of-the-century fantasy that the violent conflict taking place on the edges of the new overseas empire appeared to its own agents as highly visible spectacles of power. The reenactment's reality effects allowed audiences to delight in the impossible proximity to the distant historical processes that the reenactment appeared to grant them. Like the Wild West battles that incorporated urban audiences into the proto-modern traffic of westward manifest destiny, the war reenactment film's manufacture and orchestration of the contingencies of modern warfare incorporated film audiences into the turn-of-the-century circuits of technological modernity that were inseparable from overseas imperialism. Just as early cinematic representations of the urban street scene actuality demonstrate a "picture taking capability able to match the fugitive and accelerated temporality of American technological modernity,"[99] so too does the battle reenactment film demonstrate a picture making capability that strived to match the fugitive and accelerated history of American imperialism's expansion across a new frontier.

In 1901, the Pan-American Exposition was held to celebrate the success of the imperial endeavors of the United States; to showcase the nation's industrial and military technological progress; and to encourage the circulation of commercial traffic between the United States and the nations of Latin America. While the Pan-American Exposition displayed in official government buildings and in midway exhibits such as the "Filipino Village" the recently acquired resources and peoples found in the nation's new "possessions," it focused most of its attention on a new technology—the hydroelectric power plant—which, like the modern battleship before it, had the capacity to expand exponentially the circulation of various forms of traffic to, from, and through the United States. Just as actuality films shot before the outbreak of war in 1898 emphasized the power and pleasures of imperial traffic, actuality films shot at the Pan-American Exposition seemed to promise that American technological modernity would bring about a bright future defined by the illumination of all darkness and the absorption of everyday life into myriad forms of pleasurable, electrified traffic. The Pan-American Exposition, like the imperial wars of the United States, would bring modernity's dark underbelly into view, and the moving pictures, in turn, would provide audiences once again with the opportunity to master the shocks linked to industrialization through the reenactment film.

3

ELECTRIC MODERNITY AND THE CINEMA AT THE PAN-AMERICAN EXPOSITION

The City of Living Light

In 1895, Antonia and William Kennedy Laurie Dickson opened their *History of the Kinetograph, Kinetoscope and Kinetophonograph* with the following description: "In the year 1887, Mr. Edison found himself in possession of one of those breathing spells which relieve the tension of inventive thought. The great issues of electricity were satisfactorily under way. The incandescent light had received its finishing touches; telephonic and telegraphic devices were substantially interwoven with the fabric of international life; the phonograph was established upon what seemed to be a solid financial and social basis, and the inventor felt at liberty to indulge in a few secondary flights of fancy. It was then that he was struck by the idea of reproducing to the eye the effect of motion by means of a swift and graded succession of pictures and of linking these photographic impressions with the phonograph in one combination so as to complete to both senses synchronously the record of a given scene."[1] Given that the Dicksons were Edison employees, it is not surprising that they narrate the origins of the idea of cinema through the myth of Thomas Edison as inventive genius who with his lightning-like flashes of insight single-handedly and indefatigably mechanized illumination, communication, and representation. Crucial to this myth is the Edisonian technological landscape described by the Dicksons, which is defined primarily by the harnessed power of electricity. Preceded by the telephone, telegraph, phonograph, and incandescent light, moving picture technology emerges here as one in a series of mechanical devices brought to life by an electric current flowing through an ever-expanding circulatory system of cables and wires already "substantially interwoven with the fabric of international life." Like the other modern technologies named by the Dicksons, the moving pictures would have the power both to expand and to contract the world through the mechanical transcendence of space and time, thereby transforming electricity into yet another pleasurable attraction that derived its power to delight from the circuits and currents that increasingly incorporated modern life in the United States.

The history of early cinema, the Dicksons suggest, is bound up in and even inseparable from the history of electricity. Indeed, the most important period of electricity's development, application, and diffusion took place between 1880 and 1925 and thereby roughly coincided with the emergence and development of the cinema. Moreover, the hallmarks of modernity—the amusement park, the factory assembly line, the streetcar, the department store, and the cinema—are unthinkable without electricity. As an invisible force sensible only through touch, electricity was known and experienced at the end of the nineteenth century primarily though its effects—light, heat, and motive force—and hence by whatever (signifying) machine completed its circuit. Moving picture technology was only one of several new technologies that provided an outlet for the electric currents that revolutionized modern life by accelerating the urban and intra-urban traffic in machines, commerce, bodies, images, and communications.

Between 1880 and 1900, electricity remained for most Americans a public, urban phenomenon, and it was easily incorporated into the burgeoning sphere of commercialized leisure, commodity culture, and mechanized forms of production. Electric light first replaced gas lighting in theaters, factories, and on busy commercial thoroughfares in big cities. The Russian engineer Paul Jablochov lit Paris' boulevards with arc lights in 1867, and in so doing sparked a drive to illuminate other busy urban thoroughfares in the 1870s and 1880s—most famously on Broadway in New York City, whose luminous nightscape was popularly called the "Great White Way." Artificial light spread from the street to department store windows and interiors when Wanamakers installed electric light in its Philadelphia store in 1878. Developments in electric power and illumination spurred on production as well as consumption. Unlike the gas lighting it eventually replaced, incandescent light did not flicker and its even and bright illumination made work at night possible, thereby extending the length of the workday. As the Edison direct current system was gradually superceded by Westinghouse's alternating current system, the efficient transport of electricity across greater distances became feasible and allowed factories to be built far from generating stations. In turn, the electrification of the factory rationalized its organization into patterns of sequential production, making the assembly line possible. The electric streetcar mobilized workers and crowds to and through the electrified urban landscape and expanded the boundaries of the city by creating commuter suburbs and integrating outlying rural areas and small towns into the economies of nearby cities. It generated new forms of mechanized leisure in the shape of amusement parks, which were built at the ends of streetcar lines to generate traffic and whose rides were modeled after streetcar technology. Within the city, the electric streetcar influenced the location of cinemas in towns and cities, as venues for commercialized leisure tended to cluster around streetcar lines.[2] In short, the harnessed power of electricity greatly expanded and accelerated the circulation of modern traffic and integrated numerous technologies of communication and transportation into networks of circuits and currents that kept many forms of traffic in motion.

At the turn of the century, the modern American's experience of the power and pleasures of electricity was perhaps greatest at the world's fairs and expositions.[3] Fourteen years after Edison's remarkably productive "breathing spell" and six years after the Dicksons committed it to writing, the Edison Manufacturing Co. sent, on separate occasions, its cameramen James White and Edwin S. Porter to film the Pan-American Exposition in Buffalo, New York. The purpose of the Pan-American Exposition was to celebrate a century of technological progress in the Americas as well as the newly won position by the United States of military and economic supremacy in the Western Hemisphere. To demonstrate the nation's prowess

and progress, the organizers of the Pan-American staged nighttime spectacles using Edison incandescent light. Each night, fairgoers were treated
to a massive electric light display called the City of Living Light, which
transformed the Exposition grounds into what some observers called a
"magical fairy land" by outlining its buildings, statuary, and fountains with
350,000 incandescent lights. The City of Living Light made possible an
important social and cultural convergence between the cinema and new
technologies of artificial illumination, for the brilliance of this illumination allowed Porter to film what he described as "marvels in photography"
and what he claimed were the first moving pictures shot at night in the
United States. Through their cinematic rendering of the Pan-American's
electric light displays, these panoramic films simultaneously enacted and
aestheticized technological modernity's transcendence of the natural order
through electricity's disassociation of light from time. As visual documents
of American technological modernity, they reveal how elaborate displays
of nighttime illumination at world's fairs and expositions created idealized
forms of machine-made nighttime vision that demonstrated and celebrated
electricity's ability to extend human perception across space and time. In
short, these films reveal how parallel electric technologies merged together
at the Pan-American in the first year of the twentieth century to picture
the nation's past, present, and future and hence to teach observers and
spectators how to imagine the pleasurable power of American industry and
how to delight in one's incorporation into an expanding electric network.

Before the closing of the Pan-American, the moving pictures would
make both the vulnerability and the visibility of this power evident to moving picture spectators: while Porter was in Buffalo to shoot the City of
Living Light, Leon F. Czolgosz, described by newspapers as an unemployed laborer with ties to the anarchist movement, assassinated President
William McKinley on the grounds of the Pan-American. Porter's camera
was outside the Temple of Music when the shooting took place and, as
news of the assassination attempt rippled through the crowd, the camera
caught the reaction of the fairgoers who had gathered to shake hands with
McKinley. In the aftermath of McKinley's death, the electric chair—another technology dreamed up in the same year as the kinetophonograph
with the help of Edison—would reinforce the close association of national-
industrial progress with electric power and the boundedness of modern

life and modern death with the circuits of technological modernity. In what follows I will discuss how in the first year of the twentieth century a range of electric technologies—incandescent lighting, moving pictures, and the electric chair—helped form a picture of American modernity that charged its experience with newfound visual pleasure and displayed industry's power to contain and control the very forces it had unleashed.

Setting the Stage: The Electrified City of Light and Motion

At the turn of the century the city of Buffalo, New York, was in many respects an ideal metropolitan area for staging a spectacle of national power based on electric power, for the newly harnessed current of the Niagara River animated the cityscape with electric light and motion. To attract visitors to the Pan-American, guidebooks and advertisements promoted its host city less as a distinct locale featuring specific cultural, geographic, and social characteristics, and more as a point of transition where interconnecting lines of railway, steamship, and electric streetcar traffic converged and diverged. Many guidebooks emphasized Buffalo's historically close association with the circulation of natural resources and commodities, which began in 1825 with the completion of the Erie Canal, a transportation technology that was hailed as an example of American ingenuity's power to triumph over and control nature. By connecting Lake Erie to the Hudson River and Albany with Buffalo, the Erie Canal increased the flow of commerce between the East and regions to the west of the Great Lakes. Publicity materials from the Exposition pointed to the Erie Canal as an established form of transportation technology that had the rhizomatic effect of generating new circulatory systems running to and through Buffalo. One guidebook noted that Buffalo's position at "the head of the Erie Canal" made it "the center of a concentration of great trunk lines of railroad, *and [that it] is in [the]direct natural course of an enormous tide of traffic*," which had made it the world's fourth-largest shipping port.[4] In turn, railroad companies had "over 500 miles of trackage within the city limits, while their plans call for two hundred more." Such boosterism promoted the city as the heart of the nation's commercial-industrial circulatory system; hence, the guidebook goes on to say, "Buffalo is a great point of transhipment, and the stopping off place in the center of the continent, and may be compared to the junction of the small ends of two giant funnels, one stretching far westward, the other towards the rising sun. The products of half the continent, the mines, the forests, the fertile fields sweeping to the westward funnel" by railroad trains and waterways that pass "through the narrow neck [and] . . . out to the world beyond, through the eastern funnel, and sending in return over the same pathway the product of looms, factories, mines, and many industries which are kept unceasingly busy."[5] To sustain and showcase the city's function in perpetuating the pulsing traffic in national commerce, Buffalo required structures like the Ellicott Square Building, "the largest exclusively office building in the world" and "a city in itself."[6]

The "great tide of traffic" flowing to and through Buffalo included passengers as well as commerce. Indeed, Congress approved Buffalo as the home of the Pan-American simply because forty million people lived within a day's railway journey of the city.[7] Once inside the city, the guidebooks noted, fairgoers would find in Buffalo a model for continuous urban traffic thanks to an extensive electric streetcar system. Consisting of 315 miles of trackage, the electric streetcar "brought every section of the city within twenty minute's ride of the business center, and a single fare of five cents enables the passengers to travel from one limit of the city to another."[8] During the Pan-American, the guidebook promised, eight hundred cars would be in operation. However, should the wealthier fairgoer choose to arrive by automobile, the motorist would find 104.7 miles of stone pavement, 7.54 miles of brick, 3.08 miles of macadam, and 222.8 miles of asphalt, giving Buffalo the somewhat dubious distinction of having "more asphalt than Paris, Washington, London, or any other city in the world."[9] These paved surfaces, fairgoers were assured, made Buffalo a "wheelman's paradise" and hence an ideal destination for automobile enthusiasts. In this way, the guidebooks for the Pan-American instructed fairgoers to perceive the site of the Exposition as a key point of convergence for the orderly and continuous flow of commercial, industrial, and passenger traffic, the motion of which seemed magically to transform a limitless supply of natural resources into products enjoyed by the rest of the nation. Hence Buffalo's identity as a transitional space acted as an ideal prop for both the Exposition's celebration of modern traffic and its promotion of the broader industrial fantasy of a continuous, unhindered production and circulation of commodities spurred on by limitless natural resources and all-consuming markets.

This fascination with and promotion of the pleasurable experience of being absorbed into traffic derived from the Exposition's objective to promote and facilitate the circulation of commerce from the United States to Central America, South America, Canada, and its newly held territories in the Caribbean and in Southeast Asia. Taking place shortly after the victory by the United States in the Spanish-American War, the Pan-American was in many respects an act of commercial warfare by the United States against European manufacturers. One proposal for the Pan-American very bluntly declared in 1899 that "the United States has naturally an interest in obtaining the custom of the merchants of Latin America, and securing due appreciation for the high quality and relative cheapness of its products in contrast with the inferior grades of European manufacturers which are sold in these countries in large quantities . . . It is well known that the exports of the United States, which are increasing at the rate of 25% a year, must find an outlet."[10] Thus the Exposition was meant to promote and stimulate the north-south flow of commercial traffic in the Americas and reduce trade between European and American nations.

Despite the desire to secure "due appreciation" for U.S. exports in South and Central America, most of visitors to the Exposition were from the United States. As a result, the Pan-American labored less to teach South and Central Americans how to perceive American modernity than to teach middle- and working-class Americans to perceive themselves as part of a continuously moving and hence progressing nation united by an expanding network of transportation and communications technologies brought to life by electricity. Thus, the Pan-American was itself to be experienced in a state of motion. One pamphlet promised that the Exposition "will tell the story of civilization in such a way that he who runs may read. It will serve to awaken the young to the possibilities for achievement that surround them. It will quicken the heart beats of patriotism and stimulate the pride of the people in acquiring and maintaining a place of the highest rank among the nations. It will entertain them with refined exhibitions of skill and prowess. It will delight them with novelty and impress their minds indelibly with the deeper feeling that they are participating in the development of a wonderful age."[11] This delightful interpellation was to come about through the absorption of the fairgoer into various forms of traffic. While the government buildings exhibited commerce, material culture, and machines from the nations of the Americas, the midway attractions mobilized fairgoers on imaginary journeys to spaces and times as far flung as the moon, the antebellum South, the Philippines, and (why not?) hell. Many such attractions were based upon the same transportation technologies that brought the fairgoer to the Exposition grounds. Thus, a miniature railway ride gave passengers the experience of riding first class, while an Aquarama circulated passengers by electric boat launch through a system of canals and tunnels festooned with decorative lights. Once fairgoers tired of horizontally articulated traffic, they might enjoy vertical ascension in a mechanical captive balloon or the Thompson Aerio-Cycle, a double Ferris wheel modified to facilitate a higher turnover of passengers. Like amusement park attractions, such rides used transportation technology to create highly aestheticized and pleasurable experiences of mechanized movement that mobilized the fairgoer through predetermined paths of traffic calculated to create the illusion of freedom and mobility. As Anne Friedberg argues, the panoramic perception and imaginary mobility offered by such attractions and the films shot from them ultimately required the stasis of the amusement seeker.[12]

Electric Spectacles and the Articulation of Modern American Power

To begin to situate electricity in the history of panoramic and cinematic perception, we must first note that despite the guidebooks' emphasis on traffic, no single technology was exhibited as the primary vehicle for such mobilizations. Instead, it was through the motive force of electricity that the Exposition articulated a range of discourses on American modernity and its perception. Nearly every guidebook encouraged visitors to perceive the pulsing circulatory system running to and through the Pan-American as the effect of a greater power, the harnessing of which testified to the progress and prowess of American industry: both Buffalo and the Pan-American Exposition received power from a massive hydroelectric plant where the Niagara river current was transformed into an electric current. Hence guidebooks never failed to note that the primary motive force behind all commercial and industrial circulation in Buffalo was "the cheap electric power contributed by the forces of the current of the Niagara River transmitting it for use in Buffalo for lighting, street railway, and various industrial purposes."[13] The hydroelectric plant had made electricity a part of everyday public life in Buffalo: it mobilized streetcars, elevators, and factory assembly lines and allowed arc lights to illuminate streets, shop windows, and advertisements, and incandescent lights to illuminate the interiors of office buildings, theaters, and upper-class homes. The city and the Exposition grounds thereby served as outlets for the tremendous force of the Niagara's two currents—the river's current and the electric current it generated—making both a living model of efficient electric commercial enterprise. Electricity provided the city with a dematerialized and disembodied form of power that seemed omnipotent, omnipresent, and potentially limitless in its extension and universal in its application. Symbolizing the apotheosis of industrialization, the hydroelectric plant appeared to overcome all obstacles to the circulation of power: in an instant it transformed water into light and motion, a natural resource into a pure commodity, and the falls—traditionally an obstacle to navigation—into a "silent servant" that transcended space and time with minimal dependence upon human and animal labor. Hence the electricity that flowed to the Pan-American from the Niagara hydroelectric plant was celebrated as a form of metatraffic: it was hailed as a profitable commodity that circulated through space in order to expand further the circulation of bodies, machines, commerce, and power through cities and towns across the United States.

The Edison moving pictures that were shot from onboard rides and attractions allowed audiences to see the Exposition from a position that simulated the experience of being absorbed into the Pan-American's own system of electrified traffic. For example, shot from onboard an electric boat launch, the three-part *A Trip around the Pan-American Exposition* (Edison, 1901) visually manifests the motive force of electricity that ushered the fairgoer on a circuitous route through an extensive system of canals while at the same time making visible the other rides that fed off the same electric current, thereby bringing the enchanting electrified landscape into view. Moreover, the boat ride emphasized the important connection between the two different currents upon which the Exposition relied: the network of canals and waterways through which the electric boat moves mirrors the Exposition's own networked electric circuitry and reminds one of the current of the Niagara River, which, though more than twenty miles away, supplied power to the boats and other rides that mobilized the fairgoer through the Exposition grounds. Indeed, the smooth, continuous movement of the extended boat ride (the film is three reels long) emphasizes

FIGURE 23 *A Trip around the Pan-American Exposition* (Edison, 1901). Part of the Thompson Aerio-Cycle is visible in the background. COURTESY OF THE LIBRARY OF CONGRESS MOTION PICTURE READING ROOM

the seemingly limitless energy supplied by the electric current. Indeed, the Pan-American was organized to create an ideal impression of electrified forms of traffic, which itself relied upon the pleasurable distribution of powerful electric currents throughout the Exposition's grounds. To be sure, within the grounds of the Pan-American, electricity promised a future characterized by continuous circulation unhindered by the obstacles of space and time, natural and political boundaries, and labor strikes and distant markets. Because it was a disembodied form of energy that took no specific material shape, whatever receptacle it fed into, whatever completed the circuit or served as an end point endowed electricity with social and cultural significance. Thus the grounds and buildings of the Pan-American provided an extraordinary body or prop to make electricity signify, to make it resonate socially, and to give it new ideological power. Luther Stieringer and Henry Rustin, light designers for the Pan-American, created just such a spectacle by transforming the Exposition grounds into a City of Living Light—an ethereal urban space created by 350,000 incandescent lights that outlined every Exposition building and illuminated every pool and fountain. Like the flow of traffic that circulated to and through the Pan-

American during the day, the commodity aesthetic of the Exposition's nightime illumination stressed the streamlined, continuous, and even distribution of energy and power across space. This emphasis led Stieringer to favor incandescent over arc lighting because, as he stated, "more uniform illumination can be effected by thoroughly distributing the lighting units than by [the] intensification of light at points separated by a considerable distance" that was so characteristic of the extremely bright illumination of arc lighting.[14] To create the luminous City of Living Light, Stieringer employed a method of incandescent light design called "sketching." Louis Bell, in his 1902 work *The Art of Illumination*, described Stieringer's method in which the lines of a pencil sketch of a building serve as a guide for the placement of incandescent bulbs: "The configuration of the lights to be used in the luminous sketch that seems needful for the best artistic results may be roughly determined by making at daylight, or better, near sunset, a rough, clear, line drawing of the scene to be illuminated from a rather distant viewpoint, the further as the scale of the work increases. Then the distribution of lights following the principal points and outlines of this drawing will give the main effects that one wishes to produce. The [electric light] sketch may be filled up by adding necessary details not too brightly, and the ground illumination must be such as not to interfere with this general arrangement. Reflected light from the radiants thus distributed plays a useful part in adding to the general brilliancy of the effect without marring its artistic unity."[15]

Again the Exposition's designers favored an aesthetic that subtly reminded fairgoers of the continuity of the electric currents that pulsed through circuits and wires throughout the grounds. Indeed, the thorough distribution of light by the Pan-American's luminous sketch of "Living Light" directed the eye to the Exposition's centerpiece, the Electric Tower. Four hundred feet high and eighty square feet in circumference, the tower was studded with forty thousand lightbulbs, and highlighted by ninety-four searchlights. A waterfall that cascaded from the base of the tower and a court of fountains in front of it reminded fairgoers of the twinned currents that generated the nighttime illumination. A statue of the "Goddess of Light" and more searchlights were perched at the apex of the tower to represent the forces of power and progress central to the Exposition's vision of American modernity.

The Electric Tower was a testament to modern technology's ability to overcome the obstacles that blocked the circulation of traffic and with it the forward march of progress. One guidebook mentioned that the tower's searchlight "flashes through space with great brilliancy for many miles, embracing in its grand circle the Falls of Niagara, the harnessed energy of which operates the machinery which generates the lighting power."[16] The searchlight's reach to the falls once again emphasized that the current of electricity running to the Pan-American was the effect of the Niagara River's own current, thereby making clear that one medium for traffic's circulation created another, more expansive medium. Indeed, the self-reflexivity of this spectacle created the illusion that the falls were illuminating themselves, thereby making an attraction of the electric circuits whose currents began and ended at the power plant. In turn, the searchlight's illumination of its natural power source articulated the fantasy of modern technology's elimination of human labor, which throughout the 1890s was perceived by industry as an obstacle to the continuous and uninterrupted flow of commodities and profit. And the lightning-like flashes coming from the tower's searchlight alluded to industry's ability to overcome and harness electricity's unpredictable, instantaneous, and deadly power. The City of Living Light referred to the subordination of nature by modern technology, which had extended electricity's instantaneity into a sustained duration, converted its deadly power into life-giving energy, and transformed its arbitrariness into a highly rationalized design. Moreover, it fashioned the industrial materiality of the electric network into an aesthetic ideal. Each feature of the display showcased industry's absolute control over the forces it had first unleashed and then harnessed to create the electric current that circulated throughout the Pan-American.

With its emphasis on the control and subordination of powerful natural forces, the nighttime illumination of the Pan-American provides an extraordinary turn-of-the-century example of industry's deployment of the "technological sublime." Historians of American culture such as Leo Marx, John F. Kasson, and David Nye have analyzed the importance of the technological sublime to the formation of a specifically American sense of national identity, purpose, and destiny in the nineteenth century and early twentieth.[17] Closely related to the experience of sublime nature described by Immanuel Kant and Edmund Burke, the American version of the sublime arose from, as Nye states, "repeated experiences of awe and wonder, often tinged with an element of terror, which people have when confronted with particular natural sites, architectural forms, and technological achievements." As Nye further explains, nineteenth-century Americans increasingly organized sublime experiences around new technologies that subordinated the natural world to a degree previously thought impossible. Americans thereby modified the sublime experience in order to suit the social, political, and cultural conditions of the United States, giving each instance a specific historical resonance and politics. In this way, the sublime functioned through "emotional configurations that both emerge from and help to validate new social and technological conditions" arising from rapid industrialization and urbanization.[18] When the nation stopped to observe and celebrate the completion of the Continental Railroad, or when hundreds of thousands made an arduous and expensive pilgrimmage to Chicago in 1893 to see the illumination of its Great White Way, or when massive crowds gathered to see the opening of the Brooklyn Bridge or the Chrysler Building, they participated in the shared perception of awe-inspiring high-tech spectacles that seemed to make sense of everyday experiences typical of a rapidly changing, industrial society.

Nye argues that the experience of the technological sublime is fundamentally that of an observer's encounter with the spectacle of a manufactured object—such as the Corliss engine, Ford's massive River Rouge Plant, or the City of Living Light at the Pan-American—the sight of which provokes a sudden, "permissible eruption of feeling that briefly overwhelmed reason only to be contained by it."[19] This rupture of ordinary perception generates feelings of awe, astonishment, shock, and even terror that momentarily overpower the mental faculties and temporarily reduce the spectator to a state of dumbfoundedness, but then ultimately propel him or her into a state of mental action that allows for rational comprehension of that which initially seemed inconceivable. As new technologies were deployed as sublime objects by showmen who specialized in provoking the desired response, the sublime experience increasingly took place in urban rather than natural settings, and in the midst of crowds of spectators or tourists rather than in solitude. Moreover, the objects that inspired dumbfounded awe with their size, power, and dynamism were no longer divinely created natural phenomena but rather the products of human reason. The observer's rational processes were overwhelmed not by some awesome mysterious power but by the awesome rational power of inventors and engineers. Hence, "the awe induced by seeing an immense or dynamic technological object became a celebration of the power of human reason, and this awe granted special privilege to engineers and inventors." In turn, the privileged place granted to the engineer-inventor symbolized, by extension, the privileged place occupied by the nation, as "the American sublime transformed the individual's experience of immensity and awe into a belief in national greatness."[20] The Pan-American's aestheticized electric spectacles were calculated to inspire both awe *and* the rational comprehension of the powers of engineer-inventors, the industries they served, and the future national greatness they helped fairgoers imagine. Indeed, part of the pleasure of the Exposition was its daytime organization around what Neil Harris calls an "operational aesthetic" that explained and demonstrated the processes and principles that powered its vast machinery.[21] Hence visitors flocked both to the Exposition's massive Electricity Building (which was jammed with electrical devices, displays, and miniature power plants) and to the Niagara Power Plant to watch its day-to-day operations. In short, the pleasurable experience of new technologies did not end with shock, surprise, and astonishment (nor can such experiences be equated with passive consumption), for they constituted only one phase of the exposition-goer's experience of the "American modernity" on display.

By most accounts, the desired responses were achieved. For example, in an article entitled "Electric Dawn," a journalist for the *Chicago American* described the effect of the gradual nighttime illumination of the City of Living Light: "In the gathering darkness all the lights in the City of the Fair are turned off. Presently, low and soft as a whisper of music, the strains of 'Nearer, My God to Thee,' steals from the band stand and at that moment the lamps glow, red and dull in the darkness—about the pavillion, on the outlines of all the buildings, in the splashing waters of the many fountains. The music rises to a louder tone, and the lights brighten with music—crescendo in the band stand—avesper day—dawn through all the grounds. Clearer and higher, the hymn and the lights—until, as the closing chord lifts the song to a climax of triumph the grounds are ablaze with the clear, white light, every building and tower and fountain is luminously outlined; everything that is incomplete [or] imperfect, everything that would mar, or make a false tone, is hidden in the air—flowing steadfastly in the night sky. The deep heart applause of breathless silence tells how the picture is glowing upon every soul in the vast multitude."[22] This description recounts a near textbook example of a collective experience of the electric sublime. Stieringer's event began by placing the audience into an "ordinary" perceptual experience of the night by turning off all of the lights in and around the Exposition grounds, thereby occluding the surrounding architecture that would ultimately serve as a prop for the illumination. Ordinary nighttime perception was gradually undermined by the rather novel sight of the electric illumination, which would have been astonishing both to those unaccustomed to electric light as well as to those who experienced it in an everyday context. Indeed, one of the most distinctive features of this electric spectacle was the implementation of a rheostat that allowed electricians to control the level of the display's brightness, thus making possible an "electric dawn" that gradually began to burn and shine. The astonishment provoked by the sublime electric spectacle can be measured by the "deep heart applause of breathless silence" (the tell-tale response to the sublime) that seems to have gripped the crowd, creating the shared, public experience of a kind of quasi-religious reverence helped, undoubtedly, by the strains of "Nearer, My God to Thee," which scored the unfolding display and helped shape the crowd's interpretation of it. The journalist's account thereby suggests that fairgoers experienced the City of Living Light as an ethereal urban spectacle that concealed the imperfections of American modernity and transformed the "vast multitude" into an astonished audience, momentarily in awe of rather than at odds with industry. The particular "picture" formed in the "souls" of the crowd was that of a nation—led by the superior technical skill of its engineers— that had gloriously harnessed the power and promise of the extraordinary natural landscape of the Niagara (itself interpreted as a sublime sign of the nation's "special covenant" with God, and hence its exceptional destiny) to astounding ends. Put differently, this nighttime electric spectacle simultaneously enacted and demonstrated the *pleasurable* possibilities and effects of the modern American industry and power that fairgoers observed at work when they made their way through the streets of Buffalo each day on their way to the Exposition.

That the Edison Manufacturing Co.'s cameramàn Porter filmed the City of Living Light is unsurprising: as a skilled electrician and mechanic with expertise in motion picture exhibition, Porter had been hired by Edison in 1900 to improve the projecting kinetoscope and was later moved from the Edison laboratories to become the company's key cameraman. Not only were the designers of the City of Living Light fellow Edison employees but the Exposition also relied on Edison technology to stage its electric spectacle. Hence, there can be little doubt that Porter's cinematic articulations of the electric sublime acted as visually compelling advertisements for Edison incandescent lighting and, in turn, for the promises of a luminous future made by industry to middle-class Americans.

Indeed, Porter seems to have labored to reproduce the structural experience of the electric sublime for the crowds who watched these films beyond the confines of the Exposition. The film *Pan-American Exposition by Night* (Edison, 1901) opens with a daytime shot of the main esplanade. As the camera pans slowly it displays the fairgrounds as a utopian urban space through which middle-class fairgoers stroll arm and arm. In some respects, such an opening might have seemed quotidian to spectators expecting more than the by-then familiar sight of urban street scenes. However, when the camera reaches the Electric Tower, the image fades to black. Gradually the darkened screen is illuminated by the electric light that outlines the tower, buildings, statuary, and water displays and the camera continues to pan across the esplanade. Just as Stieringer preceded the display of his electric spectacle by turning off all lights on the Exposition grounds to cloak the Pan-American in darkness and thereby return the crowd to a state of ordinary nighttime perception, the camera's fade to black in vaudeville houses would have left spectators of Porter's film in a similar darkness. By preceding the electric dawn with darkness, both Stieringer and Porter provoked in their spectators a desire and a demand for artificial light—and herein lies the historicity of their incarnation of the electric sublime. The fade to black would have reminded spectators and fairgoers—consciously or unconsciously—of the subordination of everyday life to the inevitable alternation of night and day, and would have pulled them back, momentarily, to a relatively recent time preceding electricity, when nightfall brought not just the end of the day but the cessation of production and an end to the circulation of traffic. By transforming water into light and night into day, the Pan-American and moving pictures of the City of Living Light brought fairgoers and film audiences out from this benighted past into a

FIGURE 24 A AND B *Pan-American Exposition by Night* (Edison, 1901). The Electric Tower and its searchlight are visible in the center of the frame of the second image.
COURTESY OF THE LIBRARY OF CONGRESS MOTION PICTURE READING ROOM

comparatively bright future that promised to dissociate night and day from darkness and light.

Yet rather than simply record one instance of the technological sublime, *Pan-American Exposition by Night* constituted another, for the Edison Manufacturing Co. claimed not only that these films constituted the first in the United States to be shot at night by incandescent light but also that they were "marvels" in photography. Indeed, the catalogue description for the film quite self-consciously trades upon the structural experience of sublime technology and, in a fashion characteristic of the Pan-American's broader operational aesthetic, explained *how* the cameraman achieved the film's novel effects:

> A great feature of the Pan-American Exposition, as unanimously conceded by all visitors, was the electric illumination of the Exposition grounds at night. After a great deal of experimenting and patience, we succeeded in securing an excellent picture of the buildings at the Pan-American as they appeared when lighted up at night. All the buildings from the Temple of Music to the Electric Tower are shown, including the Electric Tower itself. The emotional and sensational effects were also secured by starting the panoramic view by daylight and revolving the camera until the Electric Tower forms the center of the field of the lens. Our camera was then stopped and the position held until night, when we photographed the coming up of the lights, an event which was deemed by all to be a great emotional climax at the Pan-American Exposition. Immediately the lights are burning to their fullest brilliancy, the camera is again set in motion and revolved until the Temple of Music is reached. The motion is then reversed and the camera goes back until it rests on the Electric Tower, thus supplying the climax to the picture. The great searchlights of the Tower are being worked during the entire time the picture is being exposed, and the effect is startling. The picture is pronounced by the photographic profession to be a marvel in photography, and by theatrical people to be the greatest winner in panoramic views ever placed before the public.[23]

This description notes Porter's canny sequencing of daytime shots with a fade to black, followed by the startling "emotional and sensational effects" of the illumination. Porter's juxtapositioning of the ordinary with the ex-traordinary had historical precedence in the early cinema, and bears striking similarity to the strategy favored by exhibitors of the first moving picture shows, who, as Tom Gunning has shown, would begin by projecting a still image that, when suddenly transformed into a moving image, provoked astonishment and surprise.[24] Just as the transformation from an all-too-familiar stillness to an entirely novel motion dramatized the capabilities of moving picture technology, the Edison Co.'s transformation of night into day dramatized the aesthetic and commercial possibilities of incandescent light—one of which was, crucially, films shot at night. Hence, the cata-logue description emphasizes the cameraman's "great deal of experiment-ing and patience" required to produce "an excellent picture of the buildings at the Pan-American as they appeared when lighted up at night." By doing so, the Edison Co. had found another way to conquer darkness—this time through film technology—and demonstrated American industry's ongoing ability to subordinate the natural order to the demands and desires of the commercial-industrial order. The emphasis on experimentation is key, for it foregrounds the idea that the technological sublime on display was based on "a communion, through the machine of man with man" which "implicitly proposed a group's experience of its own potential greatness, rather than an individual experience of the power of the non-human."[25] Moreover, the relationship between the novel electric spectacle of the City of Living Light and its cinematic counterpart foregrounds the cinema's participation in the Exposition's broader ideology of progress. The fact that one un-precedented electric spectacle could make possible another unprecedented cinematic spectacle confirmed modern technology's rhizomatic potential for the sort of self-generation and limitless extension that made one inno-vation the precursor and inevitable initiator of another. Porter's films of the Pan-American's nighttime illumination perfectly demonstrate Wolfgang Schivelbusch's contention that "every lighted image is experienced as the light at the end of the tunnel—the visual tunnel, in this case—and as a liberation from the dark."[26]

Pan-American Exposition by Night also makes visible electricity's ability to transform the urban landscape in such a way that "everything that is incomplete [or] imperfect . . . is hidden in the air—flowing steadfastly in the night sky." As this description suggests, incandescent light had the effect of both illuminating modern life and concealing the byproducts of industrialization that might undermine the Exposition's celebration of the irresistible progress of American civilization. One pamphlet described the "wonderful sensation" that emerged with "the budding of auroral lights" which "soon prick out in dotted pattern the shapes of structures which but a moment before appeared to be things of substance standing out in the full reality of daylight; now they are mere shadows slipping away into the night." Against the sky rises "a city of jewelled domes and pinnacles, with walls of flame, and a luminous tower bearing aloft the Goddess of Light who dominates the fairy-like scene."[27] The night for night images of the second shot of *Pan-American Exposition by Night* are like dream images of a dematerialized and disembodied urban landscape. In contrast with the first shot of the film, after the fade to black neither the pedestrians nor the details of the Exposition's architecture are visible. The uniform and even distribution of incandescent light gives the appearance that the buildings themselves have faded away and melted into thin air: indeed, they become nothing more than props that allow the fairgoer and the film spectator to see light itself rather than the objects it might illuminate, thereby reversing the commodity aesthetic of electricity's illumination of shop windows and street advertisements. While during the day the Pan-American celebrated the utility and use value of a range of new technologies put into motion by electric power, at night the City of Living Light abolished all use value in favor of the pure surplus value of the visually consumed electric spectacle and emphasized the magical nature of the continuous circulation of an electric current to and through the city, regardless of the hour.

Panoramas, Dioramas, and (Films of) the Pan-American Exposition

As the Exposition's publicity material stressed, the creation of electric light and motion was the culmination of an ongoing technological revolution that transformed perception and the experience of motion throughout the nineteenth century by allowing the observer to transcend spatial and temporal limits to movement and vision. Following on from the hot air balloon, the panorama, the diorama, the railway, and the gaslight, industrialized electric light made possible another technological transcendence of the horizon by separating light from time. Put differently, electric illumination promised to make the hard fact of the natural horizon and the setting sun negligible obstacles to vision—hence the ubiquity of the often-repeated promise that electricity would effectively "turn night into day." Keeping in line with the tradition of light-based media that preceded the electric spectacle, fairgoers at the Pan-American were encouraged to experience the City of Living Light "panoramically": first, encircled by the luminous horizon of "living light" on the Pan-American grounds and, second, from a distance and in motion, through the enframed view from an electric streetcar that provided nightly "twilight tours" that showed the illuminated Exposition grounds to the greatest aesthetic advantage. The streetcar that circulated the fairgoer around the grounds only emphasized the reliance of most forms of mechanical illumination and mobility on the Niagara's current, once again linking electric light to the circulation of various forms of traffic.

Armed with new technology that allowed the motion picture camera to pan fluidly on its axis, Porter shot the Pan-American and its electric spectacles almost exclusively—even obsessively—as circular panoramas. Titles listed in the Edison catalogue include *Circular Panorama of the Esplanade with the Electric Tower in the Background*, *Circular Panorama of the Base of the Electric Tower Ending Looking Down the Mall*, *Circular Panorama of the Electric Tower and Pond*, *Panoramic View of the Temple of Music and Esplanade*, *Circular Panorama of the Midway*, *Circular Panorama of the Esplanade and Forecourt*, *Circular Panorama of the Electric Tower*, and *Panoramic View of the Electric Tower from a Balloon*. That the circular panorama should have seemed the most appropriate form by which to represent the Pan-American cinematically is not surprising, for the objectives, ideologies, and desires manifest in and articulated by expositions overlapped with those of the panorama painting. Expositions tended to mimic, on a far grander scale, both the panorama's representational ambitions and its effects on spectators: both enclosed the spectator within a world bound by a strictly imposed artificial horizon that blocked out all features of the surrounding urban environment to intensify the reality effect of—and the spectator's sense of immersion in—a wondrous yet highly artificial world. Both expositions and panoramas aimed to provide an all-encompassing point of view to the observer, usually through the astonishing accumulation of detail and consequent overwhelming effect on the spectator for which both forms were famous. Gunning describes the sensory impact of Expositions as an overwhelming "dazzlement," and he explains that "the visual effect of the World Exposition . . . teeters between the rational and classifying knowledge of the object lesson and an experience of bewilderment before the intensity of technology and cultural and sensual variety."[28] Moreover, both panoramas and Expositions were premised upon the enactment and display of technology's—and the showman's—masterful subordination of nature. Expositions did so through elaborate demonstrations of old and new technologies, offered up as object lessons to curious audiences. In turn, as Stephan Oetermann notes, the "super-realism of panoramic landscapes . . . represented a visual mastery of nature symbolizing the subjugation of nature achieved by human technology in the real world." Both the industrial picture created by the exposition and technical virtuosity of the panorama yielded visually pleasurable "depiction[s] of power, in this case economic power."[29]

The convergence of electricity, the cinema, and panoramic perception at the Pan-American not only gave the Exposition grounds a new night-time visibility but also influenced the way in which industrial power was depicted through—and made pleasurable by—the moving pictures. For example, the circular panorama format of the film *Panorama of the Esplanade by Night* has a noteworthy effect on the cinematic representation of the Exposition's luminous horizon line. The gradual panning action of the camera slowly traces the tendrils of electric light that connect and unite discrete elements of the landscape, creating a visual abstraction of the power lines that were incorporating urban space street by street and block by block (above ground and below) in cities and towns across the United States. In turn, once joined to the image of the spectacular illumination, the 360-degree pan allows the camera to return to its starting point, thereby mimicking the circuitous path followed by the electric current that powered the display. Moreover, the designers' imperative to outline every architectural and decorative feature of the grounds appears in this film as the desire for an all-encompassing diffusion of electricity limitless in extension and application. The enchanting image of this diffusion, in turn, simultaneously suggests a form of benevolent incorporation that equates unification with enlightenment and leaves that which remains unincorporated in darkness and obscurity. By tracing out the illuminated horizon that surrounded and centered the look of the camera, the circular panorama format helped visu-

FIGURE 25 *Panorama of Esplanade by Night* (Edison, 1901). COURTESY OF THE
LIBRARY OF CONGRESS MOTION PICTURE READING ROOM

ally to center moving picture audiences in relation to the City of Living
Light, creating the illusion that they, too, had been incorporated into the
the Pan-American's "magical" electric circuitry.

The cultivation of a sense of benevolent incorporation into a web of enchanting currents, circuits, and light was important to the project of overcoming ambivalence toward the industrialization of light. Schivelbusch has
shown that although the efficiency and cleanliness of industrialized light
was hailed as progress by many, it was also regarded and experienced as
a loss by others. Associated with life, independence, and immediacy, the
flame of nonindustrial candlelight, lamplight, and firelight had a tangi-
bility and material presence absent from industrialized light. Not only was
the source of the illumination present and visible within illuminated space,
each household supplied and controlled its own light in a mode of self-
sufficiency. Within the home, this light would generally illuminate a room
at a single point around which a family would gather at night. In contrast,
industrialized light (first gaslight then electric light) was bright enough to
illuminate an entire room and thereby effectively dispersed the family that
had once gathered closely around the hearth. Once multiple rooms were

wired for electricity, the experience of this dispersal was even more profound.[30]

Proponents of electric light countered disenchantment with such domestic transformations by promoting the idea that the modern city's increasing dependence upon "centrally supplied" light and power effectively
united individual households and businesses into a broader urban family.
Published one year before the Pan-American, George Iles's fascinating
book *Flame, Electricity and the Camera* described electricity's capacity for
broadscale expansion and incorporation in terms of a new high-tech collectivity based on the greater good of all: "Flame, the old time servant, is
individual; electricity, its successor and heir, is collective. Flame sits upon
the hearth and draws a family together; electricity, welling from a public
source, may bind into a unit all the families of a vast city, because it makes
the benefit of each the interest of all."[31] The City of Living Light and *Panorama of Esplanade by Night* provided a visual metaphor for this principle of
benevolent incorporation into the modern collective. By placing audiences
at the center of this luminous urban horizon, the City of Living Light and
Panorama of Esplanade by Night foregrounded and made profound the collective experience of darkness made light by modern technology in a way
that momentarily eclipsed the atomized and alienated relations of industrial capitalism. Moreover, both seemed to make visible the current that
ran through urban space and bound electrified spaces together into a network. Indeed, the cinematic experience of the City of Living Light further underscored electricity's pleasurable powers of incorporation: brought
to life by electric power and a beam of light projected through darkness,
films of the Pan-American were an extension of the electric network they
pictured onscreen, and their audiences were an extension of the crowds
that gazed upon the City of Living Light from within the grounds of the
Pan-American. By dislocating the City of Living Light from its position
in space and time, the moving pictures helped expand industry's power to
bind audiences into the expanding electric collectivity. It was precisely the
urban network created by an extensive traffic in humming electric currents
that helped shape the experience of machine-made electric light into an
experience of "living" light.

Industry had to counteract another ambivalent response to artificial
illumination: accompanying electric light's effect of "dispersion" was the

perception that industrialized light had severed the relationship between light and "life." Schivelbusch argues that each new innovation in artificial illumination, from the Argand lamp to incandescent electric light, increasingly dematerialized light by transcending the "living" flame and its various byproducts.[32] Gaslight first eliminated the wick and then, in turn, electric light eliminated the flame and its byproducts such as heat, shadows, flickers, and the pollutants caused by combustion. This dematerialization of light by electricity had many beneficial outcomes for sites of production as well as sites of consumption and leisure. When used indoors, electric illumination did not give off smoke or soot, which allowed shops and department stores to utilize decorative lighting without sullying ceilings, walls, and expensive merchandise. Incandescent light did not consume oxygen—thus eliminating the "gaslight headache" suffered by theatergoers or workers who spent what was perhaps an unhealthy amount of time in rooms lit brightly by gaslight. In turn, the fact that incandescent electric light gave off a negligible amount of heat greatly reduced the risk of fire associated with gas lighting in the factory. Unlike gas and arc lighting, incandescent light did not flicker and thus its uniformly bright illumination made possible, especially after nighttime, activities that required visual acuity (such as typesetting at newspaper printshops, or needlework and newspaper reading in the parlor), thereby extending both work and leisure time. As the Edison direct current system was replaced by Westinghouse's alternating current system, the efficient transport of electricity across greater distances became feasible.[33] As a result, factories could be built far from generating stations, and broadscale electrification reorganized new factories into patterns of sequential production thus making the assembly line—and mass production—possible.

These very gains were also lamented, however, as commentators noted that incandescent light appeared too bright to the unhabituated eye, as well as too even and too extensive, its source too remote and intangible, and its effects somehow lifeless and cold. To give color and character to the industrialized light that had worked its way into the home and the workplace, decorative lamp shades and light bulbs were used to filter and aestheticize first gaslight and then electric light in order to soften it and also add the warmly colored, intimate qualities of candlelight.[34] Such compensations also took the shape of optical amusements, as light-based forms of commercialized leisure—particularly the diorama—recuperated and simulated the very qualities of natural light that industrialized light had eliminated, including the play of light and shadow, the flicker of the "living" flame, the variability of color and brightness, and, moreover, the experience of light as time. Though the influence of the circular panorama painting on the circular format of Porter's films is visible, less obvious but no less important is the relationship between the City of Living Light's electric dawn, *Pan-American Exposition by Night*, and the diorama. The mechanized light that was central to the visual pleasures of these spectacular forms of commercialized leisure worked to charge their high-tech, luminous displays with the contingencies, play, and temporality of living light at precisely the same time that industrialized light increasingly eliminated such factors from the experience of illumination.

Just as the panorama was born at roughly the same time as the Argand lamp, the diorama emerged onto the field of commercialized leisure just as gaslight was transforming optical experience in Europe in the 1820s. Like the City of Living Light did later and on a much broader and high-tech scale, the diorama both demonstrated technology's subordination of the natural while referring to and even simulating the contingencies of natural or "living light" that new technologies of illumination were in the process of displacing. To reproduce the effects of living light, the diorama's inventor, L. J. M. Daguerre, painted natural and urban landscapes on transparent linen using opaque and translucent paint. These massive canvases (71.5 feet by 45.5 feet) were illuminated from the front and above by sunlight admitted through ground-glass windows. This light was filtered through numerous colored, transparent screens and shutters that were controlled by a system of pulleys and counterweights. Reviews of Daguerre's first diorama, *The Valley of Sarnen* (1822), describe the effects of his mechanical aestheticization of natural light: "The most striking effect is the change of light, from a calm, soft delicious serene day in summer, the horizon gradually changes, becoming more and more overcast, until a darkness, not the effect of night, but evidently of an approaching storm—a murky, tempestuous blackness—discolors every object . . . This change of light upon the lake (which occupies a considerate proportion of the picture) is very beautifully contrived. The warm reflection of the sunny sky recedes by degrees, and the advancing dark shadow runs across the water—chasing, as it were, the former bright effects before it."[35] This reviewer's response to *The Valley of Sarnen* suggests that the diorama's visual pleasure was closely linked to the experience of light as time and motion, for the review emphasizes the gradual nature of the diorama's transformation of simulated sunlight through its representation of the arrival and departure of a storm. The elaboration and temporalization of mechanized light, in turn, seems to have depended on the diorama's representation of the "variable play" of natural light. Hence, another review emphasized the diorama's simulation of the contingencies of natural light: "The diversified effect produced by the varying shadows, as they become transparent or opaque, according to the approach of a storm or the clearing up of the atmosphere, cannot be surpassed . . . the varied effects of light, shade, and coloring, according to the sun's rays and passing clouds act upon its surface cannot be too highly admired; the tints of nature are in every part of the effect exquisitely portrayed."[36] The reviewer's emphasis on transparency and opacity, shade and coloring (the very principles upon which the diorama was based) suggests that pleasure of *The Valley of Sarnen* derived in part from a newly modernized understanding or perception of the natural landscape that the diorama made visible to the modern observer: it was itself a kind of filtering technology for producing an astonishing luminous view. However, the diorama's mechanization of light—its filtering of natural light through a system of screens, pulleys, windows, and painted transparencies—made the contingencies, the variability, and the fortuitous experience of the "luminous view" a standardized, repeatable experience.

Just as it did with the natural landscape, the diorama, like the City of Living Light, represented the urban landscape as a technology of the luminous view. A review of Charles Caius Renoux's *Exterior View of Notre-Dame, Paris, in Evening Light* (1843) is instructive here, for it contrasts industrialized gaslight with luminous, living light. The view begins at sunset, picturing the cathedral and "its rose window on the left and the water around its base reflecting back the last beams of the setting sun." Then, "gradually the reflections disappear, the warm tints fade from the sky, and are succeeded by the cool gray hue of twilight, and that again by night—deepening by insensible degrees till the quay and the surrounding buildings and the water are no longer distinguishable, and Notre Dame itself scarcely reveals to us its outlines against the sky. Before we have long gazed upon the scene the moon begins to emerge slowly—very slowly, from the opposite quarter of the heavens, its first rays tempering apparently rather than dispersing the gloom; presently a slight radiance touches the top of one of the pinnacles of the cathedral—and glances as it were athwart the dark breast of the stream; now growing more powerful, the projections of Notre Dame throw their light and fantastic shadows over the left side of the building, until at last, bursting forth in serene and unclouded majesty, the whole scene is lit up, except where the vast cathedral interrupts its beams, on the quay here to the left, and where through the darkness the street lamps are now seen each illuminating its allotted space. Hark! The clock of Notre Dame strikes! And low and musical come the sounds— it is midnight—scarcely has the vibration of the last note ceased before the organ is heard and the solemn service begins—beautiful, inexpressibly beautiful—we forget creeds at such a time, and think only of prayer: we long to join them."[37] Renoux's diorama represented the exterior of Notre-Dame and the surrounding urban landscape as architectural prisms that refract, reflect, and even project moonlight. The reviewer places emphasis on the moon's rays "tempering" rather than "dispersing" the gloom, on "warm tints" rather than brightness, on the "cool hues of grey" slowly deepening to darkness, once again representing light as time through transformations so gradual as to be nearly imperceptible. In turn, the industrialized light represented within the painting seems to have acted as a foil to the representation of natural light, revealing the reviewer's ambivalence toward industrialized artificial illumination even as he delights in the diorama's own mechanized light: the reviewer describes how "through the darkness the street lamps are now seen each illuminating its allotted space." In contrast to the "light and fantastic shadows" created by moonlight, streetlight is perceived as regimented light: uniform in brightness and distribution, atomized and isolated from one another, each street light illuminates only its predetermined, "allotted space." The reviewer therefore perceives industrialized light as part of the routine, the scheduled, and the homogenous, rather than the vital, the fortuitous, and the delightfully variable.

Daguerre's later double-effect diorama intensified the association of light with the living, thereby eliminating one of the uncanny effects of his first paintings. After praising the light and shadows effects of *The Valley of Sarnen*, one reviewer noted: "There is another very curious sensation which this landscape scene produces on the mind . . . You have, as far as the senses can be acted upon all these things (realities) before you; and yet in the midst of all this crowd of animation, there is a stillness, which is the stillness of the grave. The idea produced is that of a region—of a world—desolated; of living nature at an end; of the last day past and over."[38] In contrast, *A Midnight Mass at Saint-Etienne-du-Mont* used the double effect to create the illusion of human motion and hence the association of human life with living light, thereby mitigating the sensation of "a world desolated." *A Midnight Mass* began with daylight, showing the church "full of empty chairs; little by little the light waned; at the same time, candles were lit at the back of the choir; then the entire church was illuminated, and the chairs were occupied by the congregation who had arrived, not suddenly as if by scene shifting, but gradually—quickly enough to surprise one, yet slowly enough for one not to be too astonished."[39] According to *L'Artiste*, Daguerre's "discovery is all the more valuable because what the diorama paintings still lacked was life, movement and human figures which animate and complete the landscapes and monuments." The inscription of human motion within the depicted scene made its luminous view all the more lifelike, and in doing so referred the spectator back to the source of the effect, embodied in the figure of the genius-showman and his masterful manipulation of the unseen mechanical apparatus: "When one considers that such a complete transformation is produced without any scene-shifting, and by the sole modification of light, one cannot but admire the simplicity of the process and the author's great knowledge in optics and mechanics."[40] Upon seeing *The Inauguration of the Temple of Solomon*, another reviewer noted: "All of this happens in the same room, on the same canvas, with a use of colors and of light of which neither you nor I comprehend anything; for it is true to say that M. Daguerre is the only person who possesses the key to these magic operations."[41]

As the source of mechanized light in the second half of the nineteenth century became increasingly disembodied, industrialized, and distant—a process that eventually culminated with the ability to transport the alternating electric current across great distances without appreciable loss of power—the origins of the magical effects of light-based media were discursively located in living sources rather than mechanical ones. In turn, as industry gave the individual greater power over darkness and light, the diorama conjured up scenes organized around a group's shared, quasi-religious experience of the illumination of darkness by living light, which then was made available to the audience at one remove. Hence, *The Inauguration of the Temple of Solomon* culminated in the moment when "from the midst of the clouds a miraculous light illuminates the temple with its brilliance, dazzling the eyes of the people gathered in religious silence" and thereby returned the experience of mechanized light to the context and experience of the miraculous.

We can say, then, that if increasingly industrialized technologies of illumination turned luminous light into functional light, then light-based technologies of representation such as the diorama, the electric light display, and the cinema turned functional light back into an experience of "living," luminous light (indeed, the name "Vitascope" was given to Edison's first projecting mechanism). It was the abstract qualities associated with "living" luminous light that the City of Living Light recuperated in its electric spectacle. By outlining the features of the Pan-American Exposition grounds, the nighttime illumination transformed that space into a luminous structure that appeared to glow from within and give off light—much like distant stars—rather than a space or a group of buildings illuminated from without in order to be seen by observers. In turn, the Pan-American's extensive system of pools, canals, and fountains, as well as the model of Niagara Falls located at the base of the Electric Tower, fore-grounded the play and variability of light through its splashing and rippling water and reminded fairgoers of the electric current's natural, living source. Hence, as promotional material noted, "The famous cataracts, by the magic of electrical science, will turn night into day, and give to every ripple of the decorative pools, and to every spurting fountain, a fantastic brilliance that will make the courts of the Exposition a fairyland of unprecedented loveliness."[42] The aestheticization of electricity through playful light and water displays transformed industrial currents and circuits into vibrant spectacles that bubbled and glowed with "living" light. Moreover, by simulating an electric dawn, the City of Living Light temporalized light through gradual changes in color and slowly increasing brightness. Porter's *Pan-American Exposition by Night* and *Panorama of Esplanade by Night* participated in this process. Such films linked the cinematic experience of light to the pleasurable experience of the luminous as they enhanced the illusion that the Exposition's urban landscape of electrified traffic—and by extension the American landscape in general—was itself a luminous body, full of warm, benevolent, "life-like" light and living motion. Like the diorama did before it, the City of Living Light and cinematic representations of it manufactured optical experiences organized around a group's shared experience of darkness made bright by the ongoing efforts of mechanization and industry.

Modern Power, Cinema, and the Electric Chair

By concealing "all that would mar," the City of Living Light participated in the Exposition's broader sleight of hand in covering over the dystopian aspects of industrial capitalism, such as class warfare, urban poverty, economic depression, overproduction, and the immigrant slum. World's fairs and expositions were stages upon which competing "versions" or "takes" on the experience of technological modernity and industrial capitalism jockeyed for expression and position; and as with other expositions, strikes, work stoppages, and labor demonstrations marked the construction of the site. Moreover, what one Buffalo resident termed the "byproducts" of the exposition certainly tempered and even threatened to eclipse the Pan-American's quasi-religious official discourse on the ongoing advancement of American civilization. Just as the Edison Manufacturing Co. and major railroad and streetcar companies stood to profit from the Exposition, a range of lesser entrepreneurs exploited the many opportunities for profit that the Exposition created, such as selling refreshments, souvenirs, maps, and guidebooks, thus causing the official grounds of the Pan-American to contrast sharply with the jumble of advertisements, billboards, and booths that surrounded the Exposition grounds. In short, a less ideal form of commercial and at times illegitimate traffic pulsed alongside the Exposition's more controlled and aesthetically orchestrated traffic. Writing in the *Buffalo Courier* at the close of the Exposition, the local resident Mary Hart Brown observed that "the city which woos and wins a great exposition gets considerably more than it bargained for." Just as the Exposition attracted government officials, prominent engineers, inventors, industrialists, and purveyors of respectable entertainment such as John Philip Sousa, it also attracted bunco artists, thieves, and confidence men who, Brown lamented, assume "the guise of your gasman, your telephone tinkerer, and your locksmith. His feminine accomplice applies for rooms and nabs everything she can lay her fair hands on." Even worse, Brown suggests, were the highly visible effects of the efforts of numerous small entrepreneurs who used the Exposition to achieve a small measure of upward economic mobility.

> Almost immediately arrived the souvenir, small in compass, but big with menace—a symptom, prophetic of disease. From the first inno-cent little frying pan badge it spread and spread until the town was disgraced with cheap tawdriness and tinsel futilities and symbolic inanities from end to end. By mid-June the tables of them that sold the souvenirs had so choked the sidewalks of Main Street that the Common Council were driven to the extremity of enforcing the law to clear the streets. Swept from the sidewalks, the souvenir infected the reputable business houses. Banks and cigar stores and small stationers made breeches in their street walls to let in the souvenir stands. Worse than that, legitimate dealers ordered huge stocks of souvenir trash and hung their windows full of Indian heads blazoned on leather, and frying pan clocks, and brass buffaloes, and spar jewelry until the city looked like a mere annex of bazaar-ridden Niagara. The more so as the cheap Niagara photograph had by this time blossomed out in all its glory.[43]

Symptomatic of a rapidly spreading epidemic of low-end profiteers, a puls-ing traffic in cheap souvenirs first invaded the streets and sidewalks of busy commercial thoroughfares, which in turn provided an avenue into already-established legitimate businesses, ultimately making the healthiest parts of the body of the "host city" indistinguishable from the disease of cheap commerce that had infected it. Brown imbues the latter with the connota-tions of a venereal disease: "An epidemic of shameless flaming sign boards, big, bold, and bad began to break out all along the route to the exposition through the loveliest part of the residence section . . . Along with the bill-boards came an eruption of signs, speckling the faces of hitherto respectable buildings throughout the business section of town. The way to the railway station, where the cut-rate ticket offices are, turned in a day a vile yellow color, blazoned in big black letters, a combination of distressing cheapness and vulgarity. Save that it would be unfair to New York I should say it looked like the Bowery."[44] Much like other world's fairs and expositions, the Pan-American seemed to produce at every stage the dystopian inverse of each of its utopian representations of industrial capitalism. Hence the Exposition's official products (such as electric power) and advertisements (the City of Living Light) and its unofficial byproducts and advertisements occupied opposite ends of a cultural-moral spectrum that associated immateriality, homogeneity, and abstraction with virtue, on the one hand, and heterogeneity, mixture, and the lower echelons of commercial competition with vice, on the other. As with all modern traffic, it was precisely the systematic efficiency of the city's official traffic and that of the Exposition that made it possible for this less-legitimate official traffic to thrive.

Brown's invocation of the Bowery is neither surprising nor accidental, for her article appeared in the local paper following the assassination of President McKinley by Leon Czolgosz, a man who, like the Bowery itself, became an icon for ethnic heterogeneity, the so-called immigration problem, urban poverty, and criminalized class warfare. Described by newspapers as a disgruntled laborer and an anarchist with ties to Emma Goldman, Czolgosz seemed to represent the dangerous mobility and degeneration ascribed to the unskilled labor increasingly displaced and dispossesed by manufacturing technologies and served as a reminder of the violent strikes that had coincided with earlier world's fairs. Following the shooting, one newspaper described Czolgosz as "a type of dangerous class—the product of ignorance, impiety, and fanatacism. It is a transplantation from foreign soil, and is in no sense an American product. It has been called 'the army of discontent,' but it is more than probably that the failures of the discontented would have all been transformed into successes, had they worked as hard as they grumbled. Idle, aimless, without moral helm or compass, they drift about, the associates of disturbers and lawbreakers."[45] If Czolgosz seemed part of a dangerous, highly mobile working class, and hence the antithesis of the by-then mythological self-made man celebrated by Horatio Alger stories and promoted by the captains of industry, then McKinley, by contrast, seemed comparable to the same industrial technology that contributed so much to the demand for cheap unskilled labor required by the factory system. Of McKinley, *The Buffalo Express* had previously mused: "Someone called Daniel Webster a steam engine in trousers. President McKinley is of the same character, save that he does not puff and blow while he works. His machinery moves like the piston of a great Corliss engine, slowly, steadily, and irresistibly. He does the work of a dozen men, but so easily and cooly that you can hardly realize he is working at all."[46] Tellingly, the execution of McKinley's assassin in the electric chair found representation in another mechanical metaphor, when the headline of the *Auburn Daily Advertiser* announced: "Czolgosz Translated into Coal Gas."[47]

On the day before the shooting, McKinley delivered a speech at the Pan-American that constituted the most direct expression of the industrial desires and ideals celebrated by the Pan-American and the City of Living Light. In remarking upon technology's annihilation of space and time and its rapid circulation of various types of modern traffic, McKinley explained to fairgoers:

> Modern inventionists have brought into close relation widely separated peoples and made them better acquainted. Geographic and political divisions will continue to exist, but distances have been effaced. Swift ships and fast trains are becoming cosmopolitan. They invade fields which a few years ago were impenetrable. The world's products are exchanged as never before, and with increasing transportation facilities come increasing knowledge and larger trade . . . We travel great distances in a short space of time, and with more ease than was ever dreamed of . . . The same important news is read, though in different languages, the same day in all Christendom. The telegraph keeps us advised of what is occuring everywhere, and the press foreshadows, with more or less accuracy, the plans and purposes of the nations . . . Vast transactions are conducted and international exchanges are made by the tick of the cable. Every event of interest is immediately bulletined, the quick gathering and transmission made possible by the genius of the inventor and the courage of the investor.[48]

The Edison Manufacturing Co. captured the speech on film and on phonograph, making a hallmark of modern progress and order available to far-flung audiences and infinitely repeatable via the kinetophonoscope. Yet the speech was not to resonate as strongly throughout popular American culture as was the unrecorded sound of Czolgosz's pistol (another technology based on repetition and interchangeable parts) firing several times in the Temple of Music.

FIGURE 26 *The Mob Outside the Temple of Music at the Pan-American Exposition* (Edison, 1901). COURTESY OF THE LIBRARY OF CONGRESS MOTION PICTURE READING ROOM

Filmed soon after the assassination attempt, the film *The Mob Outside the Temple of Music at the Pan-American Expostion* (Edison, 1901) shows how the shooting threatened to transform the Exposition into a hallmark of modern disorder. Placed among a sea of bodies the camera captures the modern nightmare of the urban crowd on the verge of turning into a "mob," and in so doing it provides an inverse image of the controlled, broadly distributed and orderly pedestrian traffic displayed in earlier films such as *Circular Panorama of Electric Tower* (Edison, 1901) that is never concentrated enough give the impression of a crowd. Although the catalogue description for this film promises exhibitors moving pictures of a riot, neither the film itself nor contemporary records confirm this interpretation. Newspaper accounts describe over and over again scenarios in which patriotic passions that nearly transform the urban population into a lynch mob are soothed by a single voice of reason that prevailed upon the crowd to allow the civilized sensibilities of law, order, and justice to triumph over precisely those baser instincts and passions that had ostensibly motivated Czolgosz himself.[49] However, as was widely reported in newspapers and magazines, the Exposition grounds were not illuminated during the days immediately

FIGURE 27 *Circular Panorama of Electric Tower* (Edison, 1901). COURTESY OF THE LIBRARY OF CONGRESS MOTION PICTURE READING ROOM

following the shooting, and as such the darkened grounds suggested the broadscale breakdown of the ideals of American industrial capitalism.

The Pan-American's electric light display had its dystopian counterpart in the electric chair, a crude contraption that corporealized electricity in the prisoner's body and thereby helped confirm the idea that American industry had the power to contain and transform whatever forces it had unleashed. Porter filmed *The Execution of Czolgosz with Panorama of Auburn Prison* (Edison, 1901), a reenactment of the execution of Czolgosz in the electric chair that was preceded by actuality footage of the outside of Auburn Prison. This film is striking in its conversion of one of the most literally sensational and shocking modern attractions into a display of the rationalized operation of industrial power and discipline. In order to understand how this film might have resonated for turn-of-the-century audiences, we need to place it within contemporary debates around penal institutions, public executions, new technologies, and spectatorship. Indeed, it was precisely the absence of spectacle that state officials in 1889 had argued would make electrocution the ostensibly "most civilized and advanced" means of administering the death penalty. Electricity promised doubly to disembody executions. New York State then hoped that the electric chair, located inside the prison walls and tended to only by engineers, electricians, and a doctor, would eliminate the boisterous and unseemly crowds that inevitably gathered at public hangings to watch what was referred to as the "scaffold dance." Moreover, electricians claimed the administered current would bring swift death and would have no perceivable effect upon the body of the criminal. An article published in the *North American Review* claimed that in cases of execution by electric chair, once the switch had been thrown then "respiration and heart-action instantly cease. There is a stiffening of the muscles, which gradually relax after five seconds have passed; but there is no struggle and no sound. The majesty of the law has been vindicated, but no physical pain has been caused."[50]

At the time, Edison concurred with this opinion at hearings that sought to determine whether or not death by electric chair violated the Constitutional prohibition against "cruel and unusual punishment." Significantly, at the time of the hearings Edison was caught up in the "war of the currents" that pitted his direct current against Westinghouse's more industrially viable alternating current, which would be used to execute prisoners in the chair. Hoping to exploit a potential link between alternating current and swift, inevitable death in order to frighten private consumers as well as business owners from adopting the Westinghouse system, Edison testified that the electric chair would without warning or pain most certainly eliminate life. He even suggested that the verb "to Westinghouse" be used to describe death by electrocution and that the chair be named "the Westinghouse" so that newspapers would widely report of prisoners having been summarily Westinghoused in the Westinghouse.[51] Although by 1901 the Westinghouse alternating current had gained favor, Porter's film, the technologies it features, and its aesthetic mode emerged from within a complex of technological and industrial forces that competed to shape both the direction of American modernity and its perception. The Edison Manufacturing Co. was in an optimal position to achieve the latter; having recently defeated Biograph in a patents infringement lawsuit, the company was, according to Charles Musser, "virtually the only American film Manufacturer providing exhibitors with films" in the United States in summer and autumn 1901. As a result, "the McKinley films provided the Edison Manufacturing Company with a rare opportunity to derive maximum commercial benefit from its legal monopoly, and it sold more than $45,000 worth of films in the last four months of 1901—practically equal to the whole of the previous business year."[52]

Supporting the discourse on the highly civilized and humane nature of death by electrocution was the disciplinary discourse surrounding Auburn prison, which at the turn of the century was heralded as the most advanced penal institution in the nation. Inside, prisoners were subject to round-the-clock surveillance and the entire day was organized around strictly scheduled and highly regimented activities executed in absolute silence. The penologist Orlando Lewis noted that this regime gave Auburn prison "the beauty of a finely functioning machine. It had reduced the human beings within the prison to automata."[53] Such reports helped make Auburn prison one of the most popular tourist attractions in western New York at the end of the nineteenth century; indeed, it ranked second only to Niagara Falls, thanks in part to the railway line that delivered curious spectators to the prison complex. Significantly, fairgoers attending the Exposition after the assassination attempt could take a brief railway journey to Auburn to see the prison that housed the most notorious symbol of anti-industrial resistance in the nation. Hence, *Execution of Czolgosz, with Panorama of Auburn Prison* (Edison, 1901) opens with a panorama of the prison that aligns film audiences with a point of view similar to the one available to the tourists who arrived at the prison on the railway line visible within the frame, suggesting the proximate distance of those spectators who journeyed to the prison for the execution. The early cinema extended the process of disembodiment sought after by the engineers of the electric chair: initially placed on the outside of the prison's wall, the camera makes possible the visual incorporation of dispersed and relatively diverse audiences into a scopic regime that aligns them with the forces of modern power and social order: not only is this point of view comparable to the one experienced by tourists visiting the prison, it also approximates that of the twelve witnesses who were hired to supervise Czolgosz's execution and who arrived at the prison by train. The film's ensuing shift from actuality to reenactment (made visually clear by the use of a studio set and painted flats) suggested another remove from the real, a further "disciplining" disembodiment that locates the execution in the realm of the remote and the representational rather than the immediate and the actual. In this sense, the reenactment demon-

FIGURE 28 A AND B *Execution of Czolgosz, with Panorama of Auburn Prison* (Edison, 1901). COURTESY OF THE LIBRARY OF CONGRESS MOTION PICTURE READING ROOM

strated the disciplining of both the body of the prisoner and the body of the spectator via electricity: while Czolgosz is quickly dispatched by the electric current, the audience's disembodied point of view is ultimately aligned with the middle-class specialists called upon to witness the execution in an official capacity.

The film's aesthetic, I would argue, inscribes the execution as an extension of the Exposition's various object lessons: in the second tableau prison officials test the current of the electric chair with a bank of incandescent lightbulbs. As the switch is thrown the lightbulbs are illuminated, and thereby link, as Miriam Hansen observes, the deadly force of the electric chair to the generative power that illuminated the City of Living Light.[54] If Czolgosz was regarded as the embodiment of national degeneration, electric light and power promised regeneration and ongoing enlightenment through bodily incorporation into the expanding electric network. As if in response, the illumination of the lightbulbs by the electric chair testifies to the power of modern technology and its ability to redirect its forces against obstacles impeding the forward march of industrial progress. Thus the absence of anything other than the illumination of lightbulbs followed by a brief stiffening of muscles provided audiences with the visible evidence that Czolgosz had been incorporated into the circuits of modern industrial power and technology that he so earnestly resisted. Hence *Execution of Czolgosz, with Panorama of Auburn Prison* features cinematic images quite similar to those seen at the beginning of *Pan-American Exposition by Night*: it visually positions the audience among middle-class spectators and specialists gathered together in a space free of mobs or crowds both to observe the smooth functioning of modern technology and to confirm its ability to contain and control the very forces it had unleashed.

Postscript: Galvanizing the Torpid Body with *Liquid Electricity*

I would like to conclude this chapter with an analysis of a 1907 Vitagraph film, *Liquid Electricity; Or, The Inventor's Fun with Galvanic Fluid*,[55] which uses trick effects to elaborate a comic fantasy about power, electricity, and the body. Whereas *The Execution of Czolgosz* vividly displays electricity's capacity for subordinating the criminally recalcitrant body to industrial power by ending its life, *Liquid Electricity* identifies "galvanic fluid" as a revitalizing force able to solve the problem of bodily fatigue that seems to plague modern life in this film. Given the way it imagines a new relationship between electric power and the exhausted body's lifeless (in)capacity for circulation, *Liquid Electricity* serves as an important connection between the concerns of the first three chapters of this book and those discussed in the fourth chapter.

Liquid Electricity opens with a gray-haired inventor hard at work in his laboratory: he starts a generator, mixes some liquids in a beaker, and then holds the concoction up to an electric power source as sparks fly. After filling an enormous syringe with the electrified potion, the inventor squirts various inanimate objects around his office to no effect. However, after dousing himself with his "galvanic fluid," the inventor runs amuck (in fast motion) around the lab, waving his arms and spinning wildly in a chair. After expending his supply of electric energy, the inventor goes to the window and spies a group of African American workers repairing and cleaning the street at a rather leisurely pace. He squirts a dose of his galvanic fluid out the window and the workers leap into hyperkinetic motion, sweeping and fixing the street at breakneck speed. The inventor grabs his coat and leaves to recharge other lethargic bodies with his stimulating galvanic fluid.

Similar scenarios unfold in each of the tableaux that follow the opening scene. In one, three young men sit on a beach at the ocean's edge while out on the water a couple in a rowboat enters the frame. When the woman falls overboard, the lazy men make no move to help. The inventor enters the frame and sprays the men with a dose of galvanic fluid—they then jump into action and, in fast motion, save the woman in record speed. Next, a yawning shop clerk in a drugstore fills the inventor's order too slowly and is duly shot with galvanic fluid, which accelerates his rate of work to an alarming rate. Here, a new trick effect appears. During shooting, the actor playing the inventor was clearly directed to slow his own movements down to half or a third of a normal speed, which allows him to appear to move at a nearly normal rate while the "charged" clerk moves in fast motion. This trick is used throughout the rest of the film to create the illusion that the electrified bodies alone are capable of hyperkinetic speed. Hence in the next scene, a man in blackface slowly whitewashes a fence as his wife berates him for working at such a laggard pace. The inventor appears on the scene and squirts the man, and the woman and the inventor laugh as the galvanized painter finishes his whitewashing job in record time. In subsequent tableaux, the inventor appears at a construction site where he uses the galvanic fluid to energize exhausted workers; he squirts a horse and carriage, causing it to race up and down the street; and he subjects a cop found lounging against a streetlight to the same treatment, yielding similar effects. The final tableau shows the inventor running maniacally down a residential street and into a house, having shot himself with galvanic fluid to hasten his trip home. Liquid electricity enables him to move through the streets like a human motorcar.

Like the electricity that transformed inanimate streetcars into animated traffic and assembly lines into forces of rapid production, the inventor's galvanic fluid turns the human body into a mechanism able to operate with maximum efficiency at superhuman speeds. Through a sustained and comic use of fast motion, the film seems determined to bring back to life the same "restless energy of the American people" described in great detail in the *North American Review* eight years earlier by the Reverend Watson (discussed in the introduction to this book). Indeed, *Liquid Electricity* is remarkable for the way it imagines a world full of workers and even middle-class amusement seekers who seem utterly depleted of any motive force. Just as the catalogue descriptions for Spanish-American War films deemed the African American soldier to be out of step with the accelerated pace of imperial traffic, in *Liquid Electricity* African American bodies also seem to require a dose of galvanic fluid to keep urban thoroughfares in passable condition. Once energized, the workers' movements are bound only by the edges of the tableaux frame and the stylistic conventions of the cinema in 1907. In turn, like the Spanish-American war films that suggested that a new convergence between the body and modern technology had reformed the enervated body of overcivilized middle-class white masculinity into a model for dynamic heroism, so too does a dose of liquid electricity mobilize the sunbathers into action. Since the film locates the problem of fatigue in the bodies of a broad range of characters—from policemen, construction workers, and street cleaners to whitewashers, store clerks and young, middle-class men—its effect is to create an entire world defined by slowness and inefficiency. Indeed, in the film's imaginary world *all* forms of traffic circulate far too slowly: goods cross store counters at a far too slow pace, workers function at an interminably slow rate, and modern masculinity, incapable of dynamic action, fails to live up to the basic demands of manly heroism.

Spared from this epidemic of fatigue, the inventor seems to be motivated by a desire to speed up the pace of the world around him, to charge sluggish bodies with the same dynamic energy that fuels his own work and experimentation. Akin to the alternating current that flowed to and animated the Pan-American Exposition, the inventor circulates between spaces and accelerates the pace of life in each. Like a synthesis of the scientist-inventors celebrated at the Pan-American and the physician-reformers who sought cures for neurasthenia (discussed in chapter 1), this fictional inventor creates a new technology designed to increase the pace of labor, consumption, and older forms of transportation. In short, the inventor seems determined to incorporate into the rushed pace of modern traffic all those who move at a rate more appropriate to a bygone era.

Given the context of the day, in which bodies were likened to mechanisms powered, battery-like, by a limited "reserve force" of energy (discussed in greater detail in the next chapter) and in which electric power was associated with life and fluid circulation, it is not surprising that the cure for this epidemic of fatigue and torpor should be bottled electricity. Here, electricity is given the power to modernize the human body, and with it the rest of the world: a small dose magically reforms the indolent, the slow, the languid, and the fatigued. Hence like the other films discussed in this book, *Liquid Electricity* expresses a contradiction central to the experience of modern life in the early twentieth century. On one hand, it promotes the peculiarly modern fantasy of endless energy, limitless mobility, and accelerated circulation made possible by the intersection of the human body and a new technology: with the squirt of a syringe, "galvanic fluid" charges the body with new vitality. On the other hand, this fantasy arises from the peculiarly modern anxiety over an apparent deceleration in the pace of labor and the imperative that it must and can be made to move at a faster and more efficient rate. *Liquid Electricity* thereby rather comically identifies speed and fatigue as twin problems central to working bodies within modern traffic and offers a technological solution to both. However, *Liquid Electricity* focuses only on the condition of the modern male body. To understand how the female body was situated within cinematic and other discourses on technological modernity, we must turn to the circulation of the working poor woman within a specific kind of modern traffic—the so-called white slave trade—and the link that reformers made between her bodily fatigue and the "moral breakdown" that steered her into the notorious "traffic in souls."

REGULATING MOBILITY

Traffic, Technology, and
Feature-Length Narrativity

Only when human sorrows are turned into a toy with glaring colors will baby people become interested—for a while at least. The people are a very fickle baby that must have new toys every day. The "righteous" cry against the white slave traffic is such a toy. It serves to amuse the people for a little while, and it will help to create a few more fat political jobs—parasites who stalk about the world as inspectors, investigators, detectives, and so forth. What is really the cause of the trade in women? Not merely white women, but yellow and black women as well. Exploitation of course; the merciless Moloch of capitalism that fattens on underpaid labor, thus driving thousands of women and girls into prostitution. With Mrs. Warren these girls feel, "why waste your life working for a few shillings a week in a scullery, eighteen hours a day"?

EMMA GOLDMAN, "THE TRAFFIC IN WOMEN"

In 1913 a new sensation in motion picture culture, George Loane Tucker's *Traffic in Souls* (IMP, 1913), opened in New York and quickly proved to be a smash hit.[1] Not only did the film exploit a contemporary fascination with the so-called white slavery trade, but it also deployed new narrative strategies for telling feature-length stories with astonishing effect. In doing so, it seemed to spawn a series of films that played out scenarios in which otherwise virtuous young women are detoured into an inescapable life of prostitution. Such scenarios were themselves drawn from a range of factual and fictional accounts published in government reports, newspapers, and magazines about a nefarious conspiracy said to extend across the globe with the purpose of creating a clandestine trade in commercialized sex.[2] A broad range of discourses spanning a number of media identified a series of peculiarly modern formations as causing and otherwise concealing a pulsing commercial traffic in women. Some pointed toward the influx of "new" immigrants arriving en masse from Asia and Southern and Eastern Europe for bringing "foreign" procurers, victims, and morals to cities in the United States.[3] Others looked to the increased presence of women in the sectors of the commercial sphere that made them perilously vulnerable to traffickers, and they named dance halls, penny arcades, amusement parks, moving picture shows, factory floors, and department stores as dangerous places where the sexes might mix freely with little supervision and so bring innocent young women to a moral downfall.[4] Still others linked white slavery to wage slavery and industry's impoverishment of working poor women.[5] In turn, traffickers were reputed to exploit the vast network of new technologies increasing in complexity and expansive in reach: the telephone, telegraph, automobile, steamship, railroad, and streetcar were all implicated in the "slavers" efforts to locate new victims and force them into a largely unseen yet highly systematic trade. Despite the differing conclusions about how to arrest the traffic in women, discourses on white slavery express deep misgivings over the accelerated change wrought by industrial capitalism, the factory system, and the proliferation of new technologies. In short, the white slavery scandal and the cinema's relation to it provide particular insight into the way the experience of American technological modernity was imagined and articulated through the figure of traffic in the early twentieth century.

It is not surprising that the cinema played a significant role in this moral panic—whether as a site of commercialized leisure where procurers lured victims into the trade or as the source of more or less sensational (and thus more or less dangerous) representations of white slavery, particularly given the scandal's emphasis on technology and the various sorts of traffic that connected the United States to Europe, the country to the city, and the private sphere to the public sphere. Indeed, the first two decades of moving picture history offer numerous examples of films and industrial practices that give insight into the cinema's complex position within the expanding network of technological modernity and its corresponding relation to modern traffic.[6] From the cinema's initial obsession with speeding locomotives, automobiles out of control, and urban street scenes, to the nickelodeon's location as a convenient "stop" on busy urban thoroughfares, to the narration of the pleasures and horrors of technology, the moving pictures simultaneously participated in and provided representations of technological modernity's transformation of everyday life.[7] Indeed, the link between early cinema and the proliferation of new technologies went beyond the moving pictures' ability merely to represent changes in everyday life. The effectiveness of such representations often turned upon the cinema's structural affinity to other technologies—namely, relations that could be exploited in the deployment of new narrative devices whose increasingly abstract constructions of space and time placed greater demands on audiences. For example, in noting that "after 1908 the most frequent device for portraying phone conversations was parallel editing, cutting from one end of the telephone line to another," Tom Gunning argues that "the fit between the spatio-temporal form of the event and that of its portrayal has a particularly satisfying effect which one suspects rendered the innovative technique particularly legible to film audiences."[8] In what follows, I would like to explore the idea that in the process of negotiating some of the more historically significant transitions in narrativity, individual films exploited the cinema's structural affinity not just with specific technologies—such as the telephone and the railway—but with the broader, expanding network of communication and transportation technologies so central to contemporary representations of the white slave trade and, by extension, to the cinematic articulation of the experience of American modernity.

In light of this idea, "traffic" rather than "prostitution" serves as the organizing figure for this chapter simply because the multiple meanings it possessed in the early twentieth century provide a common link that ties together the various aspects of American modernity and the cinema with which this chapter is concerned. Indeed, as I indicated in the introduction to this book, "a prostitute" as well as the act of "dealing or bargaining in something which should not be made the subject of trade" was among the other, more familiar definitions of traffic provided by the OED, such as "the passing to and fro of persons, or of vehicles or vessels, along a road, railway, canal, or other route of transport." Indeed, traffic's links to immigration, transportation, commerce, prostitution, and mechanized communication allowed it to refer broadly to an aspect of modernity that seemed to many Americans increasingly difficult to escape: the absorption of everyday life into patterns of (mechanically aided) circulation. Traffic circulated natural resources to factories and transported unskilled labor from Europe, small towns, and the countryside to burgeoning cities in the United States. It brought finished products, clerks, and consumers to department stores and shuttled pleasure seekers to sites of commercialized leisure. Traffic mobilized commodities to and through the home and tied together distant spaces and times through the telephone and telegraph. And just as the term "traffic" accommodated these legitimate forms of commerce, it also accommodated less salient and more illegitimate meanings as it referred not only to prostitution and the commercialization of sex—but also, as we shall see, to the act of "trafficking" and the much-discussed modern methods for accelerating the flow of women into the trade and the flow of profits out of it.

Two feature-length films that directly address the question of prostitution and the "white slave" trade, Tucker's *Traffic in Souls* and Lois Weber's *Shoes* (Bluebird Productions, 1916), along with a number of two- and three-reel melodramas, provide important insight into the experience of modern traffic and the cinema's position within it.[9] *Traffic in Souls* and *Shoes* are as significant and striking in their similarities as they are in their differences: both feature store-clerk heroines from urban, working-class families who find themselves absorbed into the white slave trade thanks in part to a corrupt patriarch who profits from the exploitation of working poor women. However, whereas *Traffic in Souls* narrates the perils of an efficiently functioning network of streetcar, steamship, telegraph, automobile, and urban pedestrian traffic that supports and conceals the illicit traffic in women, *Shoes* focuses instead on a single unit of modern traffic—the young working poor woman who passes to and fro along city streets each day in an effort to support her family—and the impoverished existence that drains her "batteries of life" and precipitates her moral breakdown. In turn, the particular structure of modern traffic that each envisions and the model of feature-length storytelling that each employs are indicative both of new narrative strategies that emerged during the cinema's transitional era (1908–1916) and of the effects that the long feature had on film exhibition and the viewing habits of audiences defined primarily as "traffic"—that is, as the unscheduled flow of patrons into nickelodeons and moving picture theaters from surrounding commercial thoroughfares.

Traffic in Souls and the Perils and Potential of New Technologies

To greater and lesser degrees, recent scholarship identifies George Loane Tucker's *Traffic in Souls* as a threshold film that sheds light on the broader struggles that led to changes in the relationship between the cinema's technical base, its mode of address, exhibition practices, and spectatorship in the early 1910s. According to Ben Brewster, *Traffic in Souls* was the first American multi-reel feature-length film not based on a previously existing literary or theatrical source. Moreover, the film's narrative structure defied contemporary conventions for organizing multi-reel features into a linked series of relatively autonomous mini-narratives marked by denouements that correspond to reel breaks.[10] The latter structure, Eileen Bowser argues, allowed exhibitors to show individual reels separately in weekly succession and thereby preserve the variety format that guaranteed the high audience turnover rates on which their profits largely depended. Thus the utilization of the single-reel format gave exhibitors a large measure of control over how and when films were consumed, for as Bowser explains, "the longer the film, the less opportunity there was for the showman to intervene, and the less time available for nonfilmic elements. The exhibitor, perhaps unconscious of this loss of control, nevertheless strongly resisted it. As many of the exhibitors pointed out, one unsuccessful short film in the program could be offset by a good one, but if the feature was poor, the show could not be saved."[11] Moreover, as Ben Singer notes, "the inertia of standardized business practices predisposed both film exchanges and exhibitors against the multireel release. The well-established exchange system employed by the General Film Co. (the distribution arm of the Motion Picture Patents Company) and its independent competitors benefited from the stability and regularity of handling a fixed single reel length (1,000 feet) based on standing orders placed by exchanges and exhibitors."[12] As a six-reeler that had to be projected continuously or risk narrative incoherence, *Traffic in Souls* offered a model for feature-length textuality that would allow production companies to wrest a measure of control over how and when films would be consumed. Moreover, to the delight of the film's exhibitors it was a popular success, particularly with female spectators.[13]

At the same time that the film can be seen as an artifact of the struggles marking the slow and uneven shift toward the standardization of the continuously projected long feature, it also marked a struggle between the industry as a whole and the reform movement that sought to uplift it. Based on the public scandal over the white slavery trade and lurid tales of innocent girls seduced and then sold into a life of prostitution, the film provoked a struggle over censorship and female spectatorship. As Shelley Stamp has shown, some reformers warned that the film and others like it would incite in female spectators a dangerous curiosity about the formerly unseen spaces of red light districts and brothels by transporting them visually to a variety of forbidden urban spaces.[14] At the same time, uncertainty prevailed over whether white slave films would act as a gateway into the traffic or as an educational tool that might warn potential victims about the tricks of the trade. According to Stamp, one reform-minded reviewer suggested that *Traffic in Souls* should not be shown to the movie-going public but rather be reserved solely for immigrant women arriving at Ellis Island and for rural emigrés entering urban railway stations.[15] Either way, such discourse identified the cinema in general and the white slave film in particular as crucial modern formations possessing the power either to help extend or arrest the slavers' diversion of everyday commerce and traffic into the "traffic in souls."

Drawing from these and other analyses of the film, I would like to show how *Traffic in Souls* appropriates, transforms, and thematizes the structural features and effects of technologies of transportation and communication in order to produce a narrative mode and an experience of spectatorship specific to the continuously projected long feature.[16] To do this, I will focus on the film's obsession with the mobilization of bodies and identities by mechanized forms of mass transportation and the particularly modern experience of being absorbed into traffic. I will focus specifically on "traffic" in order to highlight the structural relationship between this figure—its movements, connections, detours, and destinations—and the emergence of formal strategies used to structure the cinema's increasingly abstract constructions of time and space and the multiple story lines necessary to the continuously projected, multi-reel feature-length film.

It is no coincidence, I think, that one of the earliest American long features not directly derived from a literary source dramatizes the technological mobilization of bodies between Europe and the United States, the country and the city, public space and private space, and the home and the brothel. *Traffic in Souls* makes clear connections between various kinds of traffic and the everyday, urban experience of technological modernity. The film is based on the simple premise that to participate in modern life is to be absorbed into traffic. *Traffic in Souls* therefore organizes its narrative around the unceasing mechanical mobilization of bodies through space. At the heart of the film's articulation of technological modernity is a contradiction specific to the experience of being absorbed into traffic: when one merges into the mobilized mass of bodies and machines, one constitutes traffic by acting as a single unit of its broader movement; yet, at the same time that one *constitutes* traffic, one is *constituted* by it — that is, defined by and subordinated to an already-determined path of twists and turns, forward propulsions, and arbitrary stops. *Traffic in Souls* suggests that if there is a danger linked to the subject position manufactured by traffic, it is that of simultaneously being the subject and object of a movement over which one has only illusory control. To elaborate this contradiction, the film presents us with two different kinds of traffic — the everyday traffic of commerce and mass transportation and the scandalous white slave trade, or the traffic in souls — and it links each with one of the alternating subject positions manufactured by traffic. The film suggests that once the female traveler becomes the *subject of* an apparently legitimate traffic, she also risks becoming *an object within* a dangerously illegitimate traffic.

Traffic in Souls initially presents us with an image of everyday commercial traffic: in its first third, two Swedish sisters arrive at Ellis Island via steamship to live with their brother; a country girl arrives by railway to live in the city; and two sisters traverse city streets in order to make a living as shop clerks. The film thereby provides us with an image of the broader international, national, and local mobilization of bodies and commodities necessary for the survival of American industrial capitalism and the family in the early twentieth century. Yet the film immediately connects this legitimate traffic to the scandalously illegitimate traffic of the white slave trade as the Swedish immigrants, the country girl, and the Little Sister (Ethel Grandin) are, one by one, detoured from the flow of legitimate traffic into the white slave trade by the notorious traffickers, who capture their prey at train stations, trolley stops, and in taxicabs. By repeatedly emphasizing the ease with which one might be detoured from one kind of traffic into another, *Traffic in Souls* underscores the idea that connected to every legitimate form of technological mobility is a dangerously unregulated form of mobility. Significantly, this illegitimate traffic is not figured as technological mobility out of control. In fact, the film provides us neither with an image of the hazardous speed and violent impact of mechanized movement displayed by earlier films such as *A Railway Smash-Up* (Edison, 1904) or *How It Feels to Be Run Over* (Hepworth, 1900) nor does it imagine the potential horrors of mechanical breakdown, as does, for example, *A Mother's Devotion* (Vitagraph, 1911). More precisely, this film suggests that the illegitimate traffic in souls is dangerous precisely because it exploits the highly systematic structure, schedule, and smooth efficiency of everyday traffic. That is to say, it is by attaching itself to the precise spatial and temporal coordinates of the network of everyday traffic that the slave trade detours the legitimate traffic's most precious cargo: innocent femininity. *Traffic in Souls* therefore links a hallmark of modern progress and order—the smooth functioning of technology—to an early-twentieth-century hallmark of modernity's perilous disorder—the international traffic in women.

The idea that a smoothly functioning system of mechanized transport and communication might act as a host to an inseparable unlawful system found expression in numerous one- and two-reel films made in the American cinema's transitional era. Two sequences in D. W. Griffith's *The Lonedale Operator* (Biograph, 1911) very precisely visualize the idea that just beneath the surface of everyday traffic lurk covert forces that threaten to exploit the systematic efficiency of technology for nefarious purposes. In the middle of this film, the camera provides us with an image of passengers, a payroll bag, and other cargo being loaded onto a locomotive and thereby offers a glimpse at the efficient circulation of capital, populations, and commodities by the railway system. An ensuing shot of the same train arriving at the Lonedale station appears to repeat this image.

FIGURE 29 A AND B *The Lonedale Operator* (Biograph, 1911). COURTESY OF THE
LIBRARY OF CONGRESS MOTION PICTURE READING ROOM

FIGURE 30 *A Girl and Her Trust* (Biograph, 1912). COURTESY OF THE LIBRARY OF CONGRESS MOTION PICTURE READING ROOM

Yet in this second shot, as the payroll is being deposited with the operator, two rough-looking transients emerge from the undercarriage of the train unbeknownst to the operator or anyone else, all the while keeping their eyes on her and the payroll bag. This shot makes the transients both dangerous by virtue of their undetected mobility and sinisterly illegitimate by virtue of the space from which they emerge—itself a materialization of modernity's dark underbelly. Biograph made a slightly different version of the film a year later. In *A Girl and Her Trust* (D. W. Griffith, 1912), the telegraph operator (Dorothy Bernard)—herself a facilitator of the smooth flow of traffic along the railway line—is not only perilously linked to the payroll bag left in her possession but also she and the cash are whisked down the railway lines on a handcar by two tramps (Alfred Paget and Charles Hill Mailes). This change in plot brings *A Girl and Her Trust* closer to *Traffic in Souls'* technological imaginary as it, too, suggests that traffic always carries with it the proximate threat of being displaced from one's position within the legitimate traffic into one of its illegitimate extensions.

Made in the same year, *A Beast at Bay* (Biograph, 1912) similarly underscores the terrifying ease and speed with which a dangerously illegitimate traffic might attach itself to and detour everyday traffic. Just after the heroine of this film (Mary Pickford) drops her boyfriend (Edwin August) off at a train station, she is tricked into pulling her car over to the side of the road by an escaped convict who forces her to aid him in his flight from prison guards. Here danger lurks not in the underbelly of technological modernity but at the edges of its parallel lines of traffic—for the convict (Alfred Paget) emerges from the rural landscape that borders the motorway and adjacent railway line. Once *A Beast at Bay* imagines that danger lurks at the liminal border between rural spaces and the lines of technological modernity, it goes on to exploit the utopian possibilities of the interconnecting lines of modern traffic: the heroine's boyfriend spies the kidnapping from the train station and gives chase in an engine along the railway line that runs parallel to the road.

In order to highlight the cultural and historical roots of this anxiety over railway and other traffic, I want to turn briefly to Wolfgang Schivelbusch's well-known work *The Railway Journey* because it so convincingly theorizes the idea that one of modernity's defining features is the absorption of the individual and everyday life into the movements of mechanized traffic. The book's final chapter, "Circulation," argues that the crucial link between the "panoramic perception" created by both the railway journey and the visual arrangement of the department store is their mutual dependence upon "the general motion of traffic" made possible by the mechanization of space and time in the nineteenth century.[17] I am less interested here in the salient features of the manufactured panoramic perception itself (which, as Freidberg and Kirby have shown, acted as a precursor to the mobilized vision of the moving image) than I am in the status of this particularly modern mode of perception as an *effect* of the movement of traffic.[18] For example, when defining the specific experience of the railway journey's panoramic perception, Schivelbusch notes that "as speed caused the foreground to disappear, it detached the traveler from the space that immediately surrounded him, that is, it intruded itself as an 'almost unreal barrier' between object and subject. The landscape that was seen in this way was no longer experienced intensively, discretely . . . but evanescently, impressionistically—panoramically, in fact. More exactly, in panoramic perception the objects were attractive in their state of dispersal. The attraction was generated by the motion that created this perception of the objects in the observing subject."[19]

This motion is created by the mechanized traffic upon which Schivelbusch's "more general definition" of panoramic perception depends: "It is a perception based on a specific developmental stage of the circulation of commodities, with corresponding specific stages in general, traffic technology in particular, retail merchandising, etc." Thus the panoramic perception encouraged by the display of commodities in the department store derived less from the objects themselves than it did in support of the idea that "those goods participated in the same acceleration of traffic which generated the new mode of perception on the railways and boulevards. In the department store, this meant an acceleration of turnover. This acceleration changed the relationship between customer and goods to the same degree that the railroad's accelerated speed changed the traveler's relationship with speed."[20] Just as the railway passenger's new panoramic perception depended upon his or her absorption into the general movement of railway traffic, the new relationship between customer and goods depended upon the department store's strategic absorption of—and into—the circulatory systems of urban and inter-urban traffic. While the appearance of the goods themselves depended on the railway and steamship's speedy circulation from sites of production to the sites of display and consumption, the particular specular relationship between customer and goods depended on their mutual status as "traffic." According to Schivelbusch, "If the connection with street traffic was necessary to ensure the numbers of customers and goods required by accelerated turnover, it is also true that the turnover itself depended on motion . . . The motion in the department store was a part of the general motion of traffic that generated the panoramic perception of railroad and boulevard landscapes. In the store, however, the panoramic eye was not dealing with landscapes or boulevards but with goods."[21] Thus, Schivelbusch insists that the accelerated trafficking of bodies and goods by mechanical transportation was the key to panoramic perception's distinctly modern character. In short, his study suggests that many of the phenomena now recognized as hallmarks of modernity—panoramic perception, the department store, "just looking" as a form of consumption, the experience and effects of commodity capitalism, the mechanization of transport and communication—share as common conditions of their existence the absorption of the individual into, and the transformation of public and private space by, the circulation of traffic.[22]

The narratives of *The Lonedale Operator* and *Traffic in Souls* turn on the elaboration and containment of the effects unleashed by the global circulation of technological traffic in the second decade of the twentieth century. Both films suggest that the mass mobilization of bodies, commodities, and capital by transportation technologies allow these separate types of cargo to become mixed and even dangerously confused. In *The Lonedale Operator*, mobilized capital is attached to the woman and both are imperiled by their proximity to other dangerously transient individuals; in *Traffic in Souls*, the female body itself risks becoming a commodity once absorbed into the traffic of goods and bodies crossing the city and the nation and thus of being delivered to the wrong destination—the bordello rather than the family home. Anxiety over the particular ability of traffic to collapse the distinction between passengers and parcels found its first expression decades earlier as a well-known complaint made by those alienated by railway travel. Schivelbusch mentions "that turn of phrase so well-liked by the railroad's critics—the claim that this form of travel transformed the traveler into a parcel. The realization that one no longer felt like a person but like a commodity indicates some awareness that one had been assimilated not only by physically accelerated speed but also by the generally accelerated process of the circulation of goods."[23]

Yet in *Traffic in Souls* anxiety over being absorbed into the circulation of goods extends beyond the confines in the railway car to the broader paths of circulation followed by trafficked goods and bodies. It suggests that modern traffic had so thoroughly permeated everyday existence that the act of stepping off the train, railway car, or steamship no longer necessarily guaranteed that one had exited its labyrinthine structure. Indeed, by the 1910s traffic had penetrated life to a far greater degree than in the nineteenth-century world described by Schivelbusch.[24] *Traffic in Souls* and other technological melodramas have less to do with the nineteenth-century demand upon the individual to shift away from "a traditional mode of perception, which, being still attuned to a prior development stage of circulation, found it difficult to deal with the now accelerated objects." Instead, the anxiety expressed by these films can be linked to an early-twentieth-century shift away from the nineteenth-century tendency to regard "whatever was part of circulation" as "healthy, progressive, constructive" and "all that was detached from circulation, on the other hand," as "diseased, medieval, subversive, threatening."[25] *Traffic in Souls* revises this axiom by demonstrating the

FIGURE 31 *Traffic in Souls* (George Loane Tucker, 1913). COURTESY OF THE LIBRARY OF
CONGRESS MOTION PICTURE READING ROOM

degree to which the "diseased," "subversive," and "threatening" elements
formerly outside of modernity's circulatory systems had become all the
more dangerous for having been absorbed into its traffic patterns—for the
absorption of the "threatening outside" into modern traffic made it difficult
to locate that danger and distinguish it from legitimate traffic.

Whereas *The Lonedale Operator* suggests that dangerously illegitimate
traffic lurks just beneath the surface of modern forms of mechanized transport, and *A Beast at Bay* places this danger at the edges of modernity's
permeable pathways, *Traffic in Souls* figures the dangers of modern traffic
through the technological rhizome—a structure composed of "directions
in motion" having "neither beginning nor end but always a middle from
which it grows and overspills,"[26] the multiplying extensions, connections,
and homogeneity of which render illegitimate traffic indistinguishable from
legitimate traffic. In short, *Traffic in Souls* suggests that the white slavers'
ability to plug into and thereby exploit the already-existing technological
structure of the everyday traffic allows them to elude detection and thrive.
The challenge posed to detection by the increasingly rhizomatic structure

of technological modernity is made quite clear in the sequence when Little Sister leaves the candy store with the cadet: while the couple appears to enter one black cab, they jump out and speed away in another identical cab before Officer Burke (Matt Moore) realizes what has happened, leaving him to trace the network of identical cabs spanning the urban landscape. As this sequence underscores, the lines separating legitimate traffic and its criminal counterparts are dangerously unclear precisely because they share the same technological base; thus even Little Sister fails to realize that she has been displaced into the "traffic in souls" until it is far too late. Indeed, the film suggests that technological modernity brings with it the difficulty of being able to distinguish between legitimate and illegitimate traffic and of never knowing whether one is an agent of or a commodity within traffic, and it highlights the horror of becoming permanently absorbed into its unceasing illegitimate movements.

Traffic in Souls links the illegitimate traffic's circulation through everyday traffic to the increasing interdependence between railway traffic, urban street traffic, and the commercial traffic in passengers and commodities and plays upon the dystopian effects of the interlocking structure and mutual dependence of these circulatory systems. As already noted, Schivelbusch emphasizes that the panoramic vision afforded by the department store display of goods depended on the goods' own status as traffic and their visual consumption by individuals who viewed them while in motion as an extension of the traffic traversing the urban landscape. The crucial point of intersection for trafficked goods and consumer traffic was the display window, which lured passersby to take an ambulatory detour through the store.[27] With this in mind, we can note that Little Sister becomes absorbed into the traffic in souls long before she is drugged and ushered away through the streets of New York in a black cab. Indeed, she is detoured from the everyday traffic in goods and bodies much earlier in the film—namely in the sequence when the cadet and the madam spot her through the display window of the candy store. The point here is not simply that the act of looking by a predatory consumerist gaze turns the female body into a commodified object. Rather, I would emphasize that this sequence underscores the crucial role of legitimate traffic in acting as a support for the traffic in women: the traffickers' absorption into urban pedestrian traffic and their engagement in the act of "just looking" through the display window acts as a camouflage that allows them to pose as a perfectly respectable couple moving along with the flow of everyday urban street traffic. In turn, the film plays upon contemporary anxieties over working women's increasing participation in public commercial culture by suggesting that Little Sister's own proximate position to the everyday traffic in bodies and goods allows her to be easily absorbed into the illegitimate traffic.[28] Thus the terror of modern traffic elaborated by Tucker's film derives from its elaboration of the idea that, in Schivelbusch's words, "by the end of the nineteenth century, the capitalist world's recomposition on the basis of modern traffic had been completed. From then on, traffic determined what belonged where."[29] *Traffic in Souls* translates this idea into a nightmare scenario as it repeatedly demonstrates the power of traffic to transform a "who" (the female subject) into a "what" (a commodity) and bring her to an entirely unforeseen "where" (the bordello).

It is worth noting that the rhizomatic structure and homogenizing effect of modern transportation technologies undermined similar efforts by police and immigration authorities in New York City to control what official discourse referred to as "the importation and procurement of women for immoral purposes." Importantly, public hysteria over white slavery was fueled by the scandal's status as a subset of an anti-immigration discourse that sought to place restrictions on the steady traffic in populations between Europe, Asia, and the United States—a traffic that was facilitated, in part, by efforts undertaken by steamship and railway companies to increase passenger numbers and maintain a pool of cheap labor in the United States. Indeed, one special report to the Immigration Commission on the white slave trade stated that "according to those best informed, a very large proportion of the pimps living in the United States are foreigners. Arrests made during the investigation of men violating Section 3 [a prohibition against importing or procuring women for 'immoral purposes'] include the following: Egyptian, French, Chinese, Belgian, Spanish, Japanese, Greek, Slavish, Hungarian, Italian, and Russian."[30] Jeremiah Jenks in his analysis of immigration documents came to the similar conclusion that "the investigations of the Immigration Commission seem to show very clearly that the keepers of disorderly houses and those actively engaged in the work of procuring inmates for these houses, either in this country or abroad, are either aliens or children of aliens."[31] Rather than offering any persuasive evidence that the immigrant population was any more involved in the prostitution racket than was the native white population, such conclusions simply suggest that the immigrant population was generally subject to greater surveillance, policing, and regulation than was the native white population. Indeed, one surveillance strategy devised by the Immigration Commission to arrest the trade involved posting matrons at major ports to spot girls who might be commodities in the traffic. Despite such efforts, officials lamented, "our investigations show that the matrons at some of our ports say that it is not possible for them to recognize either procurers or prostitutes when they land. Of course, identification cannot be certain, but persons familiar with people of this type would, in most instances, be able to see whether special care should be taken in the investigation of such cases before landing."[32] This observation invokes and then quickly disavows the particular challenge posed by the international traffic in women via steamships, railways, and other modes of mechanized mass transport: neither the procurers nor the girls presented themselves as distinct and detectable criminal types precisely because they were so thoroughly absorbed into and indistinguishable from the other passenger-parcels.

Indeed, the legitimate traffic in bodies and goods via steamship and railway enabled and even camouflaged the illegitimate traffic. A lawfully purchased steerage ticket was, it seems, a disguise that fooled not just those determined to arrest the circulation of the scandalous trade but also often the bearers of the tickets themselves. Stories told by girls rescued from traffickers often turn on the moment of horror when they realize that they have been absorbed into an entirely different kind of traffic circulating between cities, states, and nations.[33] Unlike other passengers who eventually arrived at a final destination, young women absorbed into the "traffic in souls" became a part of its unceasing circulation: part of the trade's ability to elude detection was to make further and continual use of the ever-expanding and interconnected forms of mechanized transport. The Immigration Commission claimed that the typical case was that of a cadet and "slave" who moved from Montreal to "Vancouver, to Prince Rupert, to Alaska and to Seattle," leading the authors to confess that "the hiding of girls and the shifting from one city and State to another makes it very difficult to keep track of an immigrant girl practicing prostitution."[34] Another popular "slaver" film, *The Inside of the White Slave Trade* (Moral

Feature Film Co., 1913), played upon reports of this type of circulation by shuttling its heroine-victim via railway from New York to New Orleans to Denver and then back again to New Orleans. Whether the white slavery scandal imagined the imperilment of an idealized Anglo-American white femininity or the secret circulation of white European prostitutes, it acted as a point of cathexis for anxieties over the impact of mechanized traffic and the mass circulation of populations on racial, national, and gendered identity. As Lee Grieveson argues, white slavery "figured as a legitimating ground for the definition of national sovereignty over and against other nations, the consolidation of national identity through the projection of deviance beyond national borders, thereby inculcating a shared sense of political community based on shared and defended space."[35]

Traffic in Souls not only plays upon the endless circulation of the traffic in women by transportation and communication technologies but also it foregrounds the arbitrariness inherent in and necessary to the systematic movement of railway, steamship, and trolley traffic. By arbitrariness, I mean that the slavers exploit the fact that mechanized forms of mass transportation never bring the traveler to her true destination or "proper place"— which the film identifies as the private space of domesticity. The traffickers always waylay their unsuspecting victims at points of transition when they must make a connection in order to reach their ultimate destination. Jane Addams concluded as much in her book on prostitution, *A New Conscience and an Ancient Evil.* Speaking, for example, of young immigrant women who arrived alone at Ellis Island, she explained: "The trafficker makes every effort to intercept such a girl before she can communicate with her relations. Although great care is taken at Ellis Island, the girl's destination carefully indicated on her ticket and her friends communicated with, after she boards the train the governmental protection is withdrawn and many untoward experiences may befall a girl between New York and her final destination. Only this year a Polish mother of the Hull House neighborhood failed to find her daughter on a New York train upon which she had been notified to expect her, because the girl had been induced to leave the New York train at South Chicago, where she was met by two young men, one of them well known to the police, and the other a young Pole, purported to have been sent by the girl's mother."[36] *Traffic in Souls* elaborates such scenarios and suggests that the failure to negotiate the multiple lines

FIGURE 32 *Suspense* (Lois Weber and Philips Smalley, 1913). COURTESY OF THE MUSEUM OF MODERN ART, NEW YORK

of movement and action demanded by the modern subject absorbed into traffic threatens the individual with a number of ancillary mobilizations, the most dangerous being the mobilization of identity. For, once detoured from the legitimate to the illegitimate traffic, innocent femininity risks being transformed into its Victorian opposite—the prostitute.

The arbitrariness of modern traffic's stops, starts, and connections, the inseparability of its criminal and lawful movements, and its power to mobilize identity—to effect a rapid shift in moral positions—is most precisely pictured and aesthetically realized in Lois Weber and Phillips Smalley's *Suspense* (Rex, 1913). This film begins with the fateful departure of a housekeeper who quits the employ of her middle-class mistress—a young wife (Lois Weber) with a baby—on the grounds that her suburban home is much too isolated. Moreover, she does so on the evening that the "man of the house," a white-collar worker (Val Paul), will not be home from work until late. As the housekeeper walks to the road leading away from the house, she is spotted by a tramp (Sam Kaufman) who traces her steps back to the family home. This untimely intersection of pedestrian traffic precipitates the crisis of the film: upon perceiving the tramp as he lurks about outside and looks for a point of entry into the home, the panicked heroine telephones her husband at work. The tramp locates the phone line, severs the connection, and thereby sets the nearly hysterical husband into motion: he commandeers a car idling outside his office and speeds to the rescue with the car's owner (Douglas Gerrard) and the police in close pursuit. In doing so, he assumes an ambivalent position in traffic: as he races to the rescue (much as the engineer does in *The Lonedale Operator*), he seeks to arrest the lawless movements of the industrial era's most pathological figure for modern transience, the tramp. In this respect, the husband represents the mobilization of the moral forces required to contain modernity's disorderly forces. Yet in the process he becomes part of the forces of disorder and enters swiftly into unlawful traffic—for not only does he steal a car, but he runs down a pedestrian. In so doing he becomes an agent of the accidental violence wrought by new technologies of transportation.[37] As a result, the husband becomes simultaneously the (criminal) object of a chase by the police and the (lawful) agent of a race to rescue his imperiled family. Ironically, if the police arrest the husband's criminal movement they will simultaneously stop his drive to save his family—a torturous possibility that Weber exploits in a shot that shows the police car pulling up alongside the husband as the officer, visible to the husband in the rear-view mirror, reaches out to grab him. Hence this film elaborates not only the rapidity with which the individual might switch (moral) positions within modern traffic—from an agent of its legitimate movements (businessman, father racing to the rescue) to an agent of its criminal mobilizations (carjacker, hit-and-run driver)—but also it visualizes the degree to which such positions might ultimately become confused and even inseparable.[38]

The very same ability of communications technology to destabilize identity is at the heart of the trafficker's own strategy in *Traffic in Souls*: that is, they actively manipulate appearance and identity by exploiting the ability of the telegraph, the dictaphone, and the electric writing pad to facilitate disembodied communication. By disembodying communication, technology aids the trafficker's manipulation of surfaces and appearances that not only threatens to transform innocent girls into prostitutes but also allows evil to pose as good: for the head of the traffic, William Trubus (William Welsh), is a wealthy socialite who also heads the Immigration Purity and Reform

League. As Tom Gunning notes, Trubus's identity remains unknown to both the police and the other traffickers precisely because his connection to the trade is purely technological: he simply listens to the proceedings of the traffickers' meetings via dictaphone and receives the day's profits on an electric writing pad.[39]

The film's conception of identity in morally schematic terms (one is either good or evil, virtuous or fallen) and its rejection of technological modernity's ability to produce false appearances derive from the fact that Tucker filters his cautionary tale through the codes and conventions of the sensation melodrama.[40] In particular, *Traffic in Souls* "starts from and expresses the anxiety brought about by a frightening new world"—in this case, the world of technological modernity—"in which the traditional patterns of moral order no longer provide the necessary social glue. It plays out the force of that anxiety with the apparent triumph of villainy, and it dissipates it with the eventual victory of virtue."[41] Moreover, the melodrama's conventional reliance on coincidence and narrative reversal offers a generic support to the film's own solution to the dangerous movements of modern traffic.[42] The melodramatic reversal of fortune that brings about the resolution of this particular film is based on the idea that the lines of technology are themselves reversible: the same technologies that initiate a dangerous mobilization of bodies and identities in the film are used to return detoured bodies to their proper place and to arrest the dangerous movement of the illegitimate traffic by fixing the seemingly ubiquitous threat of the traffickers.

The possibility of reversal is based on the idea that in order for specific technological forms of disembodied communication to find successful articulation, there *must* be a body at the other end of the line. It is worth mentioning that *The Lonedale Operator* precedes *Traffic in Souls* in turning on this idea. In the middle of the film, the besieged operator locks herself in the telegraph office while the hobos try to break down the door. Hysterically, she types out an SOS on the telegraph—yet the camera cuts to the other end of the line only to reveal that the telegraph operator has fallen asleep. By alternating between shots of the panicked Lonedale operator, the determined transients trying to break into her office, and the soporific telegraphist snoozing at his post in the other station the film elaborates the horror of finding the other end of the line unattended. Once the telegraph-

FIGURE 33 *Traffic in Souls* (George Loane Tucker, 1913). COURTESY OF THE LIBRARY OF CONGRESS MOTION PICTURE READING ROOM

ist awakens, the operator successfully communicates her SOS and sets into motion the race to the rescue, and thus the narrative reversal.

In Tucker's film the success as well as the undoing of the traffic in souls similarly turns on the bilateral structure of communications technology. At the same time that the traffickers exploit the ability of communications technology to allow them to act as a ubiquitous, floating threat, they are acutely aware that this same technology can be turned back on them to fix identity. An early sequence in the film establishes this premise and fore-shadows the film's technological resolution: as the Go-Between (Howard Crampton) calculates the week's earnings in his office, the cadets become alarmed by the presence of the dictaphone and electric writing pad. The alternation between shots of the traffickers and of Trubus in his office lis-tening to the proceedings makes the conditions of this connection clear: by disembodying communication, technology makes possible but does not guarantee anonymity, for the mere presence of the apparatus itself always implies the possibility of a body at the other end of the line. Moreover, the reciprocal structure of such systems—the fact that they facilitate *dis-cursive* communication—means that sender and receiver, observer and observed, and known and unknown can always change positions. Thus when Trubus hears the alarmed cadets' suspicious enquiries about the apparatus he is visibly worried by the possibility of being discovered; once the Go-Between calms their fears, he appears amused and relieved and continues to listen from the secret security of his office.

In this manner the film suggests that just as technology sets into motion a range of legitimate and illegitimate bodies, subjects, and objects it also has the power to arrest mobility. Thus the narrative turns when the heroine, Mary (Jane Gail), accidentally overhears the trafficker's transactions when she picks up the dictaphone in Trubus's office. Recognizing the "voice of the man who kidnapped her sister," she connects a recording apparatus into the dictaphone that links Trubus's office to the trafficker's and secures the evidence needed by the police to identify them. *Traffic in Souls* thereby assures its audience that technology carries with it the power to contain or recuperate the same dangers it unleashes, in part because a new "extension" can always be added onto the existing apparatus. Whereas the dictaphone's separation of the voice from the body helps Trubus keep the traffic in motion, the recording apparatus that Mary plugs into the system and the soundtrack that she produces link the voice back up to the body and thereby arrests the slave traders' entire system of circulation. Thus within the fiction of *Traffic in Souls* the technological restoration of the voice to the body converts fragmentation and dispersal into unity and wholeness and also subordinates a clandestine trade to lawful regulation: thanks to Mary's recording, the traffickers are jailed and Little Sister is restored to the family home. In a sense, the film anticipates the recuperative work done by the developments in film sound technology already underway in 1913.[43] But I think it makes more sense to link the function of the recording device to the textual problems precipitated by the formal demands of the multi-reel feature-length film. When the film resolves its narrative crisis through a technology that arrests dangerous mobility and converts fragmentation into unity and wholeness, it thematizes the cinema's own technical solution to the formal and structural problems associated with the multi-reel feature-length film. It is precisely the unseen work done by the cinematic apparatus to regulate multiple and intersecting story lines that converts the six-reeler's unprecedented fragmentation of space and time into a manufactured unity.

For this reason, I think it is no coincidence that this early long feature should have "traffic" as its organizing figure. Tucker's model for emergent feature-length narrativity can be likened to selected features of the mechanized traffic it represents: it is a structure whose coherence and smooth functioning requires a systematic organization of multiple lines of action and movement that converge at precisely coordinated points in time and space. At the level of form as well as fiction, *Traffic* rejects modern traffic's technological rhizome—a structure with no beginning and no end, featuring multiple extensions and complex points of transition that bring the modern individual anywhere and nowhere in particular. Thus unlike the film's dystopian vision of technological traffic, its narrative traffic works inexorably toward unity, continuity, and closure and brings the spectator to a final destination that makes the preceding twists and turns meaningful, significant, and ultimately satisfying.

Interestingly, the dystopian model of modern traffic imagined and rejected by the film bears striking similarity to the models of feature-length narrativity rejected by contemporary audiences who, as Eileen Bowser notes, were both thrilled and frustrated by the emergent five- and six-reel feature. As production companies rushed to meet the new demand for longer films, many simply padded out their shorter films. These products, however, left spectators to complain of poorly paced narratives that took too long to reach their inevitable conclusions.[44] Moreover, Bowser explains, exhibitors who attempted to preserve the short program by splitting up features and projecting individual reels in consecutive days or weeks (a practice enabled by the correspondence of narrative units to reel breaks) left spectators frustrated by a needlessly protracted journey defined by multiple and relatively arbitrary stops and starts.[45] Such practices foreground the transitional status of the long feature in the early 1910s as emergent narrative practices overlapped with dominant exhibition practices—some of which, in turn, audiences began to experience as residual. The continuous projection demanded by *Traffic in Soul*'s narrative structure did away with the arbitrariness of such stops, starts, and connections, thereby reducing both the demand on the spectator to make such connections and the accompanying risk of the spectator's quick displacement from order into disorder, pleasure into displeasure.

The Human Motor, "Moral Breakdown," and Pedestrian Traffic in *Shoes*

By focusing on the circulation of young working women to and through urban commercial thoroughfares either to work or to find employment, *Traffic in Souls* glimpses another contradiction central to working women's experience of being absorbed into modern traffic: as they entered the work-force in increasing numbers young women became important—sometimes even the primary—sources of income for their families; nevertheless, to increase profits industry paid them wages below subsistence level and based this wage slavery on the rationalization that women's income was merely supplementary to that of a father or husband. As a result, working poor women labored arduously for extremely long hours at tedious jobs that subjected them to the "speeding up process" in factories and the implemen-tation of sales quotas in stores, both of which were endemic to the "scien-tifically managed" workplace. A range of women reformers representing a broad political spectrum (from those who championed women's suffrage as the solution to the exploitation of female workers to those who argued for the return of all working women to the home) agreed that poor work con-ditions and wage slavery led to intolerable fatigue and exhaustion, which in turn had a devastating effect on "character." In the text following I examine Lois Weber's film *Shoes*, which, like *Traffic in Souls*, links unskilled labor to the traffic in women, and yet it represents that link quite differently. In *Traffic in Souls*, each of the women forced into white slavery works or has arrived in the city to find work (indeed, the Swedish immigrants are duped into the traffic by the promise of employment) and becomes the victim of the traffickers. In contrast, *Shoes* (and the source material on which it is based) links the working poor woman's marginal economic position within legitimate traffic to fatigue and "breakdown"—both of which, in turn, make her all the more easily detoured into the traffic in women.

Shoes takes place during one week in the life of Eva Meyer (Mary Mac-Laren), a young shop clerk who supports her parents and three younger sisters on her meager earnings of five dollars a week—though her mother (Mrs. Witting) takes in laundry, her father (Harry Griffith) is unemployed. In contrast to *Traffic in Souls*, which focuses on the international and na-tional traffic in women aided by the efficiency of mass transportation,

FIGURE 34
Illustration from
Stella Wynne
Herron's short
story "Shoes."
COURTESY OF THE
DOE LIBRARY,
UNIVERSITY OF
CALIFORNIA,
BERKELEY

Shoes provides a more localized view of the rather circumscribed paths of pedestrian traffic through which its heroine travels each day as she walks to and from the tenement apartment she shares with her family and the five-and-dime where she works six days a week. Eva and her family live on the impoverished margins of urban consumer culture. Mechanical transportation and access to the mass-produced goods that surround her are the structuring absences that define Eva's material and moral crisis: both are beyond her means, so her days are constituted by a scheduled alternation between walking and standing on aching feet barely covered by pitifully old shoes that threaten, as one title tells us, to "simply fall off her feet." Once they finally do so, Eva will lose her primary means for remaining within the legitimate paths of the city's commercial traffic. Burdened with the weighty responsibility of providing for her younger sisters, ill from walking through a rainstorm in shoes resoled with cardboard, and demoralized by

FIGURE 35 Illustration from Stella Wynne Herron's short story "Shoes." COURTESY OF THE DOE LIBRARY, UNIVERSITY OF CALIFORNIA, BERKELEY

her father's refusal to work, Eva is temporarily forced into prostitution to purchase the new shoes upon which her ability to continue working as a shop clerk depends.

The film is based on a short story by Stella Wynne Herron published in *Collier's Weekly* (January 1, 1916), which in turn was based on anecdotes narrated by the socialist reformer Jane Addams in her *A New Conscience and an Ancient Evil* (1912; first published in serial form in *McClure's* between 1911–1912). Eva is something of an amalgamation of the various women Addams encountered while working on behalf of poor young women in Chicago who had entered into prostitution out of dire economic need. Weber introduces Eva's story with a quotation from *A New Conscience and an Ancient Evil* about one of the women on whom the protagonist is based: "[She] first yielded to temptation when she had become utterly discouraged because she had tried in vain for seven months to save enough money for a pair of shoes. She habitually spent two dollars a week for her room, three dollars for board, and sixty cents a week for carfare, and she had found the forty cents remaining from her weekly wage of six dollars inadequate to do more than re-sole her old shoes twice. When the shoes became too worn to endure a third soling and she possessed but ninety cents toward a new pair, she gave up her struggle; to use her own contemptuous phrase, 'she sold out for a pair of shoes.'"[46] The eponymous shoes of this story help materialize the working poor woman's tenuous position within the legitimate pathways of modern industrial traffic and also foreground yet another contradiction of her plight: it is precisely her desperate effort to remain within legitimate traffic—for surely without shoes she can neither walk through the city to work nor stand behind a counter—that forces her temporarily into one of its illegitimate extensions. Hence, in this film the image of tattered shoes repeatedly reinforced with cardboard becomes emblematic of the thin and fragile barrier that separates the working poor woman's position in legitimate traffic from the proximate traffic in women. Furthermore, the battered and well-worn shoes are material analogues for the heroine's own bodily and psychological exhaustion caused by overwork, worry, and poverty: for like Eva, the shoes have been repeatedly subjected to daily forces that slowly but surely wear away at their integrity. The use of "shoes" rather than "souls" as the film's governing emblem is an indication of its focus upon the material and familial circumstances that steer the working poor woman into prostitution. For, following on from Addams, *Shoes* insistently foregrounds another axiom governing the individual's circulation through modern traffic: just as trains, streetcars, and automobiles could be expected to collapse should their motors and engines be poorly tended or their supply of energy depleted without replenishment, the same could be expected of the human motor. For example, the following description is only one of numerous and striking stories recorded sympathetically by Addams that emphasize the degree to which exhaustion and demoralizing breakdown were a part of the working poor woman's experience of technological modernity. As Addams observed, "Varicose veins and broken arches in the feet are found in every occupation in which women are obliged to stand for hours, but at any moment either one may develop beyond purely painful symptoms into crippling incapacity. One such girl returning home after a long day's work deliberately sat down upon the floor of a crowded street car, explaining defiantly to the conductor and the bewildered passengers that 'her feet would not hold out for another minute.'"[47] This anecdote about the public spectacle of the working girl's physical breakdown inverts the more familiar nineteenth-century scenario analyzed in historical detail by Schivelbusch and Kirby in which the traveler suffers (bodily and psychological) trauma as a result of the catastrophic breakdown of transportation technology. As Schivelbusch and others have noted, the speed and acceleration associated with modern transportation technologies often implied a corresponding degree of immobility on the part of the passenger: just as the railway or streetcar passenger remains relatively immobile while being shuttled through space by new transportation technologies, so too did the unskilled laborer remain fixed in space on an assembly line that sped by at ever-increasing rates or behind a sales counter over which an accelerated turnover of goods was expected. While the traveler's own bodily inertia inside the railway car made the shock of the crash all the more traumatic, the fixed, standing position of the factory girl or sales clerk as she facilitated the rapid flow of goods through the marketplace led to her own catastrophic breakdown. Forging these opposing scenarios into two sides of the same coin was the fact of modern "fatigue." While the operation of a great machine subjected its parts to stresses (jolts, vibration, pressure, temperature) that eventually caused it to break down, the processes of mass production and commerce similarly subjected the worker's body to stress that might culminate in physiological collapse. As Schivelbusch notes: "That it was the 'working' of the machine, the work performed by it which caused its component materials to suffer 'fatigue' was no mere figure of speech: there was an obvious connection between the rise of modern material testing and what Marx calls the 'intensification of labor.' Capitalist industry exploited, in fact, both material (i.e., iron, steel) and human labor power. Marx described this as 'the increased expenditure of labor in a given time, heightened tension of labor-power, and closer filling up of the pores of the working day.'"[48]

If at the end of the first decade of the twentieth century industry was symbolized by the high-tech, perpetually moving assembly line and the department store by the opulently decorated and electrically illuminated display window, then the working poor woman might best be symbolized by the image of aching feet shod in well-worn shoes that, whether she made or sold them, she could hardly afford. It is precisely this symbol that first Addams, then Stella Wynne Herron, and then Weber use to materialize the physical and moral breakdown that Addams insisted was a primary force in detouring working poor women into casual prostitution. However, before discussing *Shoes* I will first turn to the source material that informs Weber's particular incarnation of the white slave film and the "science of work" that informed Addams's understanding of the potential as well as the limits of the body absorbed into modern traffic and hence her vision of American modernity.

Modern Fatigue and Moral Breakdown

In *A New Conscience and an Ancient Evil*, Addams focuses on the conditions in which working poor women labored, the wages they received, and the socioeconomic pressures they endured at home, at work, and on the city streets. Since Addams argued that the cheapness of the working woman's unskilled labor made her an inexpensive and expendable vehicle for accelerating the circulation of products and profits to and through the commercial sphere, it is fitting that she turned her attention to the human motor and energy that powered such vehicles. Given this interest, it is important to place Addams's writings in the context of the "science of work" developed in the late nineteenth and early twentieth centuries by Hermann von Helmholtz, Etienne Marey, Frederick Winslow Taylor, and Frank Gilbreth, among others. According to Anson Rabinbach the science of work emerged in the mid-nineteenth century to provide a "vision of society powered by universal energy" that offered the rapidly industrializing West "an exhilarating explanation for its astonishing productivity . . . In that vision, the working body was but an exemplar of that universal process by which energy was converted into mechanical work, a variant of the great engines and dynamos spawned by the industrial age. The protean force of nature, the productive power of industrial machines, and the body in motion were all instances of the same dynamic laws, subject to measurement."[49]

The science of work and the inscription of the body as a mechanism had important foundations in the first law of thermodynamics (the law of the conservation of energy), formulated by von Helmholtz, which states that "the forces of nature (mechanical, electrical, chemical and so forth) are forms of a single, universal energy, or Kraft, that cannot be either added to or destroyed."[50] Though the first law of thermodynamics reconceived the universe as a vast reservoir of energy waiting to be converted into work, the process of conversion inevitably resulted in loss. Formulated at roughly the same time, the second law of thermodynamics explained the irreversibility and decline of energy in *entropy* such that "in any isolated system the transfer of energy from a warmer to a colder body is accompanied by a decrease in total available energy."[51] As Rabinbach cogently explains, "The great discoveries of nineteenth-century physics led, therefore, not only to the assumption of a universal energy, but also to the inevitability of decline, dissolution, and exhaustion. Accompanying the discovery of energy conservation and entropy was the endemic disorder of fatigue—the most evident and persistent reminder of the body's intractable resistance to unlimited productivity."[52]

The availability of energy in an isolated system, its conversion into force, and the loss that resulted from this process was widely applied to studies of the human body in the science of work. Such studies imagined the body as a mechanism akin to the steam engine powered by a limited supply of energy governed by the first and second laws of thermodynamics. These discoveries had important social implications, as studies on the various types of work undertaken by laborers, students, and soldiers sought to maximize the efficiency of the human motor and eliminate processes and conditions that needlessly depleted its reserve of energy, resulted in fatigue, and/or led to a decrease in productivity. Like any other machine, such studies concluded, the human motor was inclined to break down if needlessly taxed and improperly maintained. The clocked, photographed and measured bodies found in the works of Etienne Marey, Frederick Taylor, and Frank and Lillian Gilbreth were the outcome of a drive to limit waste and enhance the efficient functioning of the human motor so that it might conserve its limited supply of energy and yield greater productivity.[53]

To be sure, Addams did not conduct any such scientific studies herself but was instead interested in the social implications of this particularly modern understanding and use of the human body. Unlike her contemporary Frederick Taylor, Addams was less interested in questions of how to extract more work from the body by maximizing the efficiency of its movements than she was with the premature breakdown of the working poor woman's human motor due to what she called "untoward economic conditions." In this respect, Addams's concern with the effects of the accelerated pace of modern life on the body and psyche of working women paralleled, for example, the American physician George M. Beard's interest in the enervation and fatigue of white, middle-class, white-collar workers exposed to unprecedented levels of "brainwork" (see chapter 1).

Halfway through *A New Conscience and an Ancient Evil* Addams bluntly states: "The aphorism that 'morals fluctuate with trade' was long considered cynical, but it has been in Berlin, in London, in Japan as well as in several American cities, that there is a distinct increase in the number of registered prostitutes during periods of financial depression and even during the dull season of leading local industries." Boom and bust cycles, overly long workdays, the accelerated pace of the factory system, wages falling below subsistence levels, and inadequate time and opportunity for leisure conspired to create a form of wage slavery that subjected the unskilled woman worker's human motor to devastating fatigue. Hence the solution to the problem of "the social evil," Addams argued, could be found in part through the "study of industry from the point of view of the producer in a sense which has never been done before. Such a study with reference to industrial legislation will ally itself on one hand with the trades-union movement, which insists upon a living wage and shorter hours for the workers and also upon an opportunity for self-direction, and on the other hand with the efficiency of movement, which would refrain from over-fatiguing an operator as it would from over-speeding a machine."[54] Crucial for my purposes in this chapter is Addams's assertion that not only did over-fatigue and economic privation accelerate the process of entropy and result in early physical and mental exhaustion, but also it precipitated *moral* breakdown. The ever-vigilant exercise of virtue required the daily parrying of forces that constantly sought to compromise it within an urban industrial setting. When industrial work conditions and other features of modern life depleted the working poor woman's limited reserve of energy, then less was available for the exercise of virtue—resulting in moral breakdown. In short, Addams argued that moral breakdown was an effect of the working poor woman's position within modern traffic.

For example, Addams noted that in the factory women were subject to the increasingly accelerated pace of production and excessively long workdays, both of which conspired to facilitate her absorption into the traffic in women. She paints a picture in which the unskilled working woman is central to the accelerated pace of mass production and the expanded scope of consumption as she labors intensely to fill increasingly high quotas. Speaking of Taylorism's "speeding up process," Addams argues that "certainly the constant sense of haste is one of the most nerve racking exhausting tests to which the human system can be subjected. Those girls in the sewing industry whose mothers thread needles for them far into the night so they can sew without a moment's interruption during the next day; those girls who insert eyelets into shoes, for which they are paid two cents a case, each case containing twenty-four pairs of shoes, are striking victims of the overspeeding which is so characteristic of our factory system."[55] The constant acceleration of mass production meant that the factory girl's experience of modernity was overwhelmingly linked to the second law of thermodynamics: while the owner of capital might regard her as part of the supply of reserve of energy awaiting conversion into work, she experiences the processes of conversion as the depletion of her bodily energy.

The accelerated pace of production (similar to the sales quotas that department store clerks had to fill) taxes the worker's nervous system to a degree that leaves her unable to rest or enjoy the leisure activities necessary to restore her "mental balance." Addams explained that the "increasing nervous energy to which industrial processes daily accommodate themselves, and the speeding up constantly required of operators, may at any moment so register their results upon the nervous system of a factory girl as to overcome her powers of resistance. Many a working girl at the end of the day is so hysterical and overwrought that her mental balance is plainly disturbed." While the pace of assembly-line work taxed the nervous system and the body, it simultaneously "wore down her resistance" and facilitated a concomitant moral breakdown. Here Addams invokes the image of the working girl standing for hours upon aching feet to underscore the physical exhaustion and fatigue experienced by working poor women: "A humane forewoman recently said to me as she glanced down the long room in which hundreds of young women, many of them with their shoes beside them, were standing: 'I hate to think of all the aching feet on this floor; these girls all have trouble with their feet, some of them spend the entire evening bathing them in hot water.' But aching feet are no more usual than aching backs and aching heads. The study of industrial diseases has only this year been begun by the federal authorities, and *doubtless as more is known of the nervous and mental effect of over-fatigue, many more moral breakdowns will*

FIGURE 36 *Coil Winding Machines, Westinghouse Works* (AM&B, 1904). COURTESY OF THE LIBRARY OF CONGRESS MOTION PICTURE READING ROOM

be traced to this source. It is already easy to make the connection in definite cases: 'I was too tired to care,' 'I was too tired to know what I was doing,' 'I was dead tired and sick of it all,' 'I was dog tired and just went with him,' are phrases taken from the lips of reckless girls who are endeavoring to explain the situation in which they find themselves."[56]

The moral breakdown required to divert working poor woman into prostitution, Addams argues, was simply another effect of modern life: as the pace of production quickens unreasonably about her, the worker's human motor slows and eventually breaks down as would any other poorly tended machinery, resulting in "the disastrous effects of over-fatigue on character." Central to this passage is the image of shoes and women standing on aching feet, similar to that which is pictured in the 1904 film *Coil Winding Machines, Westinghouse Works* (AM&B). Shot at the Westinghouse plant in East Pittsburgh, it shows rows of women factory workers standing at their stations winding electric coils onto giant spools as a male supervisor walks up and down the factory aisles supervising the quality and speed of their work. However, while the camera's distance from the factory workers creates an orderly image of industrial productivity that makes fatigue and aching feet difficult to perceive, Addams and Weber provide visual and narrative close-ups of the body parts of individual workers to reveal the physical and moral conditions in which they toiled. Therefore, the image of women standing in place for long hours is, as we shall see, crucial to Weber's cinematic narration of the processes of fatigue, exhaustion, and, eventually, moral breakdown that lead her protagonist, Eva, to succumb to Charlie (William V. Mong), the cabaret singer who steers her into the traffic in women.

Eva is a shop clerk not a factory worker, but Weber emphasizes repeatedly that she shares the experience of standing for long hours each day. Throughout the film, we see several close-ups of Eva's feet as she stands behind the counter—one such shot shows her worn shoes so wet from a rainstorm that they create a puddle around her aching feet as she stands on the shop floor. And like the factory workers described by Addams, Eva also soaks her feet each evening upon returning home. Indeed, one reviewer found this level of detail regarding Eva's fatigue excessive: "Miss Weber has gone a step too far in showing a close-up of the girl extracting splinters from the sole of her foot. She has gone too far in showing the girl scraping mud from her feet with a pair of scissors. There is such a thing as being too realistic."[57] However this "too realistic" realism allows Weber to foreground the wear endured by the "parts" that keep Eva in motion while simultaneously stressing the dangers inherent in the shop clerk's position at the crossroads between legitimate and illegitimate commercial traffic. Even more so than the factory worker, Addams argued, the store clerk's position within traffic made her particularly vulnerable to the efforts of procurers. As crucial points in the relay of goods from producer to consumer, store clerks helped keep finished products and profits in motion; more often than not, both passed through—but rarely to—her hands. Hence, she spent each day facilitating a high turnover of goods she could not afford; was available to any customer who sought her help in the store; and stood behind a counter for long hours with little opportunity for respite from tedium and fatigue. "Such a girl," Addams explained, "May be bitterly lonely, but she is expected to smile affably all day long upon a throng of changing customers. She may be without adequate clothing, although she stands in an emporium where it is piled about her, literally as high as her head. She may be faint for want of food but she may not sit down lest she assume 'an attitude of inertia or indifference,' which is against the rules. She may have a great desire for pretty things, but she must sell to other people at least twenty-five times the amount of her own salary, or she will not be retained."[58] Poised on the threshold between production and consumption, the store clerk operates on a deficit in an atmosphere of surplus. Though fatigued from excessively long hours of standing, she is surrounded by others engaged in leisure. Though too poor to clothe and feed herself adequately, she sells myriad goods to help others meet and exceed their own needs and desires. Though placed in a milieu of social interaction, she was there to provide "service"—a function that, as William Leach has shown, required her to cater exclusively to the customer's needs in a mode of self-abnegation and deference.[59] This economy of depletion, Addams argued, made her particularly vulnerable to exhaustion and breakdown.

Most troubling to Addams, however, was the department store's policy of admitting entry to all shoppers without obligation to purchase, a practice that made the store a site where legitimate and illegitimate forms of traffic easily converged and hence an ideal site for the recruitment of young women into white slavery. Addams argued,

> It is perhaps the department store more than anywhere else that every possible weakness in a girl is detected and traded upon. For while it is true that "wherever many girls are gathered together more or less unprotected and embroiled in the struggle for a livelihood, nearby will be hovering the procurers and evil minded," no other place of employment is so easy of access as the department store. No visitor is received in a factory or office unless he has definite business there, whereas every purchaser is welcome at a department store, even a notorious woman well known to represent the demi-monde trade is treated with marked courtesy if she spends large sums of money. The primary danger lies in the fact that the comely saleswomen are thus of easy access. The disreputable young man constantly passes in and out, making small purchases from every pretty girl, opening an acquaintance with complimentary remarks; or the procuress, a fashionably dressed woman, buys clothing in large amounts, sometimes for a young girl by her side, ostensibly her daughter. She condoles

with the sales woman about her hard lot and lack of pleasure, and in the role of a kindly prosperous matron invites her to come to her own home for a good time.[60]

Here the department store functions as a crossroads where an exhausted labor force on the verge of breakdown intersects with "customers" who understand in a glance the hardships the sales clerk endures, the weaknesses such hardships cause, and precisely how such weaknesses can be "traded upon." And so the procurer is free to approach the young saleswoman in an effort to parlay a legitimate purchase into an illegitimate one. Hence, Eva's status as a store clerk helps emphasize the context of the store as a space where the "free-floating desire" provoked in the commercial sphere conspires with the fatigue experienced by the clerk to help detour her into the traffic in women.

In keeping with Addams's focus on the socioeconomic conditions that contributed to the working poor woman's displacement into the white slave traffic, Weber carefully organizes *Shoes'* temporality around the industrial time of a single workweek, during which the protagonist suffers sickness, fatigue, and, in the end, moral breakdown. The film opens on payday at the five-and-dime where Eva works behind a counter. She and other sales clerks stream out of the shop with their week's wages in hand. The shop girls provide a condensed image of the lower echelons of urban commercial traffic: dressed in ready-to-wear mass-produced clothing they walk past display windows designed to encourage them to part with whatever pittance of disposable income they possess. Indeed, as Eva walks down the street with her friend Lil (Jessie Arnold), she pauses to gaze longingly at a pair of shoes prominently displayed behind a plate glass window. As she stands outside the shop, Charlie, a "cadet" and cabaret singer who cruises shops during the day for potential victims, emerges from the shoe store as a title indicates that "he had been waiting already for a few days for the girls." Thus the film quickly visualizes the inseparability of modern life from traffic and a series of looks and movements convey the precariousness of Eva's position on the "straight and narrow path" that takes her to and from the tenement and the shop each day. As Eva looks from the shoes on display to her own poorly shod feet (which the camera does not reveal to the spectator at this point), we cut to a close-up of Charlie as a predatory grin spreads across his face. A cut to Eva reveals a worried expression as she sees Charlie, then glances at Lil, and then back down again to her shoes. Charlie regards Lil with a knowing look as Eva continues home: he sees the condition of Eva's tattered, dirty, ragged shoes and understands that the despair beneath her desiring look at the unobtainable new shoes implies the imminence of her moral breakdown. Hence, we watch Eva return home and trudge upstairs to her family's apartment with a deadened and nearly expressionless face, arms hanging motionless at her sides. Here as in the rest of the film she moves about like an automaton whose "batteries of life" are nearly drained. While *Traffic in Souls* offers a view of female bodies swept into motion by technologies of mass transportation, *Shoes* tracks a body barely kept in motion by a human motor on the verge of collapse.

Weber withholds a shot of Eva's shoes for a while longer in order to picture more precisely the precariousness of Eva's position in urban traffic and the degree to which her shoes hold her place in its more legitimate pathways. The explanation for Eva's weary, drone-like disposition becomes clear when she passes by the open door of her parents' bedroom where "as usual her father was lying, sluggishly reading on the bed," smoking a pipe and enjoying beer from a bucket that sits on the bedside table. As is done in *Traffic in Souls*, in *Shoes* the traffic in women is traced back to a corrupt patriarch who enjoys leisure and pleasure at the expense of working-class women. In this respect, the Meyer family's tenement flat becomes a microcosm for the world pictured outside, which the film suggests is divided in two: while one half seems to lead a life of toil uninterrupted by leisure, rest, or pleasure, the other leads a life of leisure, rest, and pleasure uninterrupted by toil. As Eva regards her father with careworn disgust, a title tells us, "When she saw him lying there in such a lazy manner, she longed to have the strength to take hold of him and bring him seriously to his senses that he had an obligation to work for his family." Later on in the film, when sent out of the flat to find work, Eva's father instead purchases a new novel at a newsstand and reads on a park bench, reclining as much as the bench will allow, thereby making it clear that Eva toils at the lower end of the commercial order so that her father can perpetually amuse himself at the lower end of the consumer order. Hence his recumbent stasis is the inverse of her (morally and physically) upright movements through the city streets and at the five-and-dime.

Indeed, Meyer's exploitation of his daughter's labor parallels Charlie's later commodification of Eva's body; for Charlie also seems to circulate only through the paths of commercialized leisure. While at night he sings, flirts, and drinks in a cabaret called the Blue Goose (the site of Eva's eventual downfall) during the day he circles like a shark through the world of commerce staffed by underpaid clerks, shopping for his next victim. A later shot of the interior of the Blue Goose further suggests that Eva's perilous position on the margins of legitimate traffic can be explained by patterns of consumption made possible through errant patriarchy's exploitation of working poor women: two burlesque dancers perform on stage in front of upper-class male patrons, one of whom leans back in his chair with his legs propped up on the stage, cigar in hand and goblet on the table beside him, recalling the image of Eva's father as he reclines in bed.

After Eva spies her father in his bedroom, she finds her mother in the kitchen to whom, each week, "faithfully and obediently, [she] would continuously hand over her meager salary." As Eva asks eagerly if she can purchase new shoes, her mother anticipates the inquiry that clearly has been made many times before and quickly stashes the money away with a guilty and harassed expression on her face. She explains to Eva that "this is just enough for the rent . . . the butcher will have to wait again this week," and then she promises, "next week you will certainly get it." As Eva's face falls with disappointment, Weber provides the spectator with the first close-up of Eva's shoes: they are dirty, old, and so riddled with holes that the uppers seem on the verge of peeling away completely from the tattered soles. This shot has the effect of transforming the earlier image of Eva staring longingly through the display window at the new shoes. Whereas the image might simply demonstrate the power of the plate glass display to provoke and even manufacture desire for and the consumption of mass-produced goods, the later shot of Eva's own shoes demonstrates her true and rather desperate need. In this respect, the close-up perfectly visualizes Stella Wynne Herron's description of Eva's shoes, supplemented by Eva's own description of her shoes to her mother as she begs for money to replace them: "There were great ragged holes worn through each; cracks and fissures radiated in all directions. The thin leather was disintegrating like ice in the summer sun. 'And ma, the heels are so crooked that they throw my feet all sideways, and I can hardly walk.'"[61] Much as this passage does, the close-up of Eva's shoes finally provides the spectator with the knowledge that Charlie already possesses: Eva is just days away from losing an important means for earning her pitiful wages—the shoes that enable her to circulate within legitimate traffic as she walks to work and stands behind a counter all day long. The rest of this scene quickly reveals the stakes of Eva's struggle to remain in circulation: at her mother's request she fetches her baby sister from the bedroom and her two younger sisters, hungry for dinner, gallop through the apartment.

Just as Addams argues in *A New Conscience and an Ancient Evil*, the film *Shoes* suggests that domestic space and the family contribute to the various forces that detour poor girls into the traffic in women. As part of its articulation of American modernity, *Shoes* makes clear the idea that the urban family home is a thoroughly trafficked space: in contrast to households a generation earlier, few of the goods consumed in the home—from clothing to food to furniture—are manufactured there, and most of what is purchased by Eva's mother is done so on credit. No longer is the family household a self-sufficient, independent unit of production and consumption but instead is entirely dependent upon mass production to satisfy its needs. Neither does the urban working-class family have much hope of owning the home in which they live and hence future independence from a landlord. Put differently, the working-class family home is no longer a refuge from the outside world of work and commerce, it is no longer a "space of innocence" that cloisters and protects the heroine of the melodrama from those who seek to compromise her virtue.[62] Rather, family relations in *Shoes* appear to be entirely mediated by questions of commerce and consumption: most of the scenes taking place in the tenement flat do so at mealtimes, during which Mr. Meyer reads his dime novels and Mrs. Meyer waters down her children's canned milk. And while one daughter sneaks sugar to make the thinned milk more palatable another complains about having had no meat for a week. Moreover, Eva exists in a state of homemade wage slavery: though she toils for her small salary she has no control over the income she brings home—rather, she dutifully hands each unopened pay envelope to her mother.

The fact that Eva is responsible for keeping a meager supply of canned milk, meat, and other goods trickling into the tenement flat underscores the idea that the initial absorption of the urban individual into modern traffic takes place in the family home. Indeed, Mr. Meyer's disinclination to work while he can be supported by his daughter suggests that much as the heads of industry do, the head of this household seems to regard his children as actual and potential wage earners whose differences in age simply represent a future supply of cheap, exploitable, unskilled labor. However, though Eva is the sole breadwinner in her family, she labors at a time when industry kept the wages of working poor girls below subsistence level based on what Addams called "the worn-out hypocritical pretence of employing only the girl 'protected by home influences' as a device for reducing wages."[63] *Shoes* represents precisely this historical juncture when the older, traditional family relations that made young women entirely de- pendent upon their parents intersected with newer family relations that made daughters the wage earners on whom their families often depended. Lacking economic agency, Eva is like one of the 84 percent of women wage earners discussed by Addams who turned in her entire wage to her parents, "as if the tradition of woman's dependence upon her family for support held long after the actual fact had changed, or as if the tyranny established through generations when daughters could be starved into sub- mission to a father's will continued even after the roles had changed, and the wages of the girl child supported a broken and dissolute father."[64] In turn, the narrator of Stella Wynne Herron's short story tells us: "One of the myths of the Meyers household was that Mr. Meyers's desultory labor adequately supported his family. He never admitted that Eva's money was not her own. It would have hurt his manly pride."[65] This condition of wage slavery imposed from without by industry and from within by the family ultimately made the working poor woman more vulnerable to traffickers, for, as Addams warned, "certain it is that the long habit of obedience, as well as the feeling of family obligation established from childhood, is often utilized by the slave trafficker."[66]

Ironically, though Eva labors regularly to maintain the slow circulation of goods into her home, she seems throughout much of the film to be in- capable of any form of consumption. In this respect she experiences a pecu- liar contradiction governing the working poor woman's position in traffic: the more she works without respite the less she is able to consume. She is like the "hundreds of working girls" who "go directly to bed as soon as they have eaten their suppers" because, as Addams explains, "they are too tired to go from home for recreation, too tired to read and often too tired to sleep."[67] Paralleling her inability to purchase new shoes, Eva's inability to eat and sleep is even more extreme and is thus part of the social calculus of industrial capitalism that conserves the reserve energy of a few and inevitably and irreversibly drains away the reserve energy of many. Hence, on the evening of the first payday Eva refuses to eat dinner when her father looks up from his novel only to rebuke his children for noisily clamoring for food. The next morning, we see her take a single gulp of coffee before leaving for work, having lost too much time cutting out cardboard insoles to cover over the holes in the bottoms of her shoes. On another evening, she returns home soaked with rain, too sick and feverish to eat dinner, and the next day her sore throat prevents her from eating lunch. This marked inability to engage in even the most basic forms of bodily consumption and rest (she lies awake at night worrying)—including those necessary for sustaining life—foregrounds Eva's fatigue and the impending breakdown that ushers her into the traffic in women.

Thus, if old and new shoes take on a disproportionate significance in this film, it is simply because everything depends upon them. In the lower orders of commercial traffic, Eva is (a) pedestrian in both senses of the word: she is a pedestrian (noun) in the sense that she earns her wage by walking and standing, but she is also "pedestrian" (adjective) in the sense that she is utterly common, possesses no unique skills, and is therefore utterly replaceable should she no longer possess the means of remaining in circulation. One scene is particularly important in this respect. Early one morning Eva sets off for work in a rainstorm. As others hurry past her in motorcars or protected by coats and umbrellas, we see Eva walking through the storm without such amenities—shod, of course, only in her cardboard-lined shoes. A tracking close-up of Eva's drenched feet as she walks through the puddle-filled streets conveys her bodily misery, and a title tells us that "it didn't take long before her soles were soaked, melting literally away." She quickly becomes ill that day as a result of having to stand for long hours "on her wet and swollen feet." The various close-ups of Eva's wet feet emphasize that like the tattered soles and uppers of her shoes, the membrane that separates her position within legitimate traffic from the traffic in women has grown perilously thin. At night, she cowers in bed as a hand labeled "poverty" clutches at her and her sisters and a title explains, "Often she would lie awake at night in bed with her eyes wide open . . . then she would think about the miserable existence of her family." The next day, she finally suffers a moral breakdown after being told once again that there will not be any money left from her wages to purchase the badly needed new shoes. Another title confirms that "it was just a matter of hours—the shoes would simply fall off her feet—she felt the end was near." Eva once again refuses dinner and instead goes to the Blue Goose to earn the money she needs for a new pair of shoes.

In keeping with its particular representation of modern traffic, *Shoes* suggests that the absorption of the working poor woman into the white slave trade was inevitable—or even scheduled like the workweek around which the story of Eva's "moral breakdown" is organized. In this respect, a subplot involving Charlie and Eva's friend Lil is quite important. Halfway through the film, we see her pay a nighttime visit to "that other world of luxury and leisure," the Blue Goose. On the night Lil enters the traffic in women, she approaches the cabaret haltingly from the street, checking the sign out front. A cut to the interior shows her entering quite timidly and with a degree of uncertainty that contrasts with the rather blithe revelry of the patrons inside, suggesting that this is her first visit to the cabaret. Charlie sees her, greets her with enthusiasm, and gestures for a waiter to take her order. Eva's arrival at the Blue Goose appears as a nearly identical repetition of Lil's earlier visit, creating the visual impression that she has become part of the ongoing, predictable incorporation of working poor women into casual prostitution. Hence the scene opens with the same exterior shot of the cabaret, as Eva uncertainly checks the sign above the entrance and looks about her to make sure no one sees her enter. As she does so, the doorman and another man forcibly escort a disorderly woman from the premises, suggesting that just as one woman is expelled from this trade, another is procured (indeed, Charlie gives Lil the "brush off" after their liaison and turns his attention exclusively to the pursuit of Eva). Hence, Lil and Eva seem to have the same status within modern traffic as do the goods they sell by day from behind the counter: easily and cheaply purchased, widely available, and utterly expendable, they are quickly disposed of upon satisfying the purchaser's desire. And like the mass-produced goods piled high in display cases and countertops, once consumed they simply provoke the consumer's pursuit of something new.

The film's organization around the regimented schedule of the workday and workweek is consonant with the idea of a regularly scheduled delivery of new women into the notorious traffic. Hence, it is entirely appropriate that on the next payday Lil shows Eva the elegant wristwatch that has served as payment for her liaison with Charlie. The wristwatch materializes Lil's position in traffic: visibly incompatible with wage slavery, it implies the commodification of the wearer's body during time spent in the sphere of commercialized leisure. Moreover, the wristwatch is an ornamental disciplinary device that, like the pocket watch, attaches standardized time to the body and "accompanies the individual to remind [her] of [her] temporal existence,"[68] thereby aiding industry in the abstraction of the shop girl's labor as time. As if to emphasize this idea, Lil points to her watch to remind Eva that it is time for her to punch out and take her lunch break. Throughout, *Shoes* emphasizes the strictly regimented time of the workday monitored through time cards. While earlier actuality films such as *Girls Taking Time Checks, Westinghouse Works* (AM&B, 1904) make an attraction of industry's orderly and efficient regulation of time and wages, *Shoes* melodramatizes the effects of industrial time on the worker. Hence, it is no coincidence that Eva spends her lunch break watching middle- and upper-class men and women enjoying themselves as they walk through the park. The sweeping movements of the women as they walk past Eva in bustling groups followed by a close-up of "the beautiful well-dressed feet of the rich girls" foreground both their upward socioeconomic mobility and the greater freedom that the women experience in relation to space and time as they move happily through the interconnected paths of urban leisure and consumption. Put differently, they move through the less-regimented, unscheduled flow of traffic determined by the desire that was the province of the well-heeled consumer.

As they pass by Eva she imagines her own feet transformed by new shoes (represented by a close-up dissolve) and then watches wistfully as the women part ways, some on foot, others in a taxicab. Moments later, the tolling of a clock reminds Eva that it is time for her to return to the five-and-dime. Like Lil's new wristwatch, the tolling clock visualizes the idea that the film acts as something of a stopwatch: beginning as it does with a title that announces its own unhappy ending, *Shoes'* narrative counts down toward a tragic conclusion that neither the heroine nor the spectator has the power to change. In this respect, Weber takes advantage of the cinema's tendency, in Mary Ann Doane's words, "to subject . . . its spectator to the time of its own inexorable and unvarying forward movement," its "regimentation of time in modernity, its irreversibility."[69] To emphasize the irretrievability of Eva's loss, the film concludes with the arrival home of Eva's father moments after she has confessed her downfall to her mother. Walking into the apartment with a smile that contrasts sharply with the downcast expression on Eva's face, he announces that he has finally found work—thus rendering Eva's sacrifice ultimately unnecessary. In this respect, the film dramatizes the obliviousness of industrial time to the experience and fate of the working poor woman: as one of the film's concluding titles explains, "Life and time are not disturbed by anything, ever further on does this great life go, which can often be so cruel."

In this respect, *Shoes* is similar to the other films discussed in this chapter in its suggestion that the homogenizing effects of modern traffic make its legitimate and illegitimate extensions virtually indistinguishable. *Shoes* forcefully argues that the working poor woman's position within modern traffic makes wage slavery and white slavery nearly synonymous, and for interrelated reasons. If the unskilled worker often relies on her meager wages to support herself and/or other family members, then she is nevertheless paid wages that make subsistence nearly impossible and moral breakdown, in some cases, inevitable. A brief return to Addams is helpful, for she describes the fate of another dutiful daughter who also supported her family (in this case an invalid father, an elderly mother, and a brother crippled by rheumatism) on pitifully low wages: "In her desire to earn more money, the country girl came to the nearest large city, Chicago, to work in a department store. The highest wage she could earn, even though she wore long dresses and called herself 'experienced,' was five dollars a week. This sum was of course inadequate even for her own needs and she was constantly filled with a corroding worry for 'the folks at home.' . . . The girl made an arrangement with an older woman to be on call in the evenings whenever she was summoned by telephone, thus joining that large clandestine group of apparently respectable girls, most of whom yield to temptation only when hard pressed by debt incurred during illness or non-employment, or when they are facing some immediate necessity. This practice has become so general in the larger American cities as to be systematically conducted."[70] Like Eva, this young woman finds her powers of resistance worn away by a constant "corroding worry" about her own family's poverty. And so, just as Eva abandons her pedestrian ways and takes a streetcar to the Blue Goose, this young woman depends upon the telephone to help facilitate and conceal her absorption into the "clandestine" and "systematically conducted" traffic in women, constituted in part by obedient, faithful, and hard-working daughters. Though *Shoes* suggests that Eva will remain "apparently respectable," it does not assure us entirely that her future will remain without the hardship, necessity, debt, and illness that have become prominent features of her routine workweek, making clear the idea that the hard-working, obedient daughter and the (temporary) prostitute are no longer mutually exclusive identity categories. In short, the film demonstrates the degree to which faithfulness to one's family may pave the way to prostitution. In this respect, the structure of modern traffic that the film envisions is far darker than that of *Traffic in Souls*. For while the latter suggests that the illegitimate traffic relies on legitimate traffic to cloak its nefarious movements, *Shoes* suggests that legitimate traffic profits from and perhaps depends upon the traffic in women: without it, numerous "apparently respectable" working poor women might not be able to supplement their inadequate wages and thereby remain in circulation. Within this vision of modern traffic, the illegitimate subtends the "apparently legitimate."

Feature-Length Narrativity, Spectatorship, and Exhibition

Just as these films dramatize the incorporation of everyday life into traffic, so too did the experience of attending the moving pictures underscore this facet of the experience of American modernity. The different elaborations of modern traffic by each of these films provide insight into the relation between modernity's trafficked individual and the spectator-subject that emerged with changing exhibition contexts and lengthening feature films. We can link the spectator of the continuously projected six-reeler to the individual absorbed into traffic and held under the exhilarating sway of a manufactured mobilization through space and time over which he or she has only illusory control. The success or failure to create such a position depended perhaps on the long feature's ability to translate the movements of the trafficked individual into a symbolic position by absorbing the spectator into its fictional world to a degree and duration that was relatively new—but increasingly familiar—to audiences during the cinema's transitional era.

For example, one reviewer of *Traffic in Souls* noted that "the tense atmosphere prevailing was the best indication of the holding quality of the stirring melodrama. There were no drooping heads."[71] We might link the "holding quality" of this particular film to the way in which it positioned its spectator in relation to the different kinds of traffic it narrates. Importantly, the film allows its spectator to trace the movements, transitions, and points of convergence of its multiple traffics by placing her or him in an ideal relation to everyday traffic and the traffic in souls it represents. For example, the film's opening sequences introduce its various players, and by cutting between various public and private spaces, parallel editing reveals how the paths of various traffics intersect in such a way that leads Little Sister to be absorbed into the white slave trade. The camera cuts between the Barton home (where the sisters prepare for work); the street where Officer Burke, on his beat, phones in to his precinct; the candy store, where the manager looks at his pocket watch and warns Mary, "Your sister has been late every morning for a week"; the Trubus home, where the head of the household reads a letter thanking him for agreeing to lecture on the social evil; the inside of two of Trubus's brothels; the street outside the candy store where a madame and a cadet spot Little Sister through the display window; the traffickers' office headquarters where the Go-Between collects and counts the day's profits; and back again to Trubus as he leaves for his office in a motor car. Finally, Tucker alternates between the Go-Between's office and Trubus who, arriving at the same building, pauses in the hallway, looks at the door of the Go-Between's office with a knowing smile, and proceeds to his office above where he dons headphones and watches the screen of his electric writing pad, on which he receives the figures for the traffic's daily profits.

Here I will simply note that the manner in which the film establishes the interconnecting story lines at the level of form is closely linked to its representation of technological modernity. In order to draw the spectator into its fiction, Tucker deploys crosscutting, alternation, and the organization of looks first to position each of the characters within the nexus of modern traffic and then to assign each a function within its broader movement, thereby establishing how a particular relation to modernity shapes the destiny of each character. Mary (who clocks in on time) and Officer Burke (who maintains a connection to police headquarters via a phone box) are ideal modern subjects who cannily negotiate urban traffic and are able to distinguish its legitimate extensions from its illegitimate ones (thus, they ultimately triumph); Little Sister, who fails to keep pace with the accelerated temporality and regulated schedules of modern life, is easily detoured into the slave traffic;[72] and Trubus manipulates the deceptive possibilities of technological modernity to increase the flow of capital into his clutches. In particular, he exploits the mechanically reproduced mass media that circulates throughout the diegesis, for the newspaper stories about the slave traffic, his appointment as head of an investigation of the social evil, and his daughter's impending engagement help maintain his public facade of respectability (in the end the machinery of the mass media falls into gear, and the final image of the film shows a discarded newspaper announcing Trubus's downfall). In these opening sequences and throughout the rest of the film, the camera traces the movements of various micro-traffics in order to synthesize them into a grand narrative traffic that makes scandalously meaningful connections between a range of familiar and forbidden urban spaces. In this sense, *Traffic in Souls* places its spectator in an ideal position of the trafficked individual, one that allows her to see what the imperiled protagonists fail to see—a position described by Stamp as one of recuperated surveillance, by Gunning as that of the detective, and by Lee Grieveson as omniscient.[73] With this in mind, we can suggest that the film's "holding quality" was attendant upon its narratorial inversion of the terrors of traffic it represents: whereas for the film's (good and evil) protagonists danger lies both in modern traffic's arbitrary transitions and in technology's ability to conceal identity. For its spectator, pleasure is derived perhaps from her or his alignment with the camera's own anonymous omniscience and the clear connections it makes between apparently unconnected spaces, movements, and individuals (the reformer judge and the cadet, the brothel and the family home, the traffic in commercial goods and the commercialized traffic in women). As Stamp suggests, moreover, such omniscient anonymity allowed spectators to take in the film's cautionary tale while simultaneously delighting in its scandalous scenes of titillation.[74]

Shoes similarly positions its spectator in the ideal position of the trafficked individual, but to different ends and effects. From the beginning, the spectator of *Shoes* is endowed with omniscience of a different sort: by foretelling the bad ending in the opening titles, the film gives the spectator full knowledge of Eva's dreaded destiny. And yet this knowledge does not yield the pleasurable sensation of power but instead the painful pleasure of melodramatic powerlessness as the film proceeds to harness us to a sympathetic heroine whose ultimate destiny we cannot change.[75] Indeed, Weber compounds the tragic outcome of Eva's predicament by structuring the narrative around her experience of modern life as a deadening repetition with minor variations—such as a rainstorm—that serve only to intensify her misery. Hence each day she cuts out cardboard soles for her shoes, walks to work, punches in, stands behind a counter, punches out, walks home, and soaks her feet. Over and over, Charlie approaches Eva and she rejects him, much as her mother repeatedly rejects her request for the new shoes. Reviewers suggested that the film's pattern of repetition with minor variation moving slowly toward inevitable breakdown was inseparable from its gradual development of character psychology, spectatorial identification, and absorption into the fictional world of the film. Indeed, the periodical *Wid's* indicated that something of a debate took place around the question of the film's length and whether or not a reel could be eliminated without destroying the psychological effects of the tragic story: "The story of this offering is decidedly simple but there is a big central theme and it is the very simplicity and directness of the offering which makes it register. I heard a few of the young men who are writing reviews for various publications comment upon this subject, and they revealed that they thought it might have been good in two or three reels. I seldom call attention to anything of this sort, but to make it particularly clear in the minds of all my readers that I am going on record on this subject, as feeling that it should not be trimmed more than one hundred or one hundred and thirty feet . . . It certainly should not be cut down below five reels, because if anything of the sort was attempted, the splendid psychology of the development of characters would be utterly ruined."[76] *Wid's* added only that the film's more radical narrative detour—its speculative representation of what Eva's life would have been like had she enjoyed an upper-middle-class position— should be cut. The reviewer for *Motion Picture News* similarly noted that *Shoes* is "so simple in theme that there is of necessity much repetition of incident. There is, on the other hand, a purpose to the likeness of the situations, because it makes the final step taken by the girl seem justifiable and all the more pathetic."[77]

This narrative structure of repetition is inseparable from the film's conception of modern traffic and the working poor woman's position within it. In contrast to multiple "lines of flight" so characteristic of the technological rhizome imagined by *Traffic in Souls*, *Shoes* instead places its heroine within a cul-de-sac, a closed circuit based on cyclical repetition of the workday and workweek that widens only to accommodate a single, dreaded detour taken only so that she can stay in motion. Rather than yoking the working poor woman to a linear form of time and motion based on rescue or redemption, narrative and diegetic traffic simply bring Eva—and the spectator—full circle as the film concludes with the bad ending the opening titles foretell. In this respect, the film's resolution is far less conclusive than that of *Traffic in Souls*, which ultimately restores the imperiled heroine to the family home unharmed and closes with the arrest of those responsible for the traffic in souls. In contrast, *Shoes* leaves open the possibility that in the end Eva has simply returned to the beginning of a new cycle that may very well bring her back again to the Blue Goose. In this respect, it is helpful to turn to Stella Wynne Herron's short story, which maps Eva's entry into prostitution through the figure of the "short cut." After Eva pauses on her way home to look once again upon the new shoes in the store window, she decides to walk through the red-light district that lies between the store where she works and her family's tenement flat.

> She turned away [from the shoes] with a sigh and went on to the end of the block. At the corner, she hesitated. If she turned, she could take a short cut to the side street where she lived. But the short cut led through a district which she had hitherto instinctively avoided; a district of cheap, transient hotels, of garish, late-running restaurants where food *could* be procured, but drinks and cabaret usually filled all demands; of wine shops, saloons and cigar stands, each with its quota of lazy-eyed men and boys hanging around it.
>
> But with the chill autumn rain drenching her and the pavement wearing out her stockings, Eva could not afford to be particular. She turned her head away from the even, unhurried, appraising stares of the men behind the plate glass of the hotel lobbies or gathered in from the rain in cigar-store entrances; but the women who dipped in and out under umbrellas her eyes invariably followed. These women were warmly clad and—her fascinated gaze always fixed on their feet—well shod.[78]

At the end of the story, Eva takes this "short cut" once again to get the money for the much-needed shoes she has once again been denied. Like the detour taken by Weber's Eva, the short cut taken by Herron's protagonist may very well be traversed again. For in both texts, Eva's failed rescue by her father's newfound employment arrives both too soon (if only she had held out for one more day) and too late, holding out little hope that he can be relied upon in the future. Moreover, as both the film and the short story make very clear, the new shoes, like the old ones, will wear out. *Shoes* visualizes the fact of the cyclical and circular structure of payment, debt, and the inevitable return of temporarily satisfied physical and material needs by closing with an image that repeats one seen earlier in the film: the Meyer family sits down to another meager dinner, much as they do in the film's first reel just after Eva has been refused money for shoes. The repetition of this image reminds us that Eva's position within modern traffic has not really changed and it suggests that the clearly established patterns of familial-industrial-economic relations may very well recur. Put differently, *Shoes* makes clear the idea that occasional entry into illegitimate traffic was inseparable from many working poor women's experience of modern life.

Given the focus on mechanized and pedestrian traffic and their exploitation of the pleasures of good timing and the agony of bad timing in *Traffic in Souls* and *Shoes*, it is important to note that the continuously projected long feature impacted upon the close relation between moving picture exhibition space and everyday traffic. This is quite important, for, as Miriam Hansen argues, the emergence of the category of the spectator in the early 1910s was attendant upon changes in exhibition as well as narrative practices: "In a basic sense the term 'spectator' implied a shift from a collective plural notion of the film viewer to a singular, unified but potentially universal category, the commodity form of reception. On the level of film style, this shift was epitomized in the centering of narration through the unobtrusive guidance of the omniscient camera, which implicated the viewer as a temporarily incorporeal individual. On the level of reception, it marks the dynamics by which cinematic pleasure and meaning increasingly came to depend upon the viewer's identification with the position of a textually constructed spectator, upon the viewer's desire to submerge for a spell the complexities and frustrations of everyday experience into the ordered perceptions of a fantasmatic, mobile, yet seemingly unified self."[79] The ability of the spectator to form such identifications and desires depended in part upon an increased subordination of theatrical space to the world of the fiction and thus a "minimizing [of the] awareness of theatre space—in particular the distractions attendant upon the variety format."[80] Such distractions included the constant flow of traffic in and out of theaters encouraged by the still-dominant variety program of one- and two-reelers. Industry discourse suggests that the continuously projected five- and six-reeler had an impact upon the very close relation between the moving pictures and the everyday traffic on which the very profitable quick turnover of audiences depended. For example, months after Universal distributed the commercially successful *Traffic in Souls*, Carl Laemmle publicly wished for the doom of the feature film and offered by way of anecdote the objections of one "moving picture fan" to the long feature's dislocation of the motion picture theater from the rhythms and patterns of everyday traffic: "A year or two ago, he could drop into a moving picture theatre any place in the City of Chicago and find enjoyment for an hour and leave the theatre satisfied—feeling that he had had his money's worth. As matters stand today, when the opportunity presents itself he drops into a moving picture house but is usually unfortunate enough to arrive at the end of the second or third reel of a five-reel feature and has to wait until the third, fourth and fifth are run off and then watch the part that he has missed. Under the old arrangement the worst that would happen would be that he would have had to wait five or six minutes until the reel on the screen was completed and then he could start in to enjoy himself. Today he feels that his entertainment is entirely spoiled because he has to sit through the climax of the picture before he can get an idea of what it is all about."[81]

Laemmle and his fan long for a moving picture experience modeled on and amenable to the arbitrariness and contingency of everyday traffic—one in which a patron might drop into the theater at a moment's notice and wait a few minutes before spectatorial pleasure might begin— an experience whose specific pleasures already seemed to be disrupted by emerging narrative and exhibition practices.[82] Hence, Laemmle's moving picture patron seems to confirm Schivelbusch's argument that by the early twentieth century, "only the general context of traffic assigned and dictated positions to the individual elements" of a vast circulatory system that was itself subject to historical fluctuation as its directions in motion converged and diverged, and shifted in direction and speed. Despite the fact that the continuously projected long feature increasingly addresses itself to the ideal "spectator," Laemmle's moving picture patron nevertheless resides in the place of the "audience." The frustration and loss experienced by the quoted moving picture patron derives from the liminality of his peculiar historical place within the fluctuating "contexts" of modern traffic.

In 1916, Weber herself expressed similar empathy with the film patron's encounter with the five-reeler, though she focuses more on the "transient" patron who has too little leisure time to take in a five- or six-reeler: "There will always be room for both the five-reeler and the one and two-reelers. The latter class of pictures has been disregarded of late, so great has been the demand for features, but recently the manufacturers have hearkened to the fact that if a picture is good it will always be appreciated, no matter what its footage. The short subject is, however, considerably more than a filler. A transient patronage can hardly spare the time to see a long picture, particularly when they arrive in the middle of it, and a theatre with such patronage can exist best with a program of one and two thousand foot subjects."[83] By suggesting that exhibitors tailor the offerings in their bills according to their typical patrons' position in traffic, Weber foregrounds the historical fact that the eventual standardization of the continuously projected long feature placed pressure on some exhibitors' and producers' conception of the audience as an unscheduled flow of traffic that might briefly "drop in" to theaters at will. This latter model made exhibition space an extension of urban traffic more similar to the display space of the department store described by Schivelbusch than to the exhibition space of the later classical cinema. The slow shift from the short-subject variety format to the lengthier five- or six-reel feature as the mainstay of the variety show demanded that moving picture patrons change their habits and expectations and entailed a gradual transformation of exhibition space into a site experienced as "other" to, rather than an extension of, the outside world of traffic.[84] As Laemmle's anecdote and Weber's more measured analysis suggest, this gradual shift was aided in part by the concealment of a particular component of the cinema's technical base: the single reel as a determinant of the standard length of a film's narrative unit. Thus as early as 1914, Laemmle articulates a demand to maintain a clear and tangible relation between an individual film's on-screen fiction and the cinema's technical base — that is, between the story and the reel.[85] Such a relation shaped the spectator's experience by placing limits on film lengths, thereby allowing the moving picture fan to know that he would have only "to wait five or six minutes until the reel on the screen was completed and then he could start in to enjoy himself," and thus to stop into the theater whenever "the opportunity presented itself." Ultimately, as Laemmle and Weber suggest, to derive *maximum* pleasure from absorption into the fictional world of the continuously projected five- and six-reeler, the spectator would have to begin with the first leg of the camera's fictional journey and be carried by it to a *narratively determined* final destination.

One important effect of feature-length narrativity (which was very gradually institutionalized in the 1910s) was to begin to create a clearer distinction and difference between the individual physically absorbed into everyday traffic and the spectator symbolically absorbed into narrative traffic. This shift entailed a marking out of the specificity of the moving pictures as a technology of representation that played upon the structural affinities, extensions, and connections existing between modern technologies, but whose specific pleasure depended on the gradual subordination of these affinities to the developing apparatus and, in turn, the apparatus to the narrative. For at the same time that both of these films are based on the premise that to participate in modern life is to be absorbed into traffic, their pleasure in part relies on the displacement of the spectator from modern traffic and her or his absorption into feature-length narrative traffic that provided the emerging pleasure of what the *Moving Picture World* described as "clear, well-sustained plots, carried to a full and finished ending, leaving with the audience a feeling of satisfaction and completeness."[86]

CONCLUSION

I n this book I have argued that by the end of the nineteenth century "traffic" had become a primary emblem
of modern life. As such, it was a fungible concept used to
elaborate fantasies and anxieties about the experience of
technological modernity in the United States. At stake in
this use of the concept of traffic is our understanding of
the role played by the moving pictures within this experience. As a form of commercialized leisure inseparable from
urbanization, the moving pictures represented to American
audiences the possibilities and perils of modern life. In the
cinema's early and transitional eras, moving pictures brought
into focus events and scandals that seemed to reveal much
about the nation's present and future identity and, moreover,
demanded self-conscious constructions of *American* technological modernity. Hence in 1898 the cinema thrilled audiences with compelling images of powerful new technologies
and soldiers recently mobilized for the Spanish-American
War, while in 1899 battle reenactment films represented the
shocks and trauma of American overseas expansion in the
Philippine-American War. In the early twentieth century,
moving pictures helped audiences both to celebrate the nation's technological prowess and political power at the Pan-

American Exposition and to participate in the national crisis provoked by Leon Czolgosz's assassination there of President McKinley. In the early teens, the popular white slavery films articulated the sensational idea that the nation's working poor women and newly arrived immigrant daughters were in grave peril of disappearing forever into a high-tech traffic in prostitutes run by predatory industrialists and "foreigners." Such events—and the films that represented them—inevitably involved comparisons of technological power and modern progress in the United States with older European rivals, newly subordinated colonial populations, and immigrant populations who, though important to the new industrial economy, were linked to "Old World" or "savage" sociopolitical and moral orders that contrasted sharply with the tenets of "ideal" modern American life. The cinema inserted itself into these sensational events to provide audiences with compelling visual representations of the spaces, bodies, machines, and forms of mobility that increasingly defined the experience of modern life in the United States and its new territories. Though these films were not seen by every American, they (along with newspapers, magazines, and the sensational press) nevertheless participated in the process of binding the nation into an "imagined community" as they represented events that resonated throughout the country and seemed to purport something about the changing identity and future of the United States.

In this volume I have approached such events by focusing on each as an example of the increasing incorporation of everyday life in the United States into various forms of modern traffic. As this work has shown, the American cinema's fascination with the figure of modern traffic did not end with its early (and quite popular) actualities of busy city street scenes, travelogues, or panoramic films shot from the front of trains. Rather, moving pictures framed traffic as a figure for elaborating a broad range of fantasies about the effects of new forms of mobility, speed, power, and powerlessness created by expanding networks of integrated technologies. During the Spanish-American War, imperial traffic mobilized a new generation of military recruits and machines to distant frontiers around the globe to fulfill the promise of opening overseas markets to American trade. Implementing a highly sensational version of modernity's annihilation of space and time, the new imperialism extended the nation's integrated transportation and communications networks beyond its continental borders and in the process established what Amy Kaplan describes as "vaster yet tangible networks of international markets and political influence."[1] The Spanish-American War had the effect of transforming perceptions of American modernity at home, and, importantly, the early cinema was a key source of thrilling discourses on the new empire that helped refashion the image of native white masculinity and technology for a new era of global expansion. War actualities made the agents and spaces of imperial traffic visually accessible to civilian audiences and helped promote fantasies about—and fascination with—the forms of machine-made mobility that became inseparable from imperial conquest. Moving pictures of the new fleet of battleships (the primary vehicles for setting imperial traffic into motion) provided "life-size" images of the hypermodern force of new military recruits who, like the ships they manned, appeared to fulfill American modernity's demand for endless energy and efficient circulation. Indeed, new technologies seemed to charge the body of the recruit with some of their own more celebrated qualities: soldiers and sailors appeared onscreen as ideal modern subjects able to function with the precision and drive of machines fueled by a renewed sense of national purpose and fortified by military discipline. By granting unprecedented visual access to military camps and battleships, war actualities provided moving picture audiences with the illusion of having been temporarily "mobilized" along with troops through the circuits of imperial traffic, all the while facilitating opportunities to inspect the men and machines who promised to save the nation from the ills of industrialization. In the process, the moving pictures helped visualize a highly ideological vision of American modernity based on a synthesis of human and machine motion able to counter the illnesses of "overcivilization" and neurasthenia that plagued modern life back home. Indeed, the moving pictures provided audiences with fascinating spectacles of the men and machines that kept the war driving toward its goals of accelerated mobility and the conquest of nations and new markets.

In turn, as I have shown in chapter 3, the 1901 Pan-American Exposition and the films shot there also gave expression to emerging fantasies about the newfound capacity of the United States to keep its thriving (inter)national traffic in motion. Staged as an occasion to celebrate the success of the nation's recent imperial wars and the economic and military power it exerted in the Western Hemisphere and beyond, the Pan-American's exhibits displayed thousands of new technologies designed to accelerate commercial and military forms of traffic alongside resources and inhabitants from new protectorates and colonies taken in the Spanish-American and Philippine-American Wars. Just as individual exhibits displayed new technologies able to annihilate space and time, so, too, were the Exposition grounds and its amusements designed to charge mechanical circulation with visual and physical pleasures. In short, the grounds were designed to absorb the fair-goer into idealized forms of urban traffic: a system of canals circulated visitors by electric boat launch throughout the grounds while various "rides" (and films shot from them) were based on pleasurable versions of everyday forms of mechanized transport such as elevators, streetcars, and railways. Given this pervasive emphasis on fantasy forms of machine-made mobility, it is not surprising that the primary attraction at the Pan-American was the powerful force that gave life to its myriad forms of traffic: electricity. The alternating current generated by the nearby Niagara Power Plant created an ideal form of circulation that allowed electricity to "flow" silently through underground circuits and currents to illuminate the Exposition's most popular attraction, the City of Living Light.

The astonishing moving pictures of the City of Living Light made by Edwin S. Porter symbolize the promises made by the Pan-American about the future of electricity in the United States. Such films provided audiences with pleasurable glimpses of the ongoing incorporation of modern life into a network of technologies that increasingly transformed the experience of space and time as well as darkness and light. *Pan-American Exposition by Night*, for example, creates a wondrous image of electricity's capacity to transform night into day and create new forms of machine-made nighttime vision. In turn, the camera's panning movement in films such as *Panorama of Esplanade by Night* traces the "sketched" lines of the incandescent light display that emblematized the electric network that incorporated buildings, homes, and streets into its expansive system. In doing so, films of the Pan-American contributed to its presentation of electricity as an ideal form of meta-traffic—that is, as an industrially produced commodity itself able to circulate with increasing efficiency across great distances even as it provided a motive force for the rapid circulation of other commodities and transportation technologies. By providing sublime images of electric power, films of the Pan-American helped make sense of and inspire delight in the contradictory experiences of modern life in the United States, and they promised audiences a new, bright future based upon the increasing industrialization of light, motion, and circulation. And much like Spanish-American War actualities, films of the Pan-American provided audiences with pleasurable spectacles of new forms of power that were inseparable from the absorption of everyday life into traffic.

As much as new forms of mobility—and motive force—inspired fascination and awe in Americans at the turn of the century, they also inspired anxiety. The highly pleasurable fantasies of unlimited mobility, energy, and power promoted by the Spanish-American War actualities and the films of the Pan-American Exposition had their counterpart in narrative films that translated the individual's absorption within traffic into nightmare scenarios of displacement and detour. In chapter 4, I analyzed how in such films fantasies of control over space and time give way to unease about the less salubrious mobilizations that traffic might facilitate. For example, in two-reel sensation melodramas such as *The Lonedale Operator* and *A Beast at Bay*, the very same technological networks that inspired delight give rise to terror in the face of disorderly mobilizations that foreground legitimate traffic's capacity for concealing the circulation of more illicit forms of traffic. Hence menacing hobos, thieves, and escaped convicts make use of the railway and the automobile to prey upon their unsuspecting victims and even prevent them from reaching their intended destinations. When films about white slavery began to appear onscreen in 1913, they provided a far more anxious representation of the effects of modern traffic by imagining the sudden transformation of a legitimate subject or agent within traffic into a scandalously illegitimate object of exchange—a mere commodity within a notorious and difficult-to-detect trade. The white slavery scandal, with its focus on the movement of immigrants, the circulation of women workers through the public sphere, and the exploitation of communication and transportation technologies by so-called traffickers, drew its power to thrill and terrify from its own exploitation of the movements of modern traffic. Indeed, in the sensational hit *Traffic in Souls*, traffickers spot their prey at Penn Station and Ellis Island or behind counters at commercial venues like dime stores and candy shops; they dupe unsuspecting girls at phony employment agencies for newly arrived immigrants; and they use telegrams, primitive fax machines, and taxicabs to perfect their methods.

These early feature films of the cinema's transitional era deployed new narrative strategies to reveal how the nation's pulsing system of everyday traffic might provide a source and camouflage for the slave trade's criminal traffic.

Although films like *Traffic in Souls* locate the origins of the slave trade in part in the systematic efficiency of modern technology, they also suggest that the solution to this social problem might be technological as well. Indeed, the very fact that a variety of networked technologies constituted modern traffic created the possibility that some new device might be attached to an existing apparatus in order to contain the nefarious traffic that the slightly "older" technology had set into motion. The notion that new technologies might themselves provide solutions to the ills caused by industrialization had been a compelling feature of popular discourses on American modernity. As I discussed in the third chapter of this book, for example, following Czolgosz's assassination of President McKinley at the Pan-American, the Edison reenactment *Execution of Czolgosz by Electric Chair* dramatized how the state, supported by industry, might use new technologies (of death) quite literally to incorporate into its circuits of power those who resisted the changes precipitated by industrial capitalism. Hence whether the cinema resolved the narrative crises of its urban dramas and melodramas with the latest invention of a fictional character or used painted flats and a mockup of the Auburn prison's electric chair to restage the high-tech death of an assassin, its attractions and narratives helped promote the reassuring idea that American technological modernity had the power to contain the dangerous forces it unleashed.

Other films foreground another contradictory feature of modern life: the same imperial and commercial traffic that gave rise to (sometimes paranoid) fantasies about limitless energy, power, and mobility also brought into sharp focus the limits to mobility and the bodily trauma caused by the individual's absorption into high-tech traffic. Though film production companies helped feed a fascination with imperial traffic by providing audiences with thrilling war actualities, they encountered technological and logistical limits when it came to documenting actual battles once the navy finished its work, cavalries dismounted, and soldiers moved on foot through Cuba and the Philippines. In short, the camera's ability to circulate with imperial traffic was curtailed as troops moved into what were considered to be the protomodern spaces of the new overseas frontier. And so production companies turned to a familiar form that had previously been used to satisfy the demand to see already-completed acts of expansion across a new frontier that lay beyond the scope of ordinary perception: the reenactment. Battle reenactment films, like Buffalo Bill's Wild West and other live reenactments did before them, visually incorporated audiences into otherwise inaccessible paths of imperial traffic overseas. In the late nineteenth century, live reenactments ritualistically repeated the movements of pioneer wagon trains, the Pony Express, and the Deadwood Stage Coach using "authentic" soldiers, pioneers, and scouts who established the more primitive paths of transcontinental traffic that would make way for more modern forms such as the railway. A decade or so later, battle reenactment films similarly gave audiences imaginary visual access to the movement of U.S. troops through the so-called savage spaces of the Philippines as they pictured soldiers advancing across contested spaces and overrunning the trenches of Filipino resistance fighters. Reenactment films traded the live reenactment's "authentic" artifacts and personalities for greater visual immersion in the depicted historical scene by placing the camera, and hence the spectator, in the trenches, alongside U.S. forces, or in the crossfire of two violently opposed sides. This camera placement bolstered the illusion of the spectator's status as a witness to the movements of imperial agents as they laid down and took control over the new circuits of empire.

However, even as battle reenactment films provided audiences with imaginary access to the movements of imperial traffic in the Philippines, they also foregrounded the modern shock and trauma experienced by soldiers as they battled "natives" for control over (already occupied) space. This emphasis on shock and trauma transformed those who resisted the incursions of imperialist expansion by the United States into violent aggressors against American forces who appeared to be the enemies of the efficient circulation of American troops and power. This book has argued that the recursive structure of the battle reenactment film and its tendency to replay the shocks of warfare made it an ideal form for repeating and mastering the traumatic effects of the soldier's absorption into the circuits of empire. However, when American culture's primary symbol for endless energy and mobility falls to the ground in such films, a new figure—the Red Cross nurse—rushes into motion to anneal the effects of modern warfare and to suggest that should any part of the imperial machine break down, a new mechanism would click into place in order to keep in motion the broader movement of soldiers, supplies, and ammunition.

In very different ways, I have argued, feature-length films about "casual" forms of prostitution also dramatized the bodily shock and trauma experienced in modern life by narrating the downfall of the working poor woman exhausted by her endless circulation through the lower echelons of commercial traffic. While other films discussed in this book focus on the smooth efficiency of high-tech traffic, Lois Weber's *Shoes* focuses on the impoverished, pedestrian shop clerk who walks along city streets and stands for long hours on poorly shod feet. This figure occupies yet another contradictory position within modern traffic: at work she is locked into a complex system of distribution, display, and consumption and stands for long hours behind a counter helping to keep in motion a pulsing traffic in commodities and consumers. Though her small income, in turn, channels a meager supply of goods into the family home, she is too exhausted to consume and cannot afford the basic material goods—the shoes she needs to walk to work and to stand behind her counter—that are necessary for her to maintain her tenuous position within commercial traffic. Just like a poorly tended machine, the working poor woman eventually suffers a catastrophic breakdown. As Weber and others insisted was typical in such cases, bodily fatigue and physical breakdown facilitates moral breakdown and the temporary displacement of the working poor woman into a thriving traffic of casual prostitution. In contrast to the expansive networks imagined by other films discussed in this book, *Shoes* imagines modern traffic as a closed circular system in which the working poor woman experiences an inescapable cycle of work, fatigue, and collapse, altered only by an occasional and dreaded detour into casual prostitution. And whereas *Traffic in Souls* promotes the sensational notion that the slave trade's success depended upon the traders' exploitation of the efficiency of legitimate traffic, *Shoes* far more scandalously insists that in order to stay in motion, the legitimate traffic accommodated and even depended upon the clandestine illegitimate traffic in working poor women.

In this book I use a film made in 1916 to conclude my analysis of the American cinema and its engagement with the pleasures and perils of modern life. We might readily assume that here the decision to bracket this analysis has to do with an important historical threshold in the history of American cinema: the consolidation and standardization of classical narration in 1917.[2] To be sure, increasingly efficient forms of factory-style production as well as standardized procedures for distributing and exhibiting a regular output of films provide evidence of the film industry's own absorption of—and absorption into—patterns of modern traffic that relied upon networked technologies to facilitate the mass consumption of its films in the United States and overseas. Yet my decision to conclude this project in the year 1916 was determined primarily by another factor linked to my focus on national crises and modern traffic: in the year following 1916, the United States declared war against Germany and entered into the Great War.

To be sure, there is some interesting debate about the degree to which the First World War affected production practices and the overall content of films in the American cinema. However, Kristin Thompson's research demonstrates that the war had a significant impact upon the export of Hollywood films overseas. Thanks to decreased film production in France and Italy, a ban on shipping film stock (made of gun cotton, it could be used to make explosives), and the replacement of London by New York as the center of film distribution, Hollywood was able to lay the groundwork for becoming the world's dominant location for film production.[3] And just as the Great War changed Hollywood cinema's position within commercial traffic, there can also be no doubt that it had a significant effect on popular and official discourses on technological modernity—including that of the American cinema—and that it only intensified the axiom that participation in modern life implied absorption into traffic.

Indeed, the Great War and its historically unprecedented demand for broad-scale "mass mobilization" required the mechanical circulation of bodies and machines to a degree never seen before. Contemporary observers figured the process of mass mobilization as a self-propelled war machine that seemed capable of incorporating the entire globe into its bloody operations. In turn, the invention and deployment of terrifying new military technologies and strategies (such as the submarine, poison gas, and aerial bombardment) severed notions of modern progress from machine culture and linked the latter instead to mass death and unparalleled human suffering.[4] Those who participated in the war understood that industrialization and the prior absorption of life into modern traffic not only established the conditions of possibility for the war but also prepared its combatants and victims for newly intensified forms of circulation and bodily trauma. Hence, as Charles de Gaulle observed in his reminiscences of the war: "The mass movements and mechanization to which men and women were subjected by modern life had preconditioned them for mass mobilization and for the brutal, sudden shocks which characterized the war of peoples."[5]

Stephen Kern in his book *The Culture of Time and Space* argues that the Great War constituted the apex of modernity's transformation of the experience of time, distance, and speed. Kern persuasively demonstrates that during the July Crisis of 1914 the use of the telephone and telegraph by diplomats and leaders created a "precipitous diplomacy." Instantaneous communication prompted a series of ultimatums with unreasonably short deadlines and resulted in ill-considered decisions that would affect the fate of millions. As Kern argues, "This telegraphic exchange at the highest level dramatized the spectacular failure of diplomacy, to which telegraphy contributed with crossed messages, delays, sudden surprises, and unpredictable timing. Throughout the crisis there was not just one new faster speed for everyone to adjust to, but a series of new and variable paces that supercharged the masses, confused the diplomats, and unnerved the generals."[6] To cement the relationship between the outbreak of war and modern traffic, Kern compares the July Crisis to the sinking of the *Titanic*, which can also be characterized by overconfidence in new technologies, shortsightedness, mechanically accelerated speed, and a flurry of wireless messages unable to contain a crisis moving inexorably toward mass death. As with the *Titanic* disaster, the events of the July Crisis and the ensuing war were reported rapidly around the world in the press and in newsreels thanks in part to the same technologies that helped manufacture these modern calamities.[7]

As Europe moved closer to war, the mass mobilization of its armies was determined in part by the intricate network of railways, shipping lanes, and telephone and telegraph lines that spanned countries across the globe and made it possible to set into motion tens of millions of soldiers within a moment's notice. As Kern observes, once the gears meshed and the machinery was set into motion, mobilization could not be stopped. For example, owing to the vast distances its armies needed to cover, Russia began "precautionary mobilization" once Austria declared war on Serbia on July 28, 1914; this action in turn prompted other nations to begin mobilizing in Europe. In response to Kaiser Wilhelm's request on July 30 that Russia stop mobilization, Tsar Nicholas telegraphed: "It is technically impossible to stop our military preparations which were obligatory owing to Austrian mobilization."[8] In 1914, the inexorable nature of mass mobilization charged modern military traffic with fearful systematicity and speed; this process appeared simultaneously as the ideal manifestation of modern traffic's efficient and rapid circulation of bodies and machines and of its dark underbelly. For mass mobilization resulted not in progress and the cultivation of civilization but years of chaotic warfare and terrible bloodshed.

While the United States initially remained a distant but horrified spectator of the "big show" (as the war was called by British soldiers), its soldiers were eventually subject to the war's unique mobilizations and shocks. As the war dragged on, the notion that it was taking place at a safe distance overseas was increasingly undermined by the sense that in the age of modern traffic, the United States remained profoundly connected to the war by trade agreements, economic policies, and the export of munitions to Europe. As the issue of neutrality was hotly debated within the government and in the press, Americans became increasingly aware that war profiteering—the extraordinary profits enjoyed by the U.S. banks and corporations that produced munitions—helped fuel the overseas conflict by supplying the combatants with the loans and arms needed to keep the war going. Even the plots of film comedies turned upon the circulation of weapons from the United States into the hands of the nation's potential enemies. For example, *American Aristocracy* (Lloyd Ingraham, 1916) narrates its comic romance against the backdrop of wartime intrigue that involves the protagonist, Cassius Lee (Douglas Fairbanks), in a plot to stop his romantic rival—a wealthy businessman (Albert Parker) who has secretly converted a powdered milk factory into a gunpowder plant. With the help of a Mexican spy (Artie Ortego), the traitorous industrialist schemes to ship the gunpowder south of the border (and presumably from there on to Mexico's ally, Germany). Modern traffic's ability to camouflage the circulation of illegitimate—or in this case, incendiary—industrial products thereby takes on new gravity in the context of war and foregrounds the notion that, in the years before the United States entered the war, the production and sale of munitions by American industry exacerbated the conflagration overseas. In turn, Fairbanks's use of a seaplane to stop his rival's gunpowder shipment from making it out to sea foregrounds the new spatial dynamics that the airplane would very soon contribute to perceptions of this relatively new transportation technology. While the fictional events narrated by *American Aristocracy* underscore the pleasures and possibilities of the airplane's accelerated annihilation of space and time (Fairbanks's ability to pilot the plane is linked to the hyperkinetic mobility and exuberant physicality he demonstrates throughout much of the film), the increased frequency and destruction of the bombings of London and other European cities in 1917 introduced into the popular imagination the potential terror of a new kind of modern traffic able to rain down destruction from above.

Indeed, the war seemed to link technology's annihilation of space and time to annihilation itself. For example, in *The Intrigue* (Frank Lloyd, 1916), the American scientist Guy Longstreet (Cecil Van Auker) invents a wireless X-ray gun that has the power instantaneously "to kill, with mathematical precision, at a distance of twenty-five miles." Hoping to sell the gun to the American military, Longstreet stages a demonstration of the diabolical device, which houses a small movie screen that allows him to watch his unsuspecting target (in this instance, a doomed sheep tethered to a stake). Though his gun reduces the sheep to a smoking mound of wool in a matter of seconds, the War Department decides not to purchase the weapon from him. When Longstreet looks for a European buyer, the X-ray gun nearly falls into the hands of the evil Baron Rogniat (Howard Davies)—citizen of "a certain foreign power"—who offers to make Longstreet wealthy in exchange for the gun's plans. Only after Rogniat's enemy, the Countess Sonia Varnli (Lenore Ulrich), warns Longstreet of Rogniat's plot to kill him upon acquiring the gun does the hero realize the error of trading with a potential enemy. In the end, he destroys the gun and its plans.

Anxiety over war profiteering as a new form of commerce found its way into sensation melodramas as early as 1915, when Cecil B. De Mille's *The Cheat* placed its plot concerning its wealthy heroine's excessive consumption within a wartime context. In this film a society woman, Edith Hardy (Fannie Ward), invests a $10,000 Red Cross charity fund for Belgian war refugees in a risky stock market scheme in order to keep the finest consumer goods circulating through her home (she has a taste for expensive gowns, and even spends her maid's wages in order to acquire the latest fashions). The scheme fails, and she discovers that she has lost the entire fund only moments after learning that the Red Cross plans to donate the money the next day. By using the much-needed war relief funds to satisfy her own desires, Edith becomes vulnerable to the "casual" traffic in women. When her society pal Hishuru Tori (Sessue Hayakawa) discovers her crime, he offers to pay off her debt if she agrees to "pay the price." Here war profiteering and mass mobilization overseas intersect with the traffic in commerce and women at home, and the effects are disastrous. On the night Edith is supposed to fulfill her end of the bargain, she ultimately refuses Tori and the two struggle. He brands her with his initials (transforming her from a consuming subject into an expensive object to be consumed, much like the ivory statuettes he trades and collects) and she shoots him in return, leaving her husband (Jack Dean) to take the blame. Ultimately both Edith and her husband are exonerated for the shooting in a courtroom scene that ends with the audience mobbing Tori. Despite this ending, the film functions as a cautionary tale against profiting from the war and the misery it generated for its victims in Europe.

Even before the United States formally entered into the conflict in summer 1917, most Americans were well aware of the war's power to incorporate their nation into an expanding field of military conflict. Prior to the intensification of aerial bombardments in the United Kingdom and elsewhere in Europe, the submarine gave transportation technologies a new and often terrifying vertical articulation. Throughout much of the war, Germany maintained a policy of unrestricted warfare against all merchant and passenger liners suspected of carrying munitions or supplies to its enemies, even those flying the flag of neutral nations such as the United States. With its power to approach ships undetected and to allow captains to see targets through a periscope without being seen, the submarine seemed to endow the German military with a terrifying maritime omnipresence that charged all ocean travel and coastal life with new (and sometimes imaginary) peril. Indeed, anxiety over modern traffic's powers both to conflate categories (such as subject and object, legitimate and illegitimate) and to deliver passengers to unwanted destinies took on new meaning in the wartime context. Germany's policy of unrestricted submarine warfare created a period during which all ships risked violent displacement from their intended routes. In turn, Germany's justification of its policy (i.e., that neutral countries were using passenger liners and the merchant marine to ship illegal munitions) gave new power to traffic's capacity for concealing criminal mobilizations beneath a facade of legitimacy. Passengers aboard ships attacked by submarines experienced the more deadly outcome of wartime traffic's tendency to blur the line between its passengers and its parcels: for once a passenger boarded a ship carrying (imagined or real) munitions, he or she was simply regarded as part of a shipment of arms that had to be prevented from reaching its destination. Hence the submarine underscored the war's remarkable capacity for incorporating much of the world—neutral or otherwise—into its violent mobilizations.

In *The Little American* (De Mille, 1917) De Mille further dramatized the terrors of wartime traffic shortly after the United States declared war on Germany by restaging the sinking by submarine of the passenger liner *Lusitania*. This event, which occurred on May 7, 1915, resulted in the deaths of more than one hundred Americans. Early on in the film the heroine, Angela Moore (Mary Pickford), the daughter of a U.S. senator, embarks upon the *Veritania* to bring her elderly and ailing aunt from France to the safety of the United States. Through a sustained use of crosscutting between the *Veritania* and the submarine that sinks it, De Mille foregrounds what Kern calls the war's great "drama of simultaneity" that united disparate and distant events into a single catastrophe of civilization.[9] Indeed, as I have argued elsewhere, crosscutting is deployed to melodramatize the collision of two radically different forms of modern traffic—hostile, military mobilizations and neutral, peaceful civilian travel—to suggest that the former had made the latter a thing of the past.[10] As Angela boards the *Veritania*, a shot that shows her presenting her passport to an official and kissing her family good-bye is followed by a shot of a German commander issuing the order that "all ships suspected of carrying munitions to the enemy are to be sunk." Here, crosscutting inflects the action with a profound sense that the war had collapsed the broad categories that distinguished neutral from enemy traffic. The ensuing shots of Angela sitting and reading on the deck of the *Veritania* are followed by the title "Efficient Prussianism" and a shot of the top of a submarine slicing through the surface of the water. The accelerated pace of military action contrasts with the slow temporality and leisurely pace of life onboard the ocean liner, and the submarine's swift and barely visible approach toward the *Veritania* suggests a tragic and unforeseen destination for the ship and its passengers: the bottom of the ocean.

De Mille uses the submarine's new vertical articulation of traffic to suggest that within the context of the war, technological modernity had once and for all overturned a prior historical era that seemed by comparison to be based on a far more stable moral and ethical order. In the hands of "Efficient Prussianism," new technologies convert all that seems happy, mundane, and secure into their opposites. Hence De Mille stages the submarine attack on the *Veritania* during a ball onboard the ship. He begins by alternating between images of the reveling dancers and of the crew of the submarine as they load a torpedo into a gun chamber in preparation for the attack. Once the torpedo hits the ship, the scene of joyful dancing becomes one of abject mass suffering as the vessel lists. The camera cuts to the outside of the sinking ship as the submarine's searchlight illuminates the stream of bodies plunging from the decks into the dark waters below. In increasingly eerie shots, the searchlight picks out passengers as they struggle to stay above the surface of the water: in one shot, a young child struggles toward the camera with a panicked expression; in another, more surreal image a woman in a tiara splashes helplessly as a chair floats effortlessly on the surface of the water nearby. The abrupt inversion of action from a horizontal plane to a vertical one and the contrast between the brightly lit interior of the ballroom and the darkened night illuminated only by searchlights effectively pictures the war's power to turn past happiness into a benighted world of suffering. Winsor McKay's *The Sinking of the Lusitania* (Universal, 1918) similarly dramatizes Germany's use of new military technologies to "terrorize" the modern world from beneath the surface of the sea. Animation allows McKay to represent the submarine's underwater presence as the *Lusitania* appears on the horizon and to dramatize the ship's demise. As the bow of the ship sinks and lifts the stern into the air, the passengers, lifeboats, and cargo stream from the decks to the water below. The final image of the animated film follows a young mother sinking through the dark waters as she fruitlessly tries to push her baby up to the surface. As this film makes clear, modern traffic took on new terrors in the context of the war.

A pamphlet entitled "Why We Are Fighting," published by the Wilson

Administration's Committee for Public Information, captured the sense of these films that Germany's use of technology to terrorize its enemies from above and below threatened to return the world to a past state of brutality. As the pamphlet explained: "This is a war against an old spirit, an ancient outworn spirit. It is a war against feudalism—the right of the castle on the hill to rule the village below . . . Feudalism plus science, thirteenth century plus twentieth . . . With poison gas that makes living a hell, with submarines that sneak through the seas to slyly murder noncombatants, with dirigibles that bombard men and women while they sleep, with a perfected system of terrorization that the modern world first heard of when German troops entered China, German feudalism is making war upon mankind."[11] As this passage makes clear, the Great War forced a reexamination of any necessary association of technological development with historical progress, since Germany's deployment of new military technologies seemed to be ushering in a new historical period that resurrected feudalistic domination and armed it with the latest weapons to create "a perfected system of domination." Hence the kinds of technological efficiency and military power that gave Americans cause to celebrate a new era of expansion by the nation in 1898 now provoked anxiety about the permeability of its own national borders.

It is fitting, then, that this book should end with a brief discussion of the First World War for, as with the Spanish-American War, this conflict provided further occasion to dramatize new forms of modern traffic and to compare American and European modernity and the social, political, and moral orders they seemed to embody. The cinema was to play an important role in registering transformations in the perception of technological modernity coming out of the war and what it meant to be "American" in the age of total war. Hence, as President Woodrow Wilson wrote in a letter to the head of the National Association of the Motion Picture Industry, William Brady: "It is my mind not only to bring the motion picture into the fullest and most effective contact with the nation's needs, but to give some measure of official recognition to an increasingly important factor in the development of our national life. The film has come to rank as a very high medium for the dissemination of public intelligence and since it speaks a universal language it lends itself importantly to the presentation of America's plans and purposes."[12] These "plans and purposes" concerned the mass mobilization of both troops and public sentiment, the reconfiguration of patterns of production and consumption within a wartime context, and the behavior of immigrant groups from enemy nations (particularly German Americans) who came under suspicion as their loyalty to the United States was questioned.[13] Hence the war created a new context for elaborating emerging forms of machine-made mobility, the resulting reconfiguration of spatial and temporal experience, the movements of populations, and the emergence of new national, gendered, and racial-ethnic identities.

In this conclusion I can only gesture toward some of the ways in which mass mobilization transformed the experience of modern traffic and the perception of technological modernity in the United States and Europe. Nevertheless, I hope that it has provided some sense of how the war and cinematic representations of it grew out of the prior absorption of everyday life into various forms of modern traffic. A more detailed analysis would have to take into consideration the ways in which various genres—such as film serials, battlefront films, newsreels, war melodramas, and slapstick comedies—found ways to articulate the new and often terrifying forms of mobility associated with the war. It would also have to consider the anxiety surrounding "preparedness" and the permeability of national borders as well as the new and often powerfully dynamic film bodies that emerged onto screens between 1914 and 1918 (particularly that of the serial queen). Moreover, the struggles over the representation of Germans and German Americans on movie screens, the significance of the cinema as a site for the sale of war bonds, and the Creel Committee's role in regulating the content of films during the war would also be paramount. While we would not want to overstate the impact that the war had on filmmaking (particularly film form) and on the kinds of pictures that appeared on movie screens throughout the United States, it is certain that the war made the world seem much smaller and, moreover, that it forced a further reordering of space and time; transformed bodily experience and the meanings attached to gendered, national, and ethnic identities; and foregrounded the ways in which many aspects of modern life were inseparable from the traffic circulating through small towns, large cities, and across the nation and beyond. The cinema continued not only to make sense of such changes for its audiences, but also to charge them with fascination and pleasure.

NOTES

Introduction

1. LaFeber, *The New Empire*, 8.
2. Slotkin, *Gunfighter Nation*, 88–124.
3. See especially Banta, *Taylored Lives*; Rosenzweig, *Eight Hours for What We Will*; and Peiss, *Cheap Amusements*.
4. For a fascinating discussion of the cinema's elaboration of the potentially perilous effects of communications technologies, see Gunning, "Heard over the Phone," 184–96.
5. See Jacobson, *Whiteness of a Different Color*.
6. On industrialization and urbanization in the United States, see especially Trachtenberg, *The Incorporation of America*; and Chandler, *The Visible Hand*.
7. Chandler, *The Visible Hand*, 193.
8. For an analysis of the effects of telegraphy's acceleration of the rate at which communication took place across vast distances and its elimination of face-to-face communication, see Kern, *The Culture of Time and Space*, 259–86.
9. For an analysis of the rise of the new navy, see LaFeber, *The New Empire*.
10. On the cultural and social impact of electrification, see Schivelbusch, *Disenchanted Night*; Marvin, *When Old Technologies Were New*; and Nye, *Electrifying America*.
11. Habermas, *The Philosophical Discourse of Modernity*, 5.
12. *Oxford English Dictionary* (London: Oxford University Press, 1999), online version.
13. Schivelbusch, *The Railway Journey*.
14. Karl Marx, "Speech at the Anniversary of the *People's Paper*," 577–78; quoted in Berman, *All That Is Solid Melts into Air*, 20.

15. MacLaren, "The Restless Energy of the American People," 568.

16. Ibid., 569.

17. Ibid.

18. Ibid., 573.

19. Ibid., 571.

20. For example, George M. Beard argued in *American Nervousness*, his well-known study of modern nervous disorders, that "men, like batteries, need a reserve force, and men, like batteries, need to be measured by the amount of this reserve" (11).

21. Ibid., 574.

22. Ibid.

23. Schivelbusch, *The Railway Journey*, 194.

24. Friedberg, *Window Shopping*, 2.

25. Ibid., 38.

26. Kirby, *Parallel Tracks*, 2.

27. Stamp, *Movie-Struck Girls*; Singer, *Melodrama and Modernity*; Bean, "Technologies of Stardom."

28. Singer, *Melodrama and Modernity*, 258.

29. See especially Gunning, "An Aesthetic of Astonishment"; Singer, *Melodrama and Modernity*; and Kirby, *Parallel Tracks*.

30. Simmel, "The Metropolis and Mental Life," 175.

31. Chief among these is Singer's *Melodrama and Modernity*.

32. Gunning, "Heard over the Phone," 184–96.

33. See Schivelbusch's *The Railway Journey*, in which he discusses industrial illness such as "railway spine" and "traumatic neurosis."

34. Rabinbach, *The Human Motor*.

35. Abel, *The Red Rooster Scare*, xii.

36. Musser, *The Emergence of Cinema*, 261.

37. Anderson, *Imagined Communities*.

38. Kaplan, *The Anarchy of Empire*, 92–120.

39. LaFeber, *The New Empire*, 102–49.

40. On electricity at world's fairs and expositions, see Nye, *American Technological Sublime*.

41. Friedberg, *Window Shopping*; Rabinovitz, *For the Love of Pleasure*; Bruno, *Streetwalking on a Ruined Map*.

42. Musser, *Edison Motion Pictures*, 54.

43. I borrow this phrase from Nye, who provides a history of sublime experiences of technology in the United States in *American Technological Sublime*.

44. Ohmann, *Selling Culture*, 29.

45. Ibid.

Chapter 1: Early Cinema Encounters Empire

1. Philip, "The 'Texas' at Santiago," 99.
2. Musser, *The Emergence of Cinema*, 247.
3. Edison Manufacturing Co., *War Extra Catalogue*, 2.
4. Musser, *Before the Nickelodeon*, 133.
5. For an excellent analysis of the link between overseas imperialism, the discourse of manifest destiny, and the myth of the frontier, see Slotkin, *Gunfighter Nation*. For primary examples of such discourse, see Roosevelt's *The Rough Riders* and *The Winning of the West*.
6. For analyses of the increased presence of women in the public sphere, see Peiss, *Cheap Amusements*; Rabinovitz, *For the Love of Pleasure*; and Stamp, *Movie-Struck Girls*. For an analysis of the racial politics of immigrant participation and presence in public life, see Jacobson, *Whiteness of a Different Color*.
7. For an analysis of the link between discourses on American masculinity, "civilization," and racial theories of the late nineteenth century, see especially Bederman's *Manliness and Civilization*.
8. Studlar details the late-nineteenth- and early-twentieth-century discourse on reforming masculinity in *This Mad Masquerade*, 10–89.
9. Jackson-Lears, *No Place of Grace*, 100.
10. See Hoganson, *Fighting for American Manhood*, 1–42.
11. Edison Manufacturing Co., *War Extra Catalogue*, 2.
12. Musser, *Edison Motion Pictures, 1890–1900*, 54.
13. Ohmann, *Selling Culture*, 74–75.
14. Kaplan, "Romancing the Empire," 662.
15. Mahan, *The Interest of America in Sea Power*, 6–7; this text was first published as an essay titled "The United States Looking Outward" in the *Atlantic Monthly*, December 1890.
16. Mahan, *The Interest of America in Sea Power*, 21; this text was first published as an essay titled "Hawaii and Our Future Sea Power" in *The Forum*, March 1893.
17. Mahan, *The Interest of America in Sea Power*, 52; this text was first published as an essay titled "The Isthmus and Sea Power" in the *Atlantic Monthly*, September 1893.
18. LaFeber, *The New Empire*, 197.
19. Ibid., 121–27.
20. Melville, "Our Future in the Pacific," 282.
21. Kaplan, "Romancing the Empire," 662.
22. Fullam, "The United States Naval Academy," 401, 402.
23. Bederman, *Manliness and Civilization*; Rotundo, *American Manhood*.
24. Bederman, *Manliness and Civilization*, 1–44.
25. Beard, *American Nervousness*, 26.
26. Ibid., 11.

27. See Bederman, *Manliness and Civilization*, 77–120.

28. Roosevelt, "Kidd's Social Evolution," 97, 109. For an analysis of Roosevelt's writings on race suicide see Dyer, *Theodore Roosevelt and the Idea of Race*.

29. For a discussion of the link between the "health" of native white masculinity and the "health" of what was called "the American Race" in the 1890s, see Bederman, *Manliness and Civilization*, 192–206.

30. George W. Stocking Jr.'s *Race, Culture, and Evolution* remains the most thorough and engaging analysis of the production of racial categories by scientists and pseudoscientists in the late nineteenth and early twentieth centuries. For a concise analysis of the meanings of "race" at the turn of the century, see Stocking, "The Turn-of-the-Century Concept of Race."

31. See Slotkin, *Gunfighter Nation*.

32. Bederman, *Manliness and Civilization*, 186–88.

33. Hoganson, *Fighting for American Manhood*, 49–52, 134–35.

34. For an analysis of the effects of technological breakdown on the modern individual, see Schivelbusch, *The Railway Journey*. For analyses of representations of mechanical breakdown in early cinema and its link to developments in spectatorship and film form, see Kirby, *Parallel Tracks*; and Gunning, "Heard over the Phone."

35. For an analysis of the explosion, its investigation, and the role it played in provoking hostilities between the United States and Spain, see Millis, *The Martial Spirit*, 82–139.

36. I borrow this phrase from the title of Millis's *The Martial Spirit*. Mary Ann Doane has argued that technological "catastrophe is at some level always about the body, about the encounter with death," so that "catastrophe might finally be defined as the conjuncture of the failure of technology and the resulting confrontation with death" ("Information, Crisis, Catastrophe," 223).

37. Sigsbee, "Personal Narrative of the 'Maine,'" 242.

38. Ibid., 252.

39. Singer, "Modernity, Hyperstimulus, and the Rise of Popular Sensationalism," 79–80.

40. Edison Manufacturing Co., *War Extra Catalogue*, 7.

41. Schivelbusch, *The Railway Journey*, 157–58.

42. Hollis, "The Uncertain Factors in Naval Conflicts," 728.

43. See Brown's *The Correspondents' War*.

44. Michel Foucault links the emergence of a disciplinary gaze to institutions such as the military, the school, and the prison. He argues that the "disciplinary institutions secreted a machinery of control that functioned like a microscope of conduct; the fine analytical divisions that they created formed around men an apparatus of observation, recording and training . . . The perfect disciplinary apparatus would make it possible for a single gaze to see everything constantly. A central point would be both the source of light illuminating everything, and a locus of

convergence for everything that must be known: a perfect eye that nothing would escape and a centre towards which all gazes would be turned." Rather than fulfilling the ideal of a perfect disciplinary gaze, I mean to argue that the observing points of view offered to actuality audiences and magazine articles acted like the "relays" that Foucault argues were necessary for the disciplinary gaze to function. Such relays subdivide the gaze "into smaller elements . . . in order to increase its productive function: specify the surveillance and make it functional" (*Discipline and Punish*, 173–74).

45. Edison Manufacturing Co., *War Extra Catalogue*, 7.

46. Philip, "The 'Texas' at Santiago," 90.

47. Ibid., 92.

48. Foucault offers two analyses of the disciplinary gaze relevant to the mode of looking offered by the war actuality. In his discussion of disciplinary institutions such as the military, Foucault argues that "disciplinary power . . . is exercised through its invisibility; at the same time that it imposes on those whom it subjects a principle of compulsory visibility. In discipline, it is the subjects who have to be seen. Their visibility assures the hold of the power that is exercised over them. It is the fact of being constantly seen, of being always able to be seen, that maintains the disciplined individual in his subjection." Later, when discussing Bentham's Panopticon, Foucault notes that "Bentham laid down the principle that power should be visible and unverifiable: the inmate will constantly have before his eyes the tall outline of the central tower from which he is spied upon. Unverifiable: the inmate must never know whether he is being looked at at any one moment; but he must be sure that he may always be so" (*Discipline and Punish*, 187, 201).

49. Edison Manufacturing Co., *War Extra Catalogue*, 9.

50. Taylor, "The 'Indiana' at Santiago," 63.

51. Noël Burch identifies temporal nonclosure as one of the characteristic formal features of the early preclassical film; see "Primitivism and the Avant-Garde," 488.

52. Colomb, "The Evolution of the Naval Officer," 553, 551, 553, 554.

53. Ibid., 555.

54. Fiske, "Why We Won at Manila," 132.

55. Wainwright, "The 'Gloucester' at Santiago," 86. This is one of several articles joined under the heading "The Battle at Manila Bay: The Destruction of the Spanish Fleet Described by Eye-Witnesses."

56. Kindleberger, "Narrative of Dr. Charles P. Kindleberger," 624.

57. Ibid.

58. *The Phonoscope*, September 1898, 14. Quoted in Musser, *Edison Motion Pictures, 1890–1900*, 460–61.

59. Gunning, "An Aesthetic of Astonishment," 31–43.

60. *The Phonoscope*, October 1898, 15. Quoted in Musser, *Edison Motion Pictures, 1890–1900*, 452.

61. *The Phonoscope*, October 1898, 15. Quoted in Musser, *Edison Motion Pictures, 1890–1900*, 456.

62. Gunning, "Before Documentary," 15.

63. Edison Manufacturing Co., *War Extra Catalogue*, 2.

64. Kirby, "Male Hysteria and Early Cinema," 113–31. The term "cinema of attractions" is, of course, Gunning's and is formulated in his articles "The Cinema of Attractions" and "An Aesthetic of Astonishment."

65. Edison Manufacturing Co., *War Extra Catalogue*, 3.

66. Hoganson, *Fighting for American Manhood*, 50–75.

67. Edison Manufacturing Co., *War Extra Catalogue*, 2.

68. See Kaplan, "Romancing the Empire"; and Davis, *The Cuban and Porto Rico Campaigns*.

69. Williams, *Hard Core*, 34–57.

70. Balides, "Scenarios of Exposure in the Practice of Everyday Life," 19–37.

71. Williams, *Hard Core*, 40.

72. Balides, "Scenarios of Exposure in the Practice of Everyday Life," 24.

73. Williams, *Hard Core*, 43.

74. Edison Manufacturing Co., *War Extra Catalogue*, 3.

75. Ibid., 3–4.

76. Hoganson, *Fighting for American Manhood*, 51–60.

77. See Millis, *The Martial Spirit*, 241–48; and Brown, *The Correspondents' War*, 206–12.

78. For Major General Shafter's own account of the confusion that prevailed at Tampa and the Cuban campaign and of his own nervous exhaustion, see "The Capture of Santiago de Cuba," 612–30.

79. Edison Manufacturing Co., *Edison Films Catalogue*, March 1900, 10.

80. Cooper, "Love, Danger, and the Professional Ideology of Hollywood Cinema," 85–117; Dyer, "White," 44–65.

81. Edison Manufacturing Co., *War Extra Catalogue*, 3–4.

82. Hoganson, *Fighting for American Manhood*, 118.

83. Sewell, *Congressional Report*, 6450. Quoted in Hoganson, *Fighting for American Manhood*, 122.

84. Hoganson, *Fighting for American Manhood*, 124. In June 1898 an editorial titled "The End of the War, and After" in the *Atlantic Monthly* argued that as a result of the war, "We [citizens of the United States] have recovered our own national feeling. Four months ago, we were a great mass of people rather than a compact nation conscious of national strength and unity. By forgetting even for this brief time our local differences, we have welded ourselves into a conscious unity such as the Republic has not felt since its early days. Not only have the North and South forgotten that they were ever at war—for time and industry had already wellnigh brought this result—but the Pacific states are nearer to the rest of the Union than

they ever were before, and the great middle West is no longer estranged from the seaboard. We can work out our own problems and build our own future with a steadier purpose" (432).

85. *Biograph Picture Catalogue*, November 1902, 167.

86. Bederman, *Manliness and Civilization*, 44.

87. Although African American soldiers fought heroically in battle, they were nevertheless denied the same measure of honor lavished upon the Rough Riders. In fact, although Roosevelt initially praised the heroism of the black soldiers who fought in the Battle of San Juan Hill, in his war memoir, *The Rough Riders*, he portrayed them as behaving cowardly. For an excellent analysis of Roosevelt's representation of black participation in the Cuban campaign, see Kaplan's "Black and Blue on San Juan Hill," 219–36.

88. Gatewood, *Black Americans and the White Man's Burden*. See also Gaines, *Uplifting the Race*.

89. Edison Manufacturing Co., *War Extra Catalogue*, 6.

90. Daniel Bernardi uses this phrase to describe the racial specificity of the narrator system at work in D. W. Griffith's Biograph films. He argues that the narrator system in Griffith's films deploys a range of cinematic techniques "from characterization to editing—to tell the story of the inability of non-whites to fully assimilate into white culture and society, and ultimately provide a justification for their servitude, segregation and punishment" ("The Voice of Whiteness," 112). Although Bernardi uses this term to describe narrative procedures that articulate cinematic racism from within the film text itself, I nevertheless find this formulation useful to illustrate how the catalogue description functioned to inscribe racism onto film from without.

91. Prescott, *Catalogue of New Films*, 28.

92. Rony, *The Third Eye*, 41.

93. Amy Kaplan in "Romancing the Empire" has located and described this longing for spectators for imperial masculinity in her analysis of the historical novel and journalistic representations of the war. Musser gives an account of audience enthusiasm for war programs and the Eden Musée in *Before the Nickelodeon*, 126–42.

94. Ibid., 135.

95. *Mail and Express*, September 17, 1898, 14. Quoted in Musser, *Before the Nickelodeon*, 135.

96. Kaplan, "Romancing the Empire," 661.

97. Ibid.

98. Edison Manufacturing Co., *War Extra Catalogue*, 4.

99. Hoganson, *Fighting for American Manhood*, 162–53, 174–79.

100. *Biograph Motion Picture Catalogue*, November 1902, 170.

Chapter 2: Placing Audiences on the Scene of History

1. "Pictures That Will Be Historic," *Leslie's Weekly*, January 6, 1900, 18. Part of this article is quoted in Bottomore, "'Every Phase of Present-Day Life,'" 147–211. My thanks to Giorgio Bertellini for bringing this article to my attention.

2. Holmes, "The Stereoscope and the Stereograph," 748.

3. Trachtenberg, "Albums of War," 6.

4. Ibid.

5. Sweet, *Traces of War*.

6. Abel, *The Ciné Goes to Town*, 92.

7. Hansen, *Babel and Babylon*, 30–31.

8. To trace this cultural history, this chapter focuses on reenactments of land battles and does not consider naval battle reenactments.

9. Kasson, *Amusing the Million*, 71.

10. Sarah Blackstone in *Buckskins, Bullets, and Business*, 26–27, notes that even though Cody's Wild West was set up just outside the gates at the Columbian Exposition, it nevertheless was one of the most popular attractions and grossed one million dollars in summer 1893 alone.

11. For details of features of the Wild West, see Kasson, *Buffalo Bill's Wild West*; Blackstone, *Buckskins, Bullets, and Business*; Reddin, *Wild West Shows*; and Slotkin, *Gunfighter Nation*, 29–87.

12. Edward Zane Carroll Judson (known by the pen name Ned Buntline) published the first instalment of *Buffalo Bill, King of the Border Men* in the *New York Weekly* in December 1869. See Klein, *Easterns, Westerns, and Private Eyes*.

13. For an analysis of the social, cultural, and economic transformations that made the myth of frontier life so compelling to upper-class urban easterners, see White, *The Eastern Establishment and the Western Experience*.

14. Vardac, *Stage to Screen*, 135–51.

15. Slotkin, *Gunfighter Nation*, 69.

16. Williams, *Playing the Race Card*, 43–44.

17. In his review Pomeroy noted: "I wish there were more progressive educators in this world like Wm. F. Cody" (quoted in *Buffalo Bill's Wild West: Historical Sketches and Programme*, 11).

18. Kasson, *Buffalo Bill's Wild West*, 5.

19. *Buffalo Bill's Wild West: Historical Sketches and Programme*, 5.

20. Editorial in the *New York Democrat*, June 5, 1886; reprinted in *Buffalo Bill's Wild West: Historical Sketches and Programme*, 10–12.

21. Walter Benjamin defines "aura" as "the unique phenomenon of distance, however close it may be." The decay of the aura of an artwork or of "reality" "rests on two circumstances, both of which are related to the increasing significance of the masses in contemporary life. Namely, the desire of contemporary masses to bring things 'closer' spatially and humanly, which is just as ardent as their bent

toward overcoming the uniqueness of every reality by accepting its reproduction." Technical reproduction, which around 1900 "reached a standard that not only permitted it to reproduce all transmitted works of art and thus to cause the most profound change in their impact upon the public; it also had captured a place of its own among the artistic processes" (Benjamin, "The Work of Art in the Age of Mechanical Reproduction," 219–21). The reproducibility of life on the frontier in the Wild West depended heavily on Cody's masterful orchestration of a range of technologies of transportation and representation, from the railway to electricity as well as his mobilization of authentic relics and artifacts.

22. For analyses of the waxworks museum, see Schwartz, *Spectacular Realities*; and Sandberg, *Living Pictures, Missing Persons*. On the museum life group, see Griffiths, *Wondrous Difference*. Griffiths also theorizes and historicizes the relation between reenactments and panorama paintings in her essay "Shivers Down Your Spine."

23. Mitchell, "Orientalism and the Exhibitionary Order," 304, 295.

24. *Buffalo Bill's Wild West: Historical Sketches and Programme*, 11 (my italics).

25. Ibid., 11–12.

26. Ibid., 24 (my italics).

27. This advertisement for the "Loop-the-Loop" is quoted by Kasson in *Amusing the Million*, 81.

28. *Amusing the Million*, 6–7. For Kasson's more recent analyses of Sandow and Houdini, see *Houdini, Tarzan and the Perfect Man*.

29. Harris, *Humbug*, 74.

30. Ibid., 75.

31. Ibid., 77.

32. Ibid., 8.

33. Slotkin in *Gunfighter Nation*, 81, quotes a review by David A. Curtis in the *Criterion* in 1899 that noted that the "Wild West" spectacle of "struggle and slaughter" "stirs the thinnest blood and brightens the dullest eye" in the civilized Anglo-Saxon.

34. *Buffalo Bill's Wild West: Historical Sketches and Programme*, 18.

35. Dan Streible's research on Sigmund Lubin's boxing reenactments suggests that this particular kind of reenactment might be more in line with humbug. However, Streible notes an increasing verisimilitude in the boxing reenactment. Of the *Reproduction of the Jeffries-Fitzsimmons Fight* (Lubin, 1899), he notes: "Replacing the canvas backdrop are rows of bleachers occupied by several dozen young men and boys. The sparring action between the contestants is not unconvincing, but the 'acting' of the ringside extras upstages the fighters. Playing to the camera, between rounds men stand and wave their betting money in the air" (Streible, "Fake Fight Films," 71). The placement of a ringside audience in the film suggests that the fight reenactment also enhanced its reality effect by positioning the film

spectator in the imaginary position of a witness on the scene. Such films operated in a mode of revelation by simulating a spectacular event that had been eclipsed by legal bans on prizefighting.

36. *Buffalo Bill's Wild West: Historical Sketches and Programme*, 14.

37. Ibid., 48.

38. Hoganson, *Fighting for American Manhood*, 107–32; Kaplan, *The Anarchy of Empire*, 121–45.

39. Roosevelt, *The Rough Riders*, 15–16.

40. *Buffalo Bill's Wild West: Historical Sketches and Programme* (1900), 32.

41. Roosevelt, *The Rough Riders*, 15–16.

42. Gunning, "The Cinema of Attractions," 63–70, and "An Aesthetic of Astonishment," 31–45.

43. Shivelbusch, *The Railway Journey*, 150.

44. Ibid., 153.

45. Wanger, *Organization and Tactics*, 216, 215.

46. Prescott, *Catalogue of New Films*, 22.

47. *Edison Films Catalogue*, no. 94 (March 1900): 11.

48. Ibid., 10–11.

49. Roosevelt, *The Rough Riders*, 117.

50. Schivelbusch, *The Railway Journey*, 155, 156.

51. G. H. Groeningen, *Über den Shock: Eine kritische Studie auf physiologischer Grundlage* (Wiesbaden: J. F. Bergmann, 1885), cited in Schivelbusch, *The Railway Journey*, 157.

52. Roosevelt, *The Rough Riders*, 89.

53. *Buffalo Bill's Wild West: Historical Sketches and Programme* (1900), 34.

54. Nemerov, *Frederic Remington and Turn-of-the-Century America*, 86–87.

55. Gunning, "The Whole Town's Gawking," 194.

56. Virilio, *War and Cinema*, 7.

57. Quoted in Miller, *"Benevolent Assimilation,"* 181.

58. Quoted in Gatewood, *Black Americans and the White Man's Burden*, 264.

59. Ibid., 269. One battle that might have offered such an opportunity—the Battle of Manila, in which Spain capitulated the islands to U.S. control—was itself a reenactment of sorts. Writing from the Philippines in 1899, Karl Irving Faust explained that in order to preserve their honor before the eyes of the watching world, Spain insisted on the staging of a "sham battle" before surrendering the islands to U.S. control: "By the 12th of August, the full details of the 'coming battle' had been arranged . . . In this, on the part of the American forces, such display was to be made as would satisfy an observer that further resistance on the part of the Spaniards would not only be futile, but grounds for censure by all non-combatants." Though, as Faust notes, both sides worked to "perfect the plan of a mimic battle without it verging into the real," various officers missed their visual cues due to blocked lines of sight (thanks to the contingencies of smoke,

distance, and unseen flags). Confusion ensued, resulting in an American casualty (Faust, *Campaigning in the Philippines*, 96).

60. Dickson, *The Biograph in Battle*, 124–25.

61. Dickson also noted the British soldier's experience of battlefield blindness: "The thing which chiefly demoralized our men . . . was the fact that half the time they had to fire at nothing, so cleverly were the Boers hidden, while the British were being mowed down by [their] Maxim-Nordenfeldt repeating guns, making it quite impossible for our men to escape . . . Our men shudder at the very sound . . . for the accurate shooting accomplished with the murderous weapon is something fearful to see" (*The Biograph in Battle*, 135).

62. *Edison Films Catalogue*, no. 94 (March 1900): 4.

63. Levy, "Reconstituted Newsreels, Reenactments and the American Narrative Film," 247. Levy does not directly quote the article, which was published in May in the Rochester newspaper the *Democrat and Chronicle*.

64. Freud, *Beyond the Pleasure Principle*, 14.

65. Ibid., 15.

66. Ibid., 17.

67. Quoted in Musser, *Edison Motion Pictures, 1890–1900*, 472–73.

68. Prescott, *Catalogue of New Films for Projection*, 29.

69. Schirmer, *Republic or Empire*.

70. Wexler, *Tender Violence*, 22.

71. Ibid., 21

72. Barton, *The Red Cross*, 680.

73. Kaplan, "The Birth of an Empire," 3.

74. Barton, *The Red Cross*, 519.

75. Ibid., 521.

76. Ibid., 602.

77. Ibid., 529.

78. Ibid., 406–7.

79. Ibid., 441

80. Ibid., 425.

81. In a speech delivered to the Hamilton Club in Chicago on April 10, 1899, Roosevelt argued that "the woman must be the housewife, the helpmeet of the homemaker, the wise and fearless mother of many healthy children. In one of Daudet's powerful and melancholy books he speaks of 'the fear of maternity, the haunting terror of the young wife of the present day.' When such words can be truthfully written of a nation, that nation is rotten to the heart's core. When men fear work or fear righteous war, when women fear motherhood, they tremble on the brink of doom; and well it is that they should vanish from the earth, where they are fit subjects for the scorn of all men and women who are themselves strong and brave and high-minded" (*The Strenuous Life*, 4).

82. Barton, *The Red Cross*, 447.

83. Ibid.

84. Ibid., 559.

85. Kaplan, "Birth of an Empire," 4.

86. Barton, *The Red Cross*, 557.

87. Ibid., 612–13.

88. Ibid., 613.

89. Ibid., 425

90. Prescott, *Catalogue of New Films for Projection and Other Purposes*, 24.

91. Musser, *Edison Motion Pictures, 1890–1900*, 487.

92. Ibid., 485.

93. Kaplan, "Birth of an Empire," 2.

94. "Pictures That Will Be Historic," 18.

95. Ibid.

96. Ibid.

97. Ibid. Here the author desires the erasure of the correspondent's point of view that, at the turn of the century, tended to foreground the journalist's own, often romanticized the experience of war. Indeed, during the Spanish-American War the emergent style of "yellow journalism" often narrated the journalist's own participation in highly sensationalized and dramatized events. In contrast to such forms of journalism, the "magic of the screen" achieves the illusory insertion of the spectator self into the depicted scene and the point of observation carved out in a mode of illusory, machine-made transparency. For an account of such journalism see Brown, *The Correspondent's War*.

98. "Pictures That Will Be Historic," 18.

99. Gunning, "The Whole Town's Gawking," 193.

Chapter 3: Electric Modernity and the Cinema

1. Dickson and Dickson, *History of the Kinetograph*, 6.

2. For social and cultural histories of electricity, see especially Marvin, *When Old Technologies Were New*; and Nye, *Electrifying America*.

3. For detailed historical analyses of world's fairs and expositions, see especially Rydell, *All the World's a Fair*; Greenhalgh, *Ephemeral Vistas*; and Griffiths, *Wondrous Difference*.

4. Visitor's Information Co., *Pan-American Exposition Book of 18 Special Privileges*, 16–17 (my italics).

5. Ibid.

6. Ibid., 38

7. *A General Outline of the Pan-American Exposition*, 1–2.

8. Visitor's Information Co., *Pan-American Exposition Book of 18 Special Privileges*, 53.

9. Ibid., 34–35.

10. *Pan-American Exposition: Buffalo: May 1st to November 1st*, 6.

11. *Some Information Regarding the Pan-American Exposition*, 1–2.

12. Friedberg, *Window Shopping*, 37–38.

13. Visitor's Information Co., *Pan-American Exposition Book of 18 Special Privileges*, 19–20.

14. *A General Outline of the Pan-American Exposition*, 8.

15. Bell, *The Art of Illumination*, 283–84.

16. Ibid., 59.

17. The foundational text on this subject is Marx's *The Machine in the Garden*. Kasson continues to research the meaning of technology in nineteenth-century American culture in *Civilizing the Machine*. Nye's *American Technological Sublime* focuses specifically on the sublime experience of technology in U.S. culture throughout nineteenth century and the twentieth.

18. Nye, *American Technological Sublime*, xvi, xvii.

19. Ibid., 5.

20. Ibid., 60, 43.

21. Harris, *Humbug*, 74–75.

22. Burdette, "Electric Dawn."

23. Edison Manufacturing Co., *Edison Films Catalogue* (1901). Musser, *Motion Picture Catalogs by American Producers and Distributors, 1894–1908*.

24. Gunning, "An Aesthetic of Astonishment," 52.

25. Nye, *The Technological Sublime*, 62.

26. Schivelbusch, *Disenchanted Night*, 221.

27. *Pan-American Exposition: Some of Its Special Features with Lists of Special Days, Sports, Concerts, Etc.*, 1.

28. Gunning, "The World as Object Lesson," 427.

29. Oettermann, *The Panorama*, 251.

30. Schivelbusch, *Disenchanted Night*, 158–87.

31. Iles, *Flame Electricity and the Camera*, 259.

32. Schivelbusch, *Disenchanted Night*, 4–76.

33. Platt's *The Electric City* offers an outstanding case study of the expansion of and competition between alternating current and direct current systems in the Chicago area.

34. Schivelbusch, *Disenchanted Night*, 172–78.

35. *The Times*, October 4, 1823; quoted in Gernsheim and Gernsheim, *L. J. M. Daguerre*, 17.

36. Ackerman, *Repository of Art*, November 1823; quoted in Gernsheim and Gernsheim, *L. J. M. Daguerre*, 17.

37. *London*, vol. 6 (1844); quoted in Gernsheim and Gernsheim, *L. J. M. Daguerre*, 40–41.

38. Quoted in Gernsheim and Gernsheim, *L. J. M. Daguerre*, 17.

39. Ibid., 34.

40. *L'Artiste* 10, no. 1 (1835); quoted in Gernsheim and Gernsheim, *L. J. M. Daguerre*, 36.

41. Ibid., 37.

42. *A General Outline of the Pan-American Exposition*, 7.

43. Brown, "By-Products of an Exposition."

44. Ibid.

45. *The Christian Herald and Sign of Our Times*, "One Lesson from the Tragedy," October 9, 1901.

46. "His Well-Ordered Life," *Illustrated Buffalo Express*, August 22, 1897.

47. *Auburn Daily Advertiser*, October 29, 1901.

48. Quoted from the complete transcript, available at the Buffalo and Erie County Historical Society, Buffalo, New York.

49. See especially the *Buffalo Courier*, September 7, 1901. Front-page headlines screamed, "President McKinley Shot at Public Reception in the Temple of Music; Raging Mobs Attempt to Lynch Anarchist—Sixty-Fifth Regiment Awaiting Orders."

50. Brown, "The New Instrument of Execution," 586–93.

51. Metzger, *Blood and Volts*, 111.

52. Musser, *The Emergence of Cinema*, 320.

53. Lewis, *The Development of American Prisons*, 78; quoted in Metzger, *Blood and Volts*, 121.

54. Hansen, *Babel and Babylon*, 47.

55. I am very grateful to Tom Gunning for bringing this film to my attention.

Chapter 4: Regulating Mobility

1. Shelley Stamp in *Movie-Struck Girls*, 52, estimates that *Traffic in Souls* grossed $5,000 a week at the box office and drew upward of 15,000 spectators each week in New York.

2. See for example "The Rockefeller Grand Jury Report," 471–73; Vice Commission of Chicago, *The Social Evil in Chicago*; U.S. Immigration Commission, "Steerage Conditions"; Kneeland, *Commercialized Prostitution in New York City*; Addams, *A New Conscience and an Ancient Evil* (discussed in detail in this chapter); Miner, *The Slavery of Prostitution*; and Goldman, "The Traffic in Women." Eustace Hale Ball published a novelization of *Traffic in Souls* entitled *Traffic in Souls: A Novel of Crime and Its Cure*. Stamp notes that two plays on the vice traffic, *The Lure* and *The Fight*, opened on Broadway three months before the opening of *Traffic in Souls*.

3. See especially U.S. Immigration Commission, "Steerage Conditions."

4. See especially Addams, "The House of Dreams," in *The Spirit of Youth and the City Streets*, 75–106.

5. See Addams, *A New Conscience and an Ancient Evil*; and Goldman, *Anarchism and Other Essays*.

6. For analyses of the relation between early cinema and modernity, see Charney and Schwartz's outstanding collection *Cinema and the Invention of Modern Life*.

7. For an analysis of the early railway film's link to masculinity and hysteria, see Kirby, *Parallel Tracks*. Gunning in "An Aesthetic of Astonishment," 31–44, analyzes descriptions of the first audience reactions to Lumière's *Arrival of a Train* and contextualizes them within the mode of the cinema of attractions. For an analysis of the lure and effects of the urban street on early film spectatorship, see Gunning's "From the Kaleidoscope to the X-Ray." In "Heard over the Phone: *The Lonely Villa* and the de Lorde Tradition of the Terrors of Technology" Gunning analyzes the transitional cinema's narration and exploitation of the terrifying breakdown of modern technology.

8. Gunning, "Heard over the Phone," 188.

9. My thanks to Eva Warth and Annette Forster for screening *Shoes* at the 1999 Gender and Silent Cinema Conference at the University of Utrecht; for providing English titles for the film; and for inspiring scholarly work on the film among conference participants.

10. Brewster, "Traffic in Souls," 38–39.

11. Bowser, *The Transformation of Cinema*, 192.

12. Singer, *Melodrama and Modernity*, 212. See also Singer's "Feature Films, Variety Programs, and the Crisis of the Small Exhibitor," in *American Cinema's Transitional Era*.

13. See "*Traffic in Souls* Makes Hit," *Moving Picture World*, December 6, 1913, 1157.

14. Stamp, "Is Any Girl Safe?" 12.

15. Ibid., 9.

16. Bowser in *The Transformation of Cinema*, 192, notes that in the early 1910s "there was no real precision in the use of the term" feature film. However, she notes that longer five- and six-reel pictures were often advertised as "special features" or "big features." In this chapter I am mostly concerned with the five- and six-reeler, and for consistency's sake I will use the terms "long feature" and "multi-reel feature" to designate these lengthier texts.

17. Schivelbusch, *The Railway Journey*, 192.

18. See Friedberg, *Window Shopping*; and Kirby, *Parallel Tracks*.

19. Schivelbusch, *The Railway Journey*, 189.

20. Ibid., 193, 190.

21. Ibid., 191.

22. I borrow the phrase "just looking" from Rachel Bowlby.

23. Schivelbusch, *The Railway Journey*, 193.

24. In 1890, for example, 8,123 miles of electric streetcar tracks had been laid in the

United States; by 1902 the number increased to 10,175 (U.S. Bureau of the Census, *Special Reports, Street and Electric Railways*, 34).

25. Ibid., 193–94, 195.
26. Deleuze and Guattari, *A Thousand Plateaus*, 21.
27. See Schivelbusch, *The Railway Journey*; Bowlby, *Just Looking*; and Buck-Morss, *The Dialectics of Seeing*.
28. For analyses of this anxiety, see especially Peiss, *Cheap Amusements*; Stamp, "Wages and Sin"; Hansen, *Babel and Babylon*; and Rabinovitz, *For the Love of Pleasure*.
29. Schivelbusch, *The Railway Journey*, 194.
30. U.S. Immigration Commission, "Steerage Conditions," 76.
31. Jenks and Lauck, *The Immigration Problem*, 65.
32. U.S. Immigration Commission, "Steerage Conditions," 90.
33. See the appendix of U.S. Immigration Commission, "Steerage Conditions."
34. Ibid., 67, 91.
35. Lee Grieveson, "Fighting Films," 50–51.
36. Addams, *A New Conscience and an Ancient Evil*, 26–27.
37. Ben Singer in *Melodrama and Modernity*, 59–99, details cultural responses to the violent impact of streetcar and automobile traffic on the imagination of technological modernity.
38. The unusual style of this film is analyzed by Keil in *Early Cinema in Transition*, 195–204.
39. Gunning, "From the Kaleidoscope to the X-Ray," 48–49.
40. For a detailed analysis of sensation melodrama and silent American film, see Singer, *Melodrama and Modernity*.
41. Brooks, *The Melodramatic Imagination*, 20.
42. For an analysis of these and other conventions of the stage and film melodrama, see especially Elsaesser, "Tales of Sound and Fury."
43. For an analysis of the ideological effects of the restoration of the recorded voice to the filmed body by sound technology, see especially Doane, "The Voice of the Cinema."
44. Bowser quotes a 1913 General Film advertisement that seems to address this frustration: "Some so-called features are merely single-reel stories 'padded' to fill more than a thousand feet of film. Not so, however, with General Film features. In every case the story must require more than a thousand feet to tell it clearly or it is not accepted in the form of a multiple-reel. A favorite trick with some producers of features is to use certain big scenes, as for example, a battle in a war drama, in several different pictures" (*The Transformation of Cinema, 1907–1915*, 204).
45. Ibid., 198.
46. Addams, *A New Conscience and an Ancient Evil*, 76. Here I quote directly from

the passage in the book used by Weber rather than the English retranslation of the Dutch translation of the quotation.

47. Addams, *A New Conscience and an Ancient Evil*, 75.

48. Schivelbusch, *The Railway Journey*, 127. See also Stamp, "Lois Weber."

49. Rabinbach, *The Human Motor*, 1.

50. Ibid., 3.

51. Ibid.

52. Ibid., 3–4.

53. Marey, *Animal Mechanism*; Gilbreth and Gilbreth, "The Effect of Motion Study Upon the Workers"; Taylor, *Scientific Management*.

54. Addams, *A New Conscience*, 78, 91.

55. Ibid., 74.

56. Ibid. (my italics).

57. Peter Milne, *Motion Picture News*, June 24, 1916, 3927.

58. Addams, *A New Conscience and an Ancient Evil*, 65–66.

59. Leach, *Land of Desire*, 112–34.

60. Ibid., 65.

61. Herron, "Shoes," 8.

62. I borrow this phrase from Brooks, *The Melodramatic Imagination*, 1–30.

63. Adams, *A New Conscience and an Ancient Evil*, 91.

64. Ibid., 82.

65. Herron, "Shoes," 9.

66. Adams, *A New Conscience and an Ancient Evil*, 88.

67. Ibid., 74.

68. Kern, *The Culture of Time and Space*, 105.

69. Doane, *The Emergence of Cinematic Time*, 108.

70. Addams, *A New Conscience and an Ancient Evil*, 65.

71. "*Traffic in Souls* Makes Hit," *Moving Picture World*, December 6, 1913, 1157.

72. Here I depart from Janet Staiger's argument that Little Sister represents the modern girl "who doesn't think" and therefore falls prey to the slave trade. See Staiger, *Bad Women*, 116, 134–35, 138. Indeed each of the women who we see captured by the traders are representative figures of a naïve or inexperienced relation to urban technological modernity. The costumes of the Swedish immigrants overtly mark them signifiers for the "Old Country," thereby rendering them much more visible to the traffickers (to the extent that they stand out from the Ellis Island crowds that provide the diegetic setting for the scene). Similarly, the country girl appears somewhat like a bumpkin and has trouble negotiating urban street traffic—a flaw that makes it quite easy for the traffickers to divert her into the slave trade.

73. Stamp, "Is Any Girl Safe?" 13; Gunning, "From the Kaleidoscope to the X-Ray," 41; Grieveson, "Policing the Cinema," 166.

74. Stamp, *Movie-Struck Girls*, 83–86.

75. On melodrama and powerlessness, see Neale, "Melodrama and Tears."

76. *Wid's*, "Shoes," July 15, 1916, 647–48.

77. Peter Milne, *Motion Picture News*, June 24, 1916, 3927.

78. Herron, "Shoes," 8.

79. Hansen, *Babel and Babylon*, 84.

80. Ibid., 84.

81. Laemmle, "Doom of the Long Features Predicted," *Moving Picture World*, July 11, 1914, 185. I suspect that this fan's objections indicate a response to an increased proliferation of long features in 1913–14 in general and not specifically to the effects of the popular *Traffic in Souls*, for Tucker's film was banned in Chicago.

82. Richard Koszarski in *An Evening's Entertainment*, 163, notes that Laemmle continued his short-sighted tirade against long features until 1917.

83. Weber, "Room for Long and Short Pictures," *Motion Picture News*, May 27, 1916, 3222.

84. For an analysis of the "balanced program" of short and long features during the 1910s and early 1920s, see Koszarski, *An Evening's Entertainment*, 163–90.

85. According to Bowser, the gradual unhinging of the relationship between story and reel was a process underway in 1911. She quotes an editorial from *Moving Picture World* arguing that "it would seem that the time has come when the length of the film should in no way have anything to do with the subject matter; there is too much evidence of 'cutting off' to the detriment of the continuity of the pictures and this slaughtering for the subject only increases the ambiguity of the whole. . . . Clear, well sustained plots, carried to a full and finished ending, leaving with the audience a feeling of satisfaction and completeness are demanded" (January 7, 1911, 14–15; quoted in *The Transformation of Cinema*, 198–99).

86. *Moving Picture World*, January 7, 1911, 14–15; quoted by Bowser, *The Transformation of Cinema*, 198.

Conclusion

1. Kaplan, "Romancing the Empire," 662.

2. See Bordwell, Staiger, and Thompson, *The Classical Hollywood Cinema*.

3. Thompson, *Exporting Entertainment*.

4. See especially Eksteins, *The Rites of Spring*; and Fussell, *The Great War and Modern Memory*.

5. de Gaulle, *France and Her Army*, 90; quoted in Kern, *The Culture of Time and Space*, 307.

6. Kern, *The Culture of Time and Space*, 268.

7. Ibid., 268–69.

8. Geiss, *July 1914*, 291; quoted in Kern, *The Culture of Time and Space*, 267.

9. Kern, *The Culture of Time and Space*, 294–95.

10. Whissel, "The Little American (1917)," 23–43.

11. *War Information Series*, "Why We Are Fighting," 6.

12. Woodrow Wilson, *Exhibitor's Trade Review*, July 1918, and reprinted in various newspapers and *Moving Picture World*; cited in DeBauche, *Reel Patriotism*, 109.

13. On the treatment of German Americans during the war, see Luebke, *Bonds of Loyalty*; and Kazal, *Becoming Old Stock*.

BIBLIOGRAPHY

Abel, Richard. *The Ciné Goes to Town: French Cinema, 1896–1914*. Berkeley: University of California Press, 1998.

———. *The Red Rooster Scare: Making Cinema American, 1900–1910*. Berkeley: University of California Press, 1999.

Addams, Jane. *A New Conscience and an Ancient Evil*. New York: Macmillan, 1912.

———. *The Spirit of Youth and the City Streets*. Urbana: University of Illinois Press, 1972 [1909].

Anderson, Benedict. *Imagined Communities: Reflections on the Origin and Spread of Nationalism*. London: Verso, 1991.

Balides, Constance. "Scenarios of Exposure in the Practice of Everyday Life: Women in the Cinema of Attractions." *Screen* 34, no. 1 (spring 1993): 19–37.

Ball, Eustace Hale. *Traffic in Souls: A Novel of Crime and Its Cure*. New York: G. W. Dillingham, 1914.

Banta, Martha. *Taylored Lives: Narrative Productions in the Age of Taylor, Veblen, and Ford*. Chicago: University of Chicago Press, 1993.

Barton, Clara. *The Red Cross: A History of This Remarkable International Movement in the Interest of Humanity*. Washington: American National Red Cross, 1898.

Bean, Jennifer. "Technologies of Stardom and the Extra-ordinary Body." In *A Feminist Reader in Early Cinema*, edited by Jennifer Bean and Diane Negra, 404–43. Durham: Duke University Press.

Beard, George. *American Nervousness: Its Causes and Consequences*. New York: G. P. Putnam's Sons, 1881.

Bederman, Gail. *Manliness and Civilization: A Cultural History of Gender and Race in the United States, 1880–1917*. Chicago: University of Chicago Press, 1995.

Bell, Louis. *The Art of Illumination*. New York: McGraw Publishing Company, 1902.

Benjamin, Walter. "The Work of Art in the Age of Mechanical Reproduction." In *Illuminations*, edited by Hannah Arendt, 219–21. New York: Schocken, 1968.

Berman, Marshall. *All That Is Solid Melts into Air: The Experience of Modernity*. New York: Penguin, 1988.

Bernardi, Daniel, ed. "The Voice of Whiteness: D. W. Griffith's Biograph Films (1908–1913)." In *The Birth of Whiteness: Race and the Emergence of U.S. Cinema*, 103–28. New Brunswick: Rutgers University Press, 1996.

Biograph Motion Picture Catalogue (November 1902). In *Motion Picture Catalogs by American Producers and Distributors, 1894–1908: A Microform Edition*, edited by Charles Musser. Frederick, Md.: University Publications of America, 1985.

Blackstone, Sarah. *Buckskins, Bullets, and Business: A History of Buffalo Bill's Wild West*. New York: Greenwood, 1986.

Bordwell, David, Janet Staiger, and Kristin Thompson. *The Classical Hollywood Cinema: Film Style and Mode of Production to 1960*. London: Routledge, 1985.

Botlomore, Stephen. "'Every Phase of Present-Day Life': Biograph's Non-Fiction Production." *Griffithiana* 66–67 (1999–2000): 147–211.

Bowlby, Rachel. *Just Looking: Consumer Culture in Dreiser, Gissing, and Zola*. New York: Methuen, 1985.

Bowser, Eileen. *The Transformation of Cinema, 1907–1915*. Volume 2: *History of the American Cinema*. Berkeley: University of California Press, 1990.

Brewster, Ben. "Traffic in Souls: An Experiment in Feature-Length Narrative Construction." *Cinema Journal* 31, no. 1 (fall 1991): 31–56.

Brooks, Peter. *The Melodramatic Imagination: Balzac, Henry James, Melodrama, and the Mode of Excess*. New York: Columbia University Press, 1985.

Brown, Charles H. *The Correspondents' War: Journalists in the Spanish American War*. New York: Scribner's, 1967.

Brown, Harold P. "The New Instrument of Execution." *North American Review*, November 1889.

Brown, Mary Hart. "By-Products of an Exposition." *Buffalo Courier*, October 20, 1901.

Bruno, Giuliana. *Streetwalking on a Ruined Map: Cultural Theory and the City Films of Elvira Notari*. Princeton: Princeton University Press, 1992.

Buck-Morss, Susan. *The Dialectics of Seeing: Walter Benjamin and the Arcades Project*. Cambridge: MIT Press, 1989.

Buffalo Bill's Wild West: Historical Sketches and Programme. New York: Fless and Ridge, 1896.

Buffalo Bill's Wild West: Historical Sketches and Programme (1900). Denver Public Library, Buffalo Bill Manuscript Collection, box 2, folder 34.

Burch, Noël. "Primitivism and the Avant-Gardes: A Dialectical Approach." In *Narrative, Apparatus, Ideology: A Film Theory Reader*, edited by Philip Rosen, 483–506. New York: Columbia University Press, 1986.

Burdette, Robert J. "Electric Dawn." In *The Chicago American* (1901). Buffalo and Erie County Historical Society.

Chandler, Alfred D., Jr. *The Visible Hand: The Managerial Revolution in American Business.* Cambridge: Harvard University Press, 1977.

Charney, Leo, and Vanessa Schwartz, eds. *Cinema and the Invention of Modern Life.* Berkeley: University of California Press, 1995.

Colomb, Admiral P. H. "The Evolution of the Naval Officer." *North American Review,* April 1897, 545–55.

Cooper, Mark Garret. "Love, Danger, and the Professional Ideology of Hollywood Cinema." *Cultural Critique* 39 (spring 1998): 85–117.

Davis, Richard Harding. *The Cuban and Porto Rico Campaigns.* New York: Charles Scribner's Sons, 1898.

de Gaulle, Charles. *France and Her Army.* London: Hutchinson, 1941.

DeBauche, Leslie Midkiff. *Reel Patriotism: Movies and World War I.* Madison: University of Wisconsin Press, 1997.

Deleuze, Gilles, and Felix Guattari. *A Thousand Plateaus: Capitalism and Schizophrenia.* Minneapolis: University of Minnesota Press, 1987.

Dickson, Antonia, and W. K. L. Dickson. *History of the Kinetograph, Kinetoscope and Kinetophonograph.* New York: Albert Bunn, 1895.

Dickson, W. K. L. *The Biograph in Battle: Its Story in the South African War.* London: Flicks Books, 1995 [1901].

Doane, Mary Ann. *The Emergence of Cinematic Time: Modernity, Contingency, the Archive.* Cambridge: Harvard University Press, 2002.

———. "Information, Crisis, Catastrophe." In *The Logics of Television,* edited by Patricia Mellencamp. London: BFI, 1990, 222–39.

———. "The Voice of the Cinema: The Articulation of Body and Space." In *Narrative, Apparatus, Ideology: A Film Theory Reader,* edited by Philip Rosen. New York: Columbia University Press, 1986.

Dyer, Richard. "White." *Screen* 29, no. 4 (spring 1988): 44–65.

Dyer, Thomas G. *Theodore Roosevelt and the Idea of Race.* Baton Rouge: Louisiana State University Press, 1980.

Edison Manufacturing Co. *War Extra Catalogue* (May 20, 1898). In *Motion Picture Catalogs by American Producers and Distributors, 1894–1908: A Microform Edition,* edited by Charles Musser. Frederick, Md.: University Publications of America, 1985.

———. *Edison Films Catalogue* (March 1900). In *Motion Picture Catalogs by American Producers and Distributors, 1894–1908: A Microform Edition,* edited by Charles Musser. Frederick, Md.: University Publications of America, 1985.

Eksteins, Modris. *The Rites of Spring: The Great War and the Birth of the Modern Age.* Boston: Houghton Mifflin, 1989.

Elsaesser, Thomas. "Tales of Sound and Fury: Observations on the Family Melodrama." In *Home Is Where the Heart Is: Studies in Melodrama and the Woman's Film,* edited by Christine Gledhill, 43–69. London: BFI, 1987.

Faust, Karl Irving. *Campaigning in the Philippines*. San Francisco: Hicks-Judd, 1899.

Foucault, Michel. *Discipline and Punish: The Birth of the Prison*. Translated by Alan Sheridan. New York: Penguin, 1977.

Friedberg, Anne. *Window Shopping: Cinema and the Postmodern*. Berkeley: University of California Press, 1994.

Freud, Sigmund. *Beyond the Pleasure Principle*. New York: W. W. Norton, 1989 [1920].

Fussell, Paul. *The Great War and Modern Memory*. New York: Oxford University Press, 1975.

Gaines, Kevin. *Uplifting the Race: Black Leadership, Politics, and Culture in the Twentieth Century*. Chapel Hill: University of North Carolina Press, 1996.

Gatewood, Willard B. *Black Americans and the White Man's Burden, 1898–1903*. Chicago: University of Illinois Press, 1975.

Geiss, Immanuel. *July 1914: The Outbreak of the First World War*. New York: Scribner and Sons, 1974.

General Outline of the Pan-American Exposition, May 1 to November 1, 1901 at Buffalo, New York, USA. Buffalo: Gies, 1901. Buffalo and Erie County Historical Society.

Gernsheim, Alison, and Helmut Gernsheim. *L. J. M. Daguerre: The History of the Diorama and the Daguerreotype*. London: Dover, 1968.

Gilbreth, Frank B., and Lillian M. Gilbreth. "The Effect of Motion Study upon the Workers." *Annals of the American Academy of Political and Social Science* 65 (May 1916): 272–76.

Goldman, Emma. "The Traffic in Women." In *Anarchism and Other Essays*. New York: Mother Earth, 1917.

Greenhalgh, Paul. *Ephemeral Vistas: The Expositions Universelles, Great Exhibitions, and World's Fairs, 1851–1939*. Manchester: Manchester University Press, 1988.

Grieveson, Lee. "Fighting Films: Race, Morality, and the Governing of Cinema, 1912–1915." *Cinema Journal* 38, no. 1 (fall 1998): 40–72.

———. "Policing the Cinema: *Traffic in Souls* at Ellis Island, 1913." *Screen* 38, no. 2 (summer 1997): 149–71.

Griffiths, Alison. "Shivers down Your Spine: Panoramas and the Origins of the Cinematic Re-enactment." Paper presented at the Annual Meeting of the Society for Cinema Studies, Washington, March 2001.

———. *Wondrous Difference: Cinema, Anthropology, and Turn-of-the-Century Visual Culture*. New York: Columbia University Press, 2002.

G. H. Groeningen, *Über den Shock: Eine kritische Studie auf physiologischer Grundlage*. Wiesbaden: J. F. Bergmann, 1885.

Gunning, Tom. "An Aesthetic of Astonishment: Early Film and the (In)credulous Spectator." *Art & Text* 34 (spring 1989): 31–45.

———. "Before Documentary: Early Non-Fiction Films and the 'View' Aesthetic." In *Uncharted Territory: Essays on Early Non-Fiction Film*, edited by Dan Hertogs and Nico de Klerk, 9–24. Amsterdam: Stichting Nederlands Filmmuseum, 1994.

———. "The Cinema of Attractions." *Wide Angle* 8, nos. 3–4 (1986): 63–70.

———. "From the Kaleidoscope to the X-Ray: Urban Spectatorship, Poe, Benjamin and *Traffic in Souls* (1913)." *Wide Angle* 19, no. 4 (October 1997): 25–61.

———. "Heard over the Phone: *The Lonely Villa* and the De Lorde Tradition of the Terrors of Technology." *Screen* 32, no. 2 (summer 1991): 184–96.

———. "The Whole Town's Gawking: Early Cinema and the Visual Experience of Modernity." *Yale Journal of Criticism* 7, no. 2 (1994): 189–201.

———. "The World as Object Lesson: Cinema Audiences, Visual Culture and the St. Louis World's Fair, 1904." *Film History* 6 (1994): 422–44.

Habermas, Jürgen. *The Philosophical Discourse of Modernity*. Cambridge: MIT Press, 1987.

Hansen, Miriam. *Babel and Babylon: Spectatorship in American Silent Film*. Cambridge: Harvard University Press, 1991.

Harris, Neil. *Humbug: The Art of P. T. Barnum*. New York: Little, Brown, 1973.

Hoganson, Kristin. *Fighting for American Manhood: How Gender Politics Provoked the Spanish-American and Philippine-American Wars*. New Haven: Yale University Press, 1998.

Hollis, Ira Nelson. "The Uncertain Factors in Naval Conflicts." *Atlantic Monthly*, June 1898, 728–37.

Holmes, Oliver Wendell. "The Stereoscope and the Stereograph." *Atlantic Monthly* 3 (1859): 748.

Iles, George. *Flame, Electricity and the Camera: Man's Progress from the First Kindling of Fire to the Wireless Telegraph and the Photography of Color*. New York: Doubleday and McClure, 1900.

Jackson-Lears, T. J. *No Place of Grace: Antimodernism and the Transformation of American Culture, 1880–1920*. Chicago: University of Chicago Press, 1983.

Jacobson, Matthew Frye. *Whiteness of a Different Color: European Immigrants and the Alchemy of Race*. Cambridge: Harvard University Press, 1999.

Jenks, Jeremiah, and W. Jett Lauck. *The Immigration Problem: A Study of American Immigration Conditions and Needs*. New York: Funk and Wagnalls, 1911.

Kaplan, Amy. *The Anarchy of Empire in the Making of U.S. Culture*. Cambridge: Harvard University Press, 2002.

———. "The Birth of an Empire." *PMLA* 114, no. 5 (October 1999): 1068–79.

———. "Black and Blue on San Juan Hill." In *Cultures of United States Imperialism*, edited by Amy Kaplan and Donald E. Pease, 219–36. Durham: Duke University Press, 1993.

———. "Romancing the Empire: The Embodiment of Popular Masculinity in the Popular Historical Novel of the 1890s." *American Literary History* 2, no. 4 (winter 1990): 659–90.

Kasson, John F. *Amusing the Million: Coney Island at the Turn of the Century*. New York: Hill and Wang, 1978.

————. *Civilizing the Machine: Technology and Republican Values in America, 1776–1900*. New York: Hill and Wang, 1976.

————. *Houdini, Tarzan and the Perfect Man: The White Male Body and the Challenge of Modernity*. New York: Hill and Wang, 2001.

Kasson, Joy S. *Buffalo Bill's Wild West: Celebrity, Memory, and Popular History*. New York: Hill and Wang, 2000.

Kazal, Russell. *Becoming Old Stock: The Paradox of German-American Identity*. Princeton: Princeton University Press, 2004.

Keil, Charlie. *Early Cinema in Transition: Story, Style, and Filmmaking, 1907–1913*. Madison: University of Wisconsin Press, 2001.

Kern, Stephen. *The Culture of Time and Space, 1880–1918*. Cambridge: Harvard University Press, 1983.

Kindleberger, Charles P. "Narrative of Dr. Charles P. Kindleberger, Junior Surgeon of the Flag-Ship 'Olympia.'" *Century* 58, no. 1 (August 1898): 621–26.

Kirby, Lynne. *Parallel Tracks: The Railroad and Silent Cinema*. Durham: Duke University Press, 1997.

————. "Male Hysteria and Early Cinema." *Camera Obscura* 17 (May 1988): 113–31.

Klein, Marcus. *Easterns, Westerns, and Private Eyes: American Matters, 1870–1900*. Madison: University of Wisconsin Press, 1994.

Kneeland, George. *Commercialized Prostitution in New York City*. New York: Century, 1917.

Koszarski, Richard. *An Evening's Entertainment: The Age of the Silent Feature Picture, 1915–1928*. Berkeley: University of California Press, 1990.

LaFeber, Walter. *The New Empire: An Interpretation of American Expansion, 1860–1898*. Ithaca: Cornell University Press, 1963.

Leach, William. *Land of Desire: Merchants, Power, and the Rise of a New American Culture*. New York: Vintage, 1993.

Levy, David. "Reconstituted Newsreels, Reenactments and the American Narrative Film." In *Cinema 1900/1906: An Analytical Study by the National Film Archive (London) and the International Federation of Film Archives*, edited by Roger Holman, 243–60. Brussels: Fédération Internationale des Archives du Filme, 1982.

Lewis, Orlando. *The Development of American Prisons and Prison Customs, 1776–1845; With Special Reference to Early Institutions in the State of New York*. Albany: Prison Association of New York, 1922.

Luebke, Frederick. *Bonds of Loyalty; German-Americans and World War I*. DeKalb: Northern Illinois University Press, 1974.

MacLaren, Ian [John Watson]. "The Restless Energy of the American People: An Impression." *North American Review*, no. 515 (October 1899): 564–77.

Mahan, Alfred Thayer. "Hawaii and Our Future Sea Power." *Forum*, March 1893, 1–11.

————. *The Interest of America in Sea Power, Present and Future*. London: Sampson Low, Marston, 1898.

———. "The Isthmus and Sea Power." *Atlantic Monthly*, October 1893, 459–72.

———. "The United States Looking Outward." *Atlantic Monthly*, December 1890, 816–24.

Marey, Etienne-Jules. *Animal Mechanism: A Treatise on Terrestrial and Aerial Locomotion*. New York: D. Appleton, 1874.

———. *Movement*. Translated by Eric Pritchard. New York: D. Appleton, 1895.

Marvin, Carolyn. *When Old Technologies Were New: Thinking about Communications in the Late Nineteenth Century*. Oxford: Oxford University Press, 1988.

Marx, Karl. "Speech at the Anniversary of the *People's Paper*." In *The Marx-Engels Reader*, edited by Robert C. Tucker. New York: W. W. Norton, 1978.

Marx, Leo. *The Machine in the Garden: Technology and the Pastoral Ideal in America*. New York: Oxford University Press, 1964.

Melville, George W. "Our Future in the Pacific: What We Have to Hold and Win." *North American Review*, March 1898, 281–96.

Metzger, Th. *Blood and Volts: Edison, Tesla and the Electric Chair*. New York: Autonomedia, 1996.

Miller, Stuart Creighton. *"Benevolent Assimilation": The American Conquest of the Philippines, 1988–1903*. New Haven: Yale University Press, 1982.

Millis, Walter. *The Martial Spirit: A Study of Our War with Spain*. New York: Houghton Mifflin, 1931.

Miner, Maude. *The Slavery of Prostitution*. New York: Macmillan, 1916.

Mitchell, Timothy. "Orientalism and the Exhibitionary Order." In *Colonialism and Culture*, edited by Nicholas B. Dirks, 289–317. Ann Arbor: University of Michigan Press.

Musser, Charles. *Before the Nickelodeon: Edwin S. Porter and the Edison Manufacturing Company*. Berkeley: University of California Press, 1991.

———. *Edison Motion Pictures, 1890–1900: An Annotated Filmography*. Washington: Smithsonian Institution Press, 1997.

———. *The Emergence of Cinema: The American Screen to 1907*. Berkeley: University of California Press, 1990.

———. *Motion Picture Catalogs by American Producers and Distributors, 1894–1908*. Frederick, Md.: University Publications of America, 1985.

Neale, Stephen. "Melodrama and Tears." *Screen* 27, no. 6 (December 1986): 6–23.

Nemerov, Alexander. *Frederic Remington and Turn-of-the-Century America*. New Haven: Yale University Press, 1996.

Nye, David. *American Technological Sublime*. Cambridge: MIT Press, 1994.

———. *Electrifying America: Social Meanings of New Technology, 1880–1940*. Cambridge: MIT Press, 1990.

Oettermann, Stephan. *The Panorama*. New York: Zone, 1997.

Ohmann, Richard. *Selling Culture: Magazines, Markets and Class at the Turn of the Century*. London: Verso, 1996.

Pan-American Exposition: Buffalo: May 1st to November 1st. Pan-American Exposition Co., 1899. Buffalo and Erie County Historical Society.

Pan-American Exposition: Some of Its Special Features with Lists of Special Days, Sports, Concerts, Etc. (1901). Buffalo and Erie County Historical Society.

Peiss, Kathy. *Cheap Amusements: Working Women and Leisure in Turn-of-the-Century New York.* Philadelphia: Temple University Press, 1986.

Philip, Captain John W. "The 'Texas' at Santiago." *Century,* August 1898, 87–94.

Platt, Harold. *The Electric City: Energy and Growth in the Chicago Area, 1880–1930.* Chicago: University of Chicago Press, 1991.

Prescott, F. M. *Catalogue of New Films for Projection and Other Purposes* (New York, 1899), in *Motion Picture Catalogs by American Producers and Distributors, 1894–1908,* edited by Charles Musser. Frederick, Md.: University Publications of America, 1985.

Rabinbach, Anson. *The Human Motor: Energy, Fatigue, and the Origins of Modernity.* Berkeley: University of California Press, 1990.

Rabinovitz, Lauren. *For the Love of Pleasure: Women, Movies, and Culture in Turn-of-the-Century Chicago.* New Brunswick: Rutgers University Press, 1998.

Reddin, Paul. *Wild West Shows.* Urbana: University of Illinois Press, 1999.

"The Rockefeller Grand Jury Report: Showing the Conditions of the 'White Slave' Trade in New York City," *McClure's* 35 (August 1910): 471–73.

Rony, Fatimah Tobing. *The Third Eye: Race, Cinema, and Ethnographic Spectacle.* Durham: Duke University Press, 1996.

Roosevelt, Theodore. "Kidd's Social Evolution." *North American Review* 61 (July 1895): 94–109.

———. *The Rough Riders.* New York: G. P. Putnam's Sons, 1900.

———. *The Strenuous Life: Essays and Addresses.* London: Alexander Moring, 1910.

———. *The Winning of the West.* New York: G. P. Putnam's Sons, 1907.

Rosenzweig, Roy. *Eight Hours for What We Will: Work and Leisure in an Industrial City, 1870–1920.* New York: Cambridge University Press, 1983.

Rotundo, E. Anthony. *American Manhood: Transformations in Masculinity from the Revolution to the Modern Era.* New York: Basic, 1993.

Rydell, Robert. *All the World's a Fair: Visions of Empire at American International Expositions, 1876–1916.* Chicago: University of Chicago Press, 1984.

Sandberg, Mark B. *Living Pictures, Missing Persons: Mannequins, Museums, and Modernity.* Princeton: Princeton University Press, 2003.

Schafter, William R. "The Capture of Santiago de Cuba." *Century* 57, no. 4 (February 1899): 612–30.

Schirmer, Daniel B. *Republic or Empire: American Resistance to the Philippine War.* Rochester, Vt.: Schenkman, 1972.

Schivelbusch, Wolfgang. *Disenchanted Night: The Industrialization of Light in the Nineteenth Century.* Berkeley: University of California Press, 1995.

————. *The Railway Journey: The Industrialization of Space and Time in the Nineteenth Century*. Berkeley: University of California Press, 1977.

Schwartz, Vanessa R. *Spectacular Realities: Early Mass Culture in Fin-de-Siecle Paris*. Berkeley: University of California Press, 1998.

Sewell, William J. *Congressional Report* 31, pt. 7 (June 29, 1898): 6450.

Shafter, William T. "The Capture of Santiago de Cuba." *Century* 57, no. 4 (February 1899): 612-30.

Sigsbee, Charles Dwight. "Personal Narrative of the 'Maine': By Her Commander." *Century* 57, no. 2 (December 1898): 241-64.

Simmel, Georg. "The Metropolis and Mental Life." In *Simmel on Culture*, edited by David Frisby and Mike Featherstone, 174-85. London: Sage, 1997.

Singer, Ben. "Feature Films, Variety Programs, and the Crisis of the Small Exhibitor." In *American Cinema's Transitional Era*, edited by Charles Keil and Shelley Stamp, 76-101. Berkeley: University of California Press, 2004.

————. *Melodrama and Modernity: Early Sensational Cinema and Its Contexts*. New York: Columbia University Press, 2001.

————. "Modernity, Hyperstimulus, and the Rise of Popular Sensationalism." *Cinema and the Invention of Modern Life*, edited by Leo Charney and Vanessa Schwartz, 79-80. Berkeley: University of California Press, 1995.

Slotkin, Richard. *Gunfighter Nation: The Myth of the Frontier in Twentieth-Century America*. Norman: University of Oklahoma Press, 1992.

Some Information Regarding the Pan-American Exposition. Buffalo: Bureau of Publicity, 1901. Buffalo and Erie County Historical Society.

Staiger, Janet. *Bad Women: Regulating Sexuality in Early American Cinema*. Minneapolis: University of Minnesota Press, 1995.

Stamp, Shelley. "Lois Weber, Progressive Cinema, and the Fate of 'The Work-a-Day Girl' in *Shoes*." *Camera Obscura* 19, no. 2 (2004): 140-69.

————. *Movie-Struck Girls: Women and Motion Picture Culture after the Nickelodeon*. Princeton: Princeton University Press, 2000.

————. "Is Any Girl Safe? Female Spectators at the White Slave Films." *Screen* 37, no. 1 (1996): 1-15.

————. "Wages and Sin: Traffic in Souls and the White Slavery Scare." *Persistence of Vision* 9 (1991): 90-102.

Stocking, George W., Jr. *Race, Culture, and Evolution: Essays in the History of Anthropology*. Chicago: University of Chicago Press, 1983.

————. "The Turn-of-the-Century Concept of Race." *Modernism/Modernity* 1, no. 1 (1993): 4-16.

Streible, Dan. "Fake Fight Films." In *Le Cinéma au Tournant du Siècle*, edited by Claire Dupre la Tour, André Gaudreault, and Roberta Pearson, 63-79. Lausanne: Payot, 1999.

Studlar, Gaylyn. *This Mad Masquerade: Stardom and Masculinity in the Jazz Age*. New York: Columbia University Press, 1996.

Sweet, Timothy. *Traces of War: Poetry, Photography, and the Crisis of the Union.* Baltimore: Johns Hopkins University Press, 1990.

Taylor, Frederick Winslow. *Scientific Management: Comprising Shop Management; The Principles of Scientific Management: The Testimony before the Special House Committee.* New York: Harper, 1947.

Taylor, Henry C. "The 'Indiana' at Santiago." *Century* 58, no. 1 (August 1898): 62–77.

Thompson, Kristin. *Exporting Entertainment: America and the Film Market, 1907–34.* London: BFI, 1985.

Trachtenberg, Alan. "Albums of War: On Reading Civil War Photographs." *Representations*, no. 9 (winter 1985): 1–32.

———. *The Incorporation of America: Culture and Society in the Gilded Age.* New York: Hill and Wang, 1982.

U.S. Bureau of the Census. *Special Reports: Street and Electric Railways.* Washington: Government Printing Office, 1903.

U.S. Immigration Commission. "Steerage Conditions; The Importation and Harboring of Women for Immoral Purposes; Immigration Homes and Aid Societies; Immigrant Banks." *Reports of the Immigration Commission*, vol. 37. Washington: Government Printing Office, 1911.

Vardac, A. Nicholas. *Stage to Screen: Theatrical Origins of Early Film: David Garrick to D. W. Griffith.* New York: Da Capo, 1949.

Vice Commission of Chicago. *The Social Evil in Chicago.* Chicago: Gunthorp-Warren, 1911.

Virilio, Paul. *War and Cinema: The Logistics of Perception.* London: Verso, 1989.

Visitor's Information Co. *Pan-American Exposition Book of 18 Special Privileges and Guide for the Comfort and Accommodation of Visitors to Buffalo.* Buffalo: G. M. Hauser and Son, 1901. Buffalo and Erie County Historical Society.

Wainwright, Richard. "The 'Gloucester' at Santiago." *Century* 58, no. 1 (August 1898): 77–87.

Wanger, Arthur. *Organization and Tactics.* New York: B. Westermann, 1895.

War Information Series. "Why We Are Fighting," no. 2. Washington: Committee on Public Information, August 1917.

Wexler, Laura. *Tender Violence: Domestic Visions in an Age of U.S. Imperialism.* Chapel Hill: University of North Carolina Press, 2000.

Whissel, Kristen. "*The Little American* (1917)." In *America First: Naming the Nation in U.S. Film*, edited by Mandy Merck, 23–43. London: Routledge, 2007.

White, G. Edward. *The Eastern Establishment and the Western Experience.* New Haven: Yale University Press, 1968.

Williams, Linda. *Hard Core: Power, Pleasure. and the Frenzy of the Visible.* Berkeley: University of California Press, 1991.

———. *Playing the Race Card: Melodramas in Black and White from Uncle Tom to O. J. Simpson.* Princeton: Princeton University Press, 2001.

INDEX

Biograph, 61, 63, 65, 92–93, 113–15, 170.
  See also specific film titles
Boer War, 63, 93, 115
Bowser, Eileen, 165, 184, 247 n. 16, 250
  n. 85
Breakdown: mechanical, 8, 33–34, 85,
  168; moral, 159, 164, 185, 188–98,
  202–3, 205, 209, 222; technological,
  10–11, 30, 51, 189
Brewster, Ben, 165
Brown, Mary Hart, 147–48
Buffalo Bill's Wild West: American war
  influence on, 83–84, 89, 91, 93, 96, 98;
  "Attack on the Deadwood Stage",
  74–75; compared to Barnum's hoaxes,
  76–79; "Congress of Rough Riders
  of the World", 81, 85; historical
  simulations, 67–69, 71, 82, 240 n. 21;
  Pomeroy on, 73; programs/guide-
  books, 15, 18–19, 70, 72, 80–81, 87;
  spectators, 74, 76, 99, 112, 114–16,
  221

Camera operators (cameramen), 15, 22,
  60, 65, 89, 95, 119, 131–32, 134–35
Capitalism. *See* Industrial capitalism
Capture of the Trenches at Candaba
  (Edison, 1899), 96–97
Century magazine, 19, 37, 40
Cinema: African Americans in, 55–57,
  239 n. 90; American culture and, 1,
  11–12, 119, 216, 222–23, 230–31; audiences and, 10, 41, 57, 63, 114, 165,
  206, 211, 215; early (*see* Early cinema);
  catalogues, 18; modern traffic and, 9,
  17, 164–65, 213–14, 216, 219–20, 223;
  modernity and, 8, 163; Pan-American
  Exposition and, 16, 19, 120, 132, 135–
  38, 140, 146–47; reenactments and,
  85–88, 102, 116; technology, 183, 213;
  war actualities as, 14–15, 24–25, 60–

61, 65, 93, 104; white slavery in (*see*
  White slavery: in films); women in,
  158, 195. *See also* Actualities; Feature-
  length films; Moving pictures; Re-
  enactments; *specific film titles*
Circular panoramas. *See* Panoramas
Circular Panorama of Electric Tower
  (Edison, 1901), 151–52
City of Living Light, The, 16, 19, 120,
  126–32, 135–7, 139–43, 146–47, 156,
  218. *See also* Pan-American Exposi-
  tion
Civilization: American, 30–31, 41, 59,
  69, 84, 123, 136, 147; catastrophes of,
  225, 228; "over", 23, 27, 29, 217; Western, 72, 74–75, 78, 112
Civil War (U.S.), 63–65, 110
Cody, William F. *See* Buffalo Bill's Wild
  West
*Coil Winding Machines, Westinghouse
  Works* (AM&B, 1904), 194
Colomb, Admiral P. H. (Royal Navy),
  38–39
Colonialism (Spanish), 14, 21–22, 30,
  33–34, 39, 41, 106, 109, 123
Colored Invincibles (1898), 56
Colored Troops Disembarking (Edison,
  1898), 55–56
Commercialized leisure, 2, 13, 18–19, 22–
  23, 25, 109, 141–42, 162, 164; reenact-
  ment as a form of, 95; urban, 1, 67,
  68, 118–19, 215
Communication: disembodied, 4, 180–
  82; mechanized, 6, 118, 164, 168, 172;
  technologies, 4, 10, 44, 123, 163, 166;
  telegraphic, 3–4, 9, 17, 26, 28, 77, 117,
  162, 224–25; traffic and, 7, 13, 119,
  178, 219
Cooper, Mark, 51
Cuba. *See* Colonialism (Spanish);
  Spanish-American War

masculine ideals and, 32, 43, 49, 51, 56, 158; women within, 104, 108–9, 111

Inauguration of the Temple of Solomon, The (Daguerre), 145–46

Industrial capitalism, 4, 17, 22, 28, 140, 147, 149, 152, 154, 167, 202, 220

Industrial power, 16, 86, 138, 152, 156

Industrialization: ills of, 217, 220; of light, 136, 139, 219; United States, 2–3, 11, 25–26, 73, 116, 125, 129, 224

Industry: American, 14, 36, 120–21, 124, 131–32, 152, 226; electric light, 16, 128, 140, 145, 147; film and, 9, 11, 14, 18, 19, 22, 223, 230; wage slavery and, 162, 166, 185, 201, 204

Intrigue, The (Lloyd, 1916), 226

Jim Crow laws, 53–54, 57

Johnston, Frances, 103

July Crisis (of 1914), 224

Kaplan, Amy, 14, 26, 27, 57–58, 104, 217, 239 n. 93

Kasson, John F., 68, 76, 128

Kern, Stephen, 224, 228

Kirby, Lynne, 8, 44, 171, 189

Labor, 3, 19, 28, 128, 159, 189; strikes, 2, 126, 147; unskilled, 149, 164, 185, 190, 201

Laemmle, Carl, 212–14

Lears, T. J. Jackson, 23

Leisure. *See* Commercialized leisure

Leslie's Weekly, 63, 113, 114

Levy, David, 95

Light: bulbs, 127, 156; designers, 126; electric, 16, 118–21, 131–32, 136–38, 140, 152; gas-, 139, 141–42; incandescent, 117–20, 127, 134, 135–36; industrialized, 139, 144, 218–19; living,

145–47; natural, 143. *See also* City of Living Light, The; Electricity

Liquid Electricity (Vitagraph, 1907), 156–59

Little American, The (De Mille, 1917), 228

Lonedale Operator, The (Griffith, 1911), 11, 168–70, 172–74, 180–81, 219

Lonely, Villa, The (Biograph, 1909), 11

Lusitania (passenger ship, 1915) 228–29

MacLaren, Mary (as Eva Meyer in *Shoes*), 185–88, 195, 197–205, 209–11

Magazines, 18, 19, 23, 25, 38, 105, 151, 162, 216

Mahan, Alfred Thayer, 26

Maine (U.S. battleship), 24, 30–33, 38, 106

Major General Shafter (Edison, 1898), 49–50

Manila Bay (Philippines), 39–40, 108, 242 n. 59

Markets, 3, 122; Asian, 14, 26; international, 216–17

Marx, Karl, 5, 189

Masculinity, 14, 21–34, 38–40, 43–49, 51, 56, 59–60, 158, 217; degeneration of, 110; heroic, 103–5

McKay, Winsor, 229

McKinley, William, 12, 16, 67, 120, 149–50, 153, 216, 220

Midnight Mass at Saint-Etienne-du-Mont, A (Daguerre), 145

Military: campaign, 101, 106; camps, 12, 14, 22, 42–43, 49, 59–60; displays (Wild West), 67–68, 70, 79, 81–83, 89, 112; drill (films), 85, 87; everyday life, 35–36, 38, 40, 55; German, 227–30; masculinity, 21, 23, 25, 32, 39, 44, 50–51; *mise-en-scène*, 45–46; parades, 113; power (American), 30, 34, 86,

10th US Infantry Disembarking from Cars (Edison, 1898), 47–48

10th US Infantry, 2nd Battalion, Leaving Cars (Edison, 1898), 48, 51–52, 55–56

Trachtenberg, Alan, 64–65

Traffic: circulation of, 4–8, 16, 128, 132, 137, 164, 172–73, 178, 219; commercial, 10–14, 27, 40, 60, 109, 116, 123, 222–23; electric streetcar, 3, 121; everyday, 167–68, 211–12, 220; frontier, 73–74, 76, 84; illegitimate and legitimate, 147, 167–68, 170, 174–77, 179, 181, 185, 188, 199–202, 206, 222; imperial (*see* Imperial traffic); military, 38, 66, 86, 95–96, 107, 114, 115, 225; modern (*see* "Modern traffic"); narrative, 184, 208, 214; *Oxford English Dictionary* definition of, 4, 5, 13, 17, 164; pedestrian, 151, 175, 179, 186, 211; street, 98, 175–76, 249 n. 72; urban, 6, 8, 118, 122, 172, 198, 207, 213, 218; of women, 161–64, 177–78, 192, 195–200, 202–3, 206–8, 227

Traffickers, 17, 162, 168, 175, 177–78, 180–85, 201, 207, 219

Trafficking, 164, 172

Traffic in Souls (Tucker, 1913): modern traffic in, 11, 17, 172–76, 181, 184, 206–8, 211; success of, 212, 219, 246 n. 1; technology in, 166–67, 180–83, 220; women's role in, 12, 159, 164, 68, 173, 176–78, 185, 198, 209–10, 222

Trained Cavalry Horses (Edison, 1898), 44

Transportation: communication and, 4, 9–10, 119, 216, 219; Erie Canal, 121; mass, 166–67, 178, 185, 198; mechanical, 172, 186; modernity and, 150, 159, 164, 176; railway, 5–6, 8–9, 44, 73, 75, 86, 168, 171–73, 189, 221, 241 n. 21; streetcar, 2, 3, 17, 118–19, 121–22, 124, 137, 158, 188; submarine, 227–30;

technologies, 2–3, 123–24, 163, 173, 180, 189, 218, 226

Trip around the Pan-American Exposition, A (Edison, 1901), 125–26

Troops Making Military Road in Front of Santiago (Edison, 1898), 42

Tucker, George Loane, 17, 161, 164–65, 176, 181–82, 184, 207. See also *Traffic in Souls* (Tucker, 1913)

Twain, Mark, 81, 102

Urban: consumers, 81, 83, 186; landscapes, 6, 10–11, 119, 135–36, 142–44, 147, 163, 175; leisure, 1, 67–68, 95, 204; life, 2, 16–17, 69, 118; population/families, 151, 164, 200; space, 126, 129, 131, 132, 138, 140, 166, 208; technological modernity, 44, 249 n. 72; traffic (*see* Traffic: urban); transit, 3, 8

US Battleship "Indiana" (Edison, 1898), 36–37

US Battleship "Iowa" (Edison, 1898), 35

U.S. Cavalry, 42–44, 51, 55, 85–86. *See also* Actualities

U.S. Cavalry Supplies Unloading at Tampa, Florida (Edison, 1898), 43

US Infantry Supported by Rough Riders at El Caney (Edison, 1899), 87–88

U.S. Naval Academy, 27–28

US Troops and Red Cross in the Trenches before Caloocan (Edison, 1899), 104–5. *See also* Red Cross

Valley of Sarnen, The (Daguerre, 1822), 142–44

Victorious Squadron Firing Salute (Edison, 1898), 41

Wanger, Arthur, 86

War. *See* Boer War; Civil War (U.S.);